Praise for *Uninvited*

"A rollicking tale about a bunch of social wannabes busting down Holly-wood's closed-door industry, pushing boundaries, confronting obstacles, and nonstop risk-taking. Witty and illuminating . . . priceless moments and scenes. A grand narrative more bizarre than any movie script."

—**Rick King**, film producer, *Point Break*

"Adrian Maher's *Uninvited* is an uproarious account of his party-crashing adventures—and the quirky characters that shared his compulsions. It's also a forthright exploration of his own motives, a keen commentary on celebrity culture, and an offbeat anthropology of contemporary Los Angeles. Consider this your formal invitation to enjoy his madcap memoir."

—**Peter Richardson**, author of *No Simple Highway:*
A Cultural History of the Grateful Dead

"Adrian Maher's gatecrasher capers would make any paparazzi proud: an ear for confrontation, a nose for action, and an eye for exquisite details. Nervy, amusing, and surreal. His Hollywood is a ceaseless and hair-raising series of nightly exploits and daily reckonings."

—**Jennifer Buhl**, author of *Shooting Stars:*
My Unexpected Life Photographing Hollywood's Most Famous

"Used to think great gonzo journalism was dead until I picked up this magnificent trip through the world of hilarious party-crashing wackos and their obsessive weekly tango with class, fame, and hors d'oeuvres. I feel better now about gonzo journalism, though the country may be doomed."

—**Sam Quinones**, author of *Dreamland:*
The True Tale of America's Opiate Epidemic

UNINVITED

CONFESSIONS OF A
HOLLYWOOD
PARTY CRASHER

ADRIAN MAHER

CHICAGO
REVIEW
PRESS

Copyright © 2020 by Adrian Maher
All rights reserved
Published by Chicago Review Press Incorporated
814 North Franklin Street
Chicago, Illinois 60610
ISBN 978-1-64160-114-6

Library of Congress Cataloging-in-Publication Data
Names: Maher, Adrian, author.
Title: Uninvited : confessions of a Hollywood party crasher / Adrian Maher.
Description: Chicago : Chicago Review Press, 2020. | Summary: "The first
    book to chronicle a unique subterranean culture in Los Angeles: the
    gate-crashers who routinely infiltrate Tinseltown's celebrity party
    circuit"— Provided by publisher.
Identifiers: LCCN 2019030365 (print) | LCCN 2019030366 (ebook) | ISBN
    9781641601146 (paperback) | ISBN 9781641601153 (adobe pdf) | ISBN
    9781641601177 (epub) | ISBN 9781641601160 (kindle edition)
Subjects: LCSH: Maher, Adrian—Anecdotes. | Maher, Adrian—Friends and
    associates—Anecdotes. | Hollywood (Los Angeles, Calif.)—Biography—
    Anecdotes. | Hollywood (Los Angeles, Calif.)—Social life and customs—
    21st century—Anecdotes. | Parasitism (Social sciences).
Classification: LCC F869.H74 M34 2020 (print) | LCC F869.H74 (ebook) |
    DDC 979.4/94054092 [B]—dc23
LC record available at https://lccn.loc.gov/2019030365
LC ebook record available at https://lccn.loc.gov/2019030366

All photos by Adrian Maher unless otherwise indicated

Cover design: Preston Pisellini
Typesetting: Nord Compo

Printed in the United States of America
5 4 3 2 1

CONTENTS

Part III: On the Road

Part IV: Pushing Limits

AUTHOR'S NOTE

THE NAMES OF SOME INDIVIDUALS mentioned in this book have been changed and a few identifying characteristics altered to protect the socially opportunistic. All changed names are indicated by the use of SMALL CAPS on first appearance. Any similarity between fictionalized names and the names of real people is strictly coincidental.

ACKNOWLEDGMENTS

I AM MOST GRATEFUL to the following for their generous assistance and for all favors large and small: Carolyn Jones, Duane Flanigan, Paul Perelman, Charles Rappleye, Mark Cromer, David Cogan, Damon Aper, Jeff Swimmer, Nur Nur Cummings, Michael Klubock, Denny Cline, and Elizabeth Johnson. I'm especially thankful to my literary agent Andy Ross and my siblings Toody, Ashley, and Mike for their inestimable support. And I dedicate this book to Mary Moore and Avi Fisher, who provided endless encouragement, advice, and that most precious resource, their time.

INTRODUCTION

THE PINK PALACE

WITH A SLIGHTLY TREMULOUS HAND I picked up a bottle of Patrón Silver tequila and filled two neat shot glasses—one for me and the other for Avi Fisher, my main party-crash partner. It was early evening in Avi's spacious apartment in L.A.'s Pico-Fairfax neighborhood, and we needed a little liquid spine, a booster shot to proceed with the night's daunting itinerary.

After several years of ginning up the courage and months of planning, we'd decided to penetrate the grounds of the Beverly Hills Hotel for the Night Before party, a lush Hollywood affair for past Oscar winners and current nominees. It was the Everest of party-crash capers, a social gathering more prestigious than most movie premieres or even other awards shows in its opulence, exclusivity, and concentration of Tinseltown power. Many interlopers considered the gala impregnable, and we'd never known another trespasser who'd made it in. It was always held on the Saturday night preceding the Sunday evening Academy Awards ceremony.

Over the years Avi and I had both taken advantage of countless "self-invitations" to a variety of extravaganzas. We considered ourselves street pros, toughened and even coarsened by hundreds of side-door entries and backdoor escapades. Our backgrounds, mine as a former hard-charging reporter for the *Los Angeles Times* and Avi's as an ex-member of the Israeli intelligence services, also provided us with the skills and chutzpah to pull off this epic stunt. But for one of the few times in our partnership, we needed a preliminary drink.

As Avi and I sat on his living room couch, resplendent in Hugo Boss and Giorgio Armani respectively, we clinked glasses a bit too aggressively.

"Here's to making a few new friends . . . celebrity friends," I offered.

"Hopefully, not new friends in the Big House," countered Avi as we simultaneously drained the jet fuel.

All crashers know that the most high-stakes festivities involve celebrities. There's something about a concentrated gathering of the famous that sparks a steely zealotry in local sentries. Security at the star-studded Night Before party is particularly oppressive and ramps up to supermax prison levels, although they're trying to keep you out instead of in.

The event attracts hordes of paparazzi, broadcast news trucks, helicopters, wire and newspaper reporters, foreign correspondents, and mobs of looky-loos. With the intense media coverage, any security mishap is guaranteed viewing for millions of eyeballs around the globe.

No manager of a venue's security detail ever wants to be responsible for a breach like the November 24, 2009, gatecrash by Tareq and Michaele Salahi at a White House state dinner for the prime minister of India, Manmohan Singh. The Salahis were social strivers from Virginia horse country who arrived at the world's most important official residence with camera crews in tow to film an episode of Bravo's *The Real Housewives of D.C.* The camera crew never made it in, but the Salahis passed through two security checkpoints and entered the White House complex where they posed for photographs with President Barack Obama, Vice President Joe Biden, and Chief of Staff Rahm Emanuel. Their caper exploded across the Internet when they posted the photos on Michaele's Facebook page the next day. Their stealth exploits consumed the media for months and led to a presidential spanking of the Secret Service and subsequent investigations and legal inquiries.

While of a different landscape than the parade of political power at a White House function, the Night Before extravaganza has its own luster. The annual event is hosted by the Motion Picture & Television Fund and raises money for aging veterans of the entertainment industry to provide social and financial services. The combination of a good cause and spectacular venue, the Beverly Hills Hotel, a lodging world famous for its film luminaries, rock stars, and other celebrity guests, brings out *le tout* Hollywood.

The pink palace with its trademark green trim, palm trees, and deep-blue pool has the feel of a desert oasis amid L.A.'s gray, concrete megalopolis. The hotel's 208 guest rooms, twenty-three bungalows, and surrounding grounds are the site of innumerable Hollywood tales, capers, and peccadilloes. Elizabeth Taylor spent six honeymoons in one of the back bungalows. Katharine Hepburn performed a backflip into the pool, still wearing her tennis outfit. Humphrey Bogart and the Rat Pack wet their beaks in the ornate Polo Lounge. For decades, Old Hollywood has retreated to this exclusive watering hole to write screenplays, partake in secret love affairs, and recover from the ravages of plastic surgery or dissolved marriages.

The place exudes wealth and privilege—a spot where careers can be launched or broken by a quick handshake or potent cocktail.

But like all power spots, it's got a sinister, dark side: a cubbyhole where producers routinely trade starlets for sexual sacrifice, a hangout where rent boys are ferried along hedge paths to backdoor bungalows for unholy assignations, a favorite nook for Donald Trump to meet his extramarital paramours.

Despite the historic locale, intimidating guards, and high-wattage attendees, Avi and I felt ready to pierce the palace moats. We originally met a decade earlier working on several documentaries for the History Channel. After spending months in a dark, dank editing bay, he editing and me writing, we developed an easy synergy and functioned well together under deadline pressure. As our partnership morphed into high-pressure social blowouts, we developed a coded language, a dual intuition and feral awareness between each other. We had a keen understanding of our corresponding strengths, weaknesses, and idiosyncrasies after years of stealth shenanigans, incidents, and accidents. And we would need all our abilities and experience for this Night Before spectacular.

After fortifying ourselves with a last nip of Mexican firewater, we soon found ourselves on Sunset Boulevard heading east, and as we approached the party site, we noticed a long line of black Suburbans with tinted windows inching toward the driveway entrance. Security had already fanned out in three concentric rings several blocks out. My car at the time was a barely functioning 1984 Toyota Corolla that was already on its third paint job—a conspicuous color called "Grabber Blue" that's prevalent on American cars from the 1950s still operating in Cuba. I thought it best to get out of the line of fire, so I turned up Benedict Canyon Drive seeking a hidden street to park behind the hotel. We found a space, and I ditched my rusty contraption in front of a lamppost that had a sign restricting parking to local residents.

In a prior week, Avi and I had mapped out the back entrance to the hotel, and we began sauntering down the hill. Hotels are always the best venues for illicit entry. Their honeycomb structures have dozens of exits and entrances—janitorial doors, garden pathways, underground garages, freight elevators, bathrooms, and kitchen facilities.

Out of nowhere—it might have been some thick shrubbery on the side of the road—popped LAVANDA FRANTIGLIONI. She was an Italian national working as a freelance production assistant in the film industry and a ubiquitous crasher. Lavanda was in her midforties and spoke with a heavy but charming Italian accent. Of average height, she had an explosion of thick, reddish hair atop a zaftig figure and a face with a look of perpetual surprise.

"Where are you doing tonight?" she asked in her fractured syntax as we stood on the side of the nearly vacant road.

"We are going bowling, Lavanda," I said. "Would you like to join us and make this a competitive threesome?"

She responded with her trademark guffaw. I'd always liked her. Though somewhat high-strung, she was absolutely fearless and always party-traveled alone. She got into *every* shindig. I'd never seen her turned away or walking around in dazed circles like other crashers I know after being unceremoniously catapulted. She was also infamous for one key trait: she had an absolutely ravenous appetite. I'd often spot her with a teetering pyramid of buffet food piled on her plate, only to watch it quickly disappear and see her return for another round of chomping. Her bulky steel-wool mane was always encrusted with bits of food caused by her hunching over too many chow trays.

We exchanged condolences about the heavy security and compared notes about points of entry. My plan was to head for an opening in the back parking structure, but Lavanda decided to try the check-in table out front. She'd researched the names of a few past award winners and was confident about her chances. We parted, promising to stay on our cell phones for reciprocal updates.

Avi and I continued our march downhill but slowed perceptibly as we spotted two security guards standing sentry. We looked at each other and picked up the pace, sticking to our agreed plan. Avi put his phone to his ear and started to faux-giggle hysterically. We handed the phone back and forth as if talking to our mother.

"Hey you two, where you goin'?" barked a guard, impervious to our giggling ploy.

"We are just picking up our car in the back garage," I said, pointing toward the back of the hotel, not breaking stride.

The guards gave us a quizzical look, but our formal black outfits and determined gait propelled us through. Few security guards want to firmly challenge two dressy Hollywood big-shots a couple of blocks from party venues. If only they could have seen my car hidden up the hill.

I then spotted BRADLEY BLEAT, a crasher I knew well. We instantly acknowledged each other with a quick nod, though we were a block apart. He was easily recognizable with that classic gout pouch from scarfing way too much free food and drink—the typical silhouette of a devoted middle-aged freeloader, horrified by the idea of exercise.

He was hoofing it up the hill, sweating heavily and breathing irregularly and seemed about to A-fib from the uncommon exertion.

"You guys will never make it in—it's like the Kremlin down there," he said wearily. "Trust me, I'm just being a loyal time-saver. Best to just turn around now before you get detained. The security is absolutely insane."

The admonition gave us pause. But Avi and I were not deterred. We were already jacked up and blinded by adrenaline and testosterone, hybrid hormones not easily turned off.

We waved off the flailing crasher and soon arrived at the back parking structure. It had a manacled gate with a slim opening—just enough to wiggle my six-foot-three frame and 230 pounds of *Schweine-fleisch* right through. Avi followed and had no problem.

We were on the property. We'd heard the party was always held at the pool, which was boarded over for the occasion. Now, how to get past security?

After walking the perimeter of the building for a few minutes, we started seeing more guards and decided it was best to get out of the sun and into darker environs. We spotted a trusty fire-exit door and ducked in. We clattered down two stories of stairs, opened a door, and emerged into a long, shoddy, fluorescent-lit hallway. We passed office personnel doing paperwork at their dingy desks, a few plumbers heading to their next assignment, and a couple of maids. We got nary a side look.

We turned right, then left, then right, constantly moving in the direction of the ever-elusive pool. We were in an interminable warren of hallways—like two rabbits looking for a carrot. Were we just circling the inside of the building? The tension escalated as I inadvertently smashed my shoulder into a fire extinguisher on the wall while frantically looking for a clear easement. Suddenly we heard the lurch of a freight elevator and the door opened. We side-hopped in. Up it went for several floors. The door slid open and we walked straight into the kitchen—a very large kitchen for banquets.

We were getting closer. Dozens of cooks, waiters, and supervisors milled about. We noticed massive assembly lines chopping, dicing, and slicing elite cuisine. I picked up a large silver tray and carried it officiously behind a waiter burdened with several platters of freshly braised lobster and lamb. I asked if he needed help, but he declined. Avi picked up a basket of apples and huddled behind.

We finally turned a corner and heard an enormous din ahead. A row of security stood with their backs to us at the door entrance. I motioned to Avi to duck off to the side, down another hallway. Soon we popped out into a vacant ballroom, and we both bent over, holding our props, hyperventilating and sweating profusely. We'd found a quiet cranny at last but seemed trapped inside a beehive of law enforcement and security personnel. "Our late fathers would be proud," said Avi as we looked at each other sideways, both wondering if all this violent anxiety was worth the price of admission.

We walked to the edge of the ballroom and poked our heads out into a lush garden surrounded by bougainvillea, a cluster of palm trees, and giant topiaries. Off to the side was an open gate. We saw throngs of guests breezing past one last security guard directly into the pool area and the party.

"Follow my lead and just run with me—play with what I say," Avi hissed at me as he ditched his basket of apples and I discarded my silver tray.

He strode purposefully into the garden and toward the open gate and I dutifully followed. Then he whirled on me suddenly.

"You've fucked it all up again. I told you not to reach out to the folks at Paramount!" Avi barked at me in his authoritative Israeli baritone. "You've screwed up the whole deal. It's over. What chance have we got now?"

"Hey, hey, I've got a quick meeting lined up here tonight with Steve at Castle Rock," I spat back. "They're probably a better home for the script anyway."

"You're a numbskull—months of work down the drain," Avi shouted, looking like he was about to hit me. He continued raining put-downs. The guard gave us one look and wanted no part. When two dogs are fighting on the side of the freeway, the last thing anyone wants to do is get in the middle and try to break it up.

Within a few seconds we were in. I quickly noticed that Avi and I were virtually the only non-celebrities in attendance, making our civilian status highly conspicuous. Hollywood is a notoriously exclusive town with a layered hierarchy enforced with rope lines, unreturned phone calls, sycophants, private security, and German shepherds. Half the rush of crashing an A-list event like this was piercing the hardened edifice that reliably keeps out intruders like me. I couldn't get a Hollywood meeting to save my life, but I could get in here. And the only people in here were people with last names like Spielberg, Pitt, or silver screen power brokers willing to donate $25,000 for entry.

I quickly surveyed the lush scene. A huge pink tent was outfitted with multiple bars and buffets. Waiters scurried to and fro, replenishing serving tables with endless trays of scallion pancakes, poached salmon, and buttery sushi. Roving attendants quickly topped off wine glasses and vodka tumblers. And of course, there was Lavanda, assiduously strip-mining the barbecue area.

Soon I was moving through the crowd, rubbing shoulders with multiple famous faces. I complimented Eddie Murphy on his work in *Dreamgirls* as he edged by me, holding a drink. He gave a quick nod. I said hello to Tyler Perry, who didn't respond. I bumped into Michael Douglas, who politely let me pass. Everywhere I looked there was another recognizable mug—Emily Blunt, Philip Seymour Hoffman, Jeffrey Katzenberg, Jennifer Lopez, Sacha Baron Cohen. It all started to feel a bit disconcerting—something out of a Rod Serling *Twilight Zone* episode where everyone is famous but you.

I stepped to the outskirts of the crowd to get my breath and bearing. I felt a pointed tap on the shoulder from behind and almost leapt out of my skin. "Would you like a tuna tartar?" said one of the tuxedo-clad waiters offering me some Wolfgang Puck finger food. "*Ugghhh . . .* yes," I said with some irritation.

Avi acknowledged my hinky manner and suggested we fortify ourselves at the bar with some bubbly. As we stood drinking at one of the standing tables, I noticed Jennifer Aniston quizzically staring at Avi from only a few feet away.

"I know you," she said as she approached Avi with a smile.

"You do?" said Avi. "I have a common face and a very common accent."

Aniston chuckled and her interest immediately went up. At this point in his fashion career, Avi had a full head of dyed-blonde hair and looked vaguely like an Israeli Billy Idol. Gone was the shaved head of yore from his days in the military. Avi had indeed met Aniston a few times when dating his ex, a famous actress on a popular television crime series who was a friend of Aniston. But his new look was cause for confusion.

"No, no, I do know you," said Aniston. "But I just can't place you," her voice trailing off.

"I must owe you money," replied Avi, reverting to his classic mode of gamesmanship that always kept people guessing, back on their heels.

He then peeled off and returned to the bar. Aniston couldn't stop staring at him.

"Chase them until they catch you," whispered Avi to me as he tippled another shimmering flute of champers.

At one point, I looked over and saw my former boss at a television production company hunched over the sushi bar. I recognized his grayish straw hair, rangy figure, and deliberative manner. He seemed focused on a spread of yellow sashimi splayed out before him. By this time, I was well secured with adult beverages and eager to talk with

Avi (right) and two friends at a Star Wars sequel after-party. *Courtesy of Nur Nur Cummings*

someone I knew. Even though I'd made it into Hollywood's inner sanctum, I still felt like an outsider, and my anxiety was escalating. Better to calm down with a quick chat with a familiar face.

I skipped up behind my ex-boss, gave him a giant double-handed shoulder slap, gripped his shoulders, and started rocking him. At one point I remembered his head whipping back and forth. Then I began massaging his neck. "Great to see you, big boy!" I bellowed. He turned to me, slightly startled, inches from my grinning, howling face. It was Clint Eastwood. *Ooops!* The last thing you ever want to do as a social interloper is put your hands on an A-list celebrity, let alone one who was now in his late seventies.

I quickly tried putting him at ease, telling him how great he looked as if we were old pals. I even gave his bicep a quick squeeze. Clint offered a weak grin, played along and said, "Thanks, fella," in that whispery voice so well known to millions. I noticed a significant uptick in security radio traffic and decided to defer more intimate conversation with Clint until the party was over. I bowed briefly, ducked down, and disappeared into the crowd. I ripped off my blue blazer and flung it into a poolside beach chair and kept moving. From afar, I noticed Clint shrugging when talking to one of his security rescuers.

When in hell, keep moving. I galloped over to the ice cream bar and grabbed a double scoop, thinking the melting confection would provide cover. As it liquefied on my shoes, I chucked it at a garbage bin but missed. A waiter gave me a scowl and began cleaning it up. I scampered toward the barbecue pit, wishing to chat with Lavanda to uncork my exploding angst. It never looks good to be friendless in such a situation—a single, male, middle-aged crasher traveling alone looks like a single, male, middle-aged crasher traveling alone. Like Raskolnikov in *Crime and Punishment*, I even returned to the scene of the crime: the sushi table.

Avi witnessed the whole encounter and, after avoiding me for twenty minutes, finally sidled up to me at a safe moment outside the temporary bathroom stalls.

"Do you realize you just assaulted an icon?" he said.

Indeed I had. It was a major crasher faux pas. I couldn't help ruminating on Clint's anxious reaction and the crease of fear on his face at being accosted by an exuberant stranger. Here he was, the lion in his den, finally able to relax among his peers in a safe space, only to be man-grabbed by a blustery intruder whom he'd never seen before.

I told Avi to wait while I ducked into the Andy Gump to relieve myself. The insides were plush with carpeting, towels, and running water. It was drenched in industrial perfume—quite unlike the malodorous messes that typically line concert and carnival sites. I looked in the mirror and saw a slightly intoxicated, hapless outcast with furrowed brow and darting eyes. My mind was beginning to pancake. I seemed to ooze guilt, and a wave of the jitters gnawed my insides. I took care of business and popped outside.

Avi seemed uncharacteristically skittish, and as I looked around I saw a security guard on the party perimeter peering at me through binoculars. Was his detail the bathroom area, or was he homing in on prime crasher prey? I flinched and realized it was time to bolt. I had no interest in consuming additional food and drink, cavorting with any more celebrities, grabbing raffle tickets for a free MacBook Air, or retrieving my jacket.

Avi intuitively agreed, and we began a jagged retreat to our entry gate. We cantered through the garden and into the ornate ballroom whence we had come and found a fire exit that spat us out into the street. We began tramping back up the hill.

"Guess you didn't find your car?" said one of the guards elliptically. I just shook my head. The whole escapade felt a bit like

Disneyland—hours of planning, waiting, and pulsing anxiety for a three-minute ride.

Soon, I saw the comforting contours of my Grabber Blue claptrap. It was unmolested by any parking tickets, tire chalk marks, or towing services. Just waiting patiently for its disheveled owner to turn the trusty key and flee the area.

We hopped in and I began revving the engine in neutral, a reflection of my agitated state and an action that always irritated Avi. I made things worse by pulling out with tires squealing and then took a roundabout route back to Sunset Boulevard. Soon we were gliding down a hill with a coastal breeze sweeping through the car, and we both began unwinding.

"Do you think we were ever in their sights?" I asked.

"You mean, were *you* ever in their sights?" countered Avi.

I began to consider that maybe I had overreacted to the whole spectacle—the endless food, the parade of celebrities, the hyper-exclusivity of the crowd, the overwhelming feeling of being an outsider and not knowing anyone. Maybe it really was just me with too many wrenches rattling around in my head.

"Maybe we should go back?" I suggested. "As I think about it, I never really got a question from anybody, and there was lots of time for security to draw down on me. Jeez, let's go back!"

"No man, let it go. Let's move on," said Avi. "It's not worth the headache. Do you really think you'll meet your wife there? Do a deal with a big-shot? Win an award? Let's just hit a local bar and have a beer. We've had enough fun tonight."

Our inane chatter was interrupted by a phone call. It was Lavanda, and I put her on speakerphone. She sounded enthralled, giddy, and confident.

"I just won a free MacBook Air, and it seems they're handing them out like candy!" she exclaimed. "The party's really going, and I've been chatting with everyone. Meg Ryan says hello. Where are you guys?"

"We *uugghhh*, we stepped out to take a break but should be back soon," I said, gamely trying to save face. "I'll call you back shortly."

I hung up and looked at Avi, whose face had changed considerably. "Turn around," he said. "Let's go back."

PART I

ROOKIE

Adrian in trademark pose with flamenco dancer at L.A. hat store opening.

1

WHO ARE THESE PEOPLE?

A S A REPORTER for the *Los Angeles Times* and other media outlets in
the 1990s, I roved L.A. hunting for stories and covering a variety
of events. It might be a screening for the UCLA Film & Television
Archive, a restaurant opening, or an animal rights fundraiser.

At some point, I started seeing the guy everywhere. I'd arrive pen
and notebook in hand, scan the venue, and there he'd be.

In his late forties, he was of medium height, lean and hyper with
a shock of ink-black hair. Usually wearing a blue blazer, dark slacks,
and a crisp white shirt, he looked entirely respectable. That is, until
the food and drink arrived. Then he'd become conspicuously wolfish,
grabbing two plates and lunging at the victuals, occasionally boxing
out elderly couples, the hosts, or even the VIP guests themselves who
were ostensibly first in line.

He'd soon have a pile of lasagna, a pyramid of salami, Brie, celery
sticks, olives, and bread, while double-fisting cups of pinot. He'd
quickly sit and begin inhaling the bounty. I thought his behavior odd
at the time, but I'd rapidly return to my reporting duties without giving him another thought.

Through the haze of more than two decades, I seem to remember first meeting him as I walked by a nondescript bar in Santa Monica and noticed a small gathering. It was an informal social for the Santa Monica Chamber of Commerce. Fusty peanuts, cheese, and crackers were the offerings. Sure enough, there was the same fellow tearing away at the food crumbs, wearing a red plastic wristband. He introduced himself as BARTON WHITAKER, and after a few pleasantries and questions, I soon realized that Mr. Whitaker had no connection to Santa Monica or its business affairs—or to the UCLA Film Archive, animal rights, or the restaurant industry, for that matter.

He was chatty and friendly, and after the Chamber event we walked back to his car and he opened the trunk. Out popped an enormous jack-in-the-box full of splashy items—hundreds of multicolored wristbands, pens, stickers, lanyards, ultraviolet inks, hand stamps, name tags, generic tickets, baseball hats, earpieces, clipboards, wine glasses, eyeglasses, and champagne flutes.

"These are the tools of the trade—the golden tickets for entry," Barton said, laughing. "Dime-store items that penetrate rings of security costing thousands of dollars and provide access to inestimable goods and services!"

Out of swelling curiosity, intrigued by his brio and rash of self-invitations, I began following Barton (maybe a good reporter story?) as he made his nocturnal rounds to a variety of events and activities. I soon began meeting other social infiltrators who were part of his tight network of gatecrashers.

There was Dr. Al Barrios, a former philosophy professor at UCLA. Now in his midseventies with time on his hands, he had an affinity for flashy events like the Grammys and Golden Globes and always played the part well. Blessed with a thick helmet of swept-back grayish hair, he was invariably attired in a freshly pressed Armani tuxedo and assumed a regal posture that allowed him to breeze by security.

Dr. Barrios was a fiend for overflowing buffets stocked with thick meats, preferably catered by Wolfgang Puck. After choking down enough tri-tip to send anyone to a vomitorium, he would pluck a dozen of the juiciest chunks and stuff them into large Ziploc bags. Then, ever so gingerly, he'd open his dinner jacket and line his pockets with the contraband, later to be devoured by Ruckus, his pet Chihuahua. He often left events looking like a Michelin Man. We joked that he was the most physically fortified driver on the Westside of L.A. No airbag could ever compete.

I also made the acquaintance of CLARA VESTERGAARD, an attractive, earnest Danish émigré in her late twenties who was obsessed with glamorous events that she was often terrified of crashing. One routinely saw her on the periphery of various extravaganzas circling the block, cell phone in hand desperately pleading with Dr. Barrios (who was already inside tending to his carnivorous needs) to find a semi-legitimate way to get her in. Maybe he could read a name off the list for her? Scamper out with an extra wristband? Tell her what the hand stamp looked like?

Dr. Barrios, like many party crashers, was a lonely figure. As an aging gentleman he'd been badly fleeced by a young Russian mail-order bride that he'd found in an ad in L.A.'s *Recycler* newspaper, more of a publication for used cars and refrigerators. On arrival in America, she stripped his finances and left him romantically bereft. He was partial to the attentions of younger women and doted on Clara religiously. I often witnessed him frantically bolting from a party, covered in flecks of meat and sundry sauces to tend to his damsel in distress outside. Eventually they'd waltz in together playing off the stereotype of the much older Hollywood power mogul and his latest ingénue.

Once inside, Clara often couldn't shake her paranoia and once spent two hours squatting with her feet atop a toilet seat in a bathroom cubicle to avoid what she thought was patrolling security.

I was subsequently introduced to MIKE MULLEN, a high school teacher in his late twenties obsessed with event swag. Also known as

"Ten-Minute Mike," he'd always show up at the very end of a party and hover around the gifting table, desperate to nab a free bag of cosmetics, movie posters, or T-shirts. Mike cared nothing for industry networking or women or alcohol, the usual motives of typical self-inviters. His usual salutation, either on the phone or in person, was, "Is there a gift bag?" Then, "What's in it?" The answer would quickly determine his plans for the remainder of the night.

Ten-Minute Mike lived alone in a two-bedroom apartment in the San Fernando Valley, and no one in the party-crasher network had ever seen the interior. Once, a mutual friend was outside, desperate to use the bathroom. After frantic entreaties, Mike finally relented. After using the toilet the friend peeked in one room—all looked normal, nothing to report. Then, he pushed open the door to the master bedroom. Inside were floor-to-ceiling gift bags dating back to the *Top Gun* movie premiere in 1986. After studying the tableau, the friend noticed the outline of a full-body imprint in the center of the clump of bags. The body profile looked like Mike's.

And who can forget Burt Goldenberg? Burt had the look of a former boxer from the boroughs of New York City with cauliflower ears and a ruddy face, but he was actually a savvy stock investor who'd been crashing parties in L.A. since he'd migrated here in the early 1970s. We called him an OC—an original crasher. Now in his late sixties and still sharp-witted, he always employed the same opening salvo: "Where are the pretty girls?" delivered in a heavy *Nooo Yaawwwk* accent. His clothes were straight off the rack from Goodwill—usually a shoddy blazer and faded slacks, often covered with food and wine stains. He always wore a baseball hat and bright white sneakers, no matter how formal the occasion.

In the days before cell phones, Burt would staple large Thomas Guide maps of L.A. to his home walls. As daily party tips came in, he'd prioritize the locations with multicolored pins, moving them around like soldiers on a dynamic battlefield. At the appointed evening hour, he'd peruse his custom-made map and head out to the choice venues.

Burt Goldenberg and Adrian Maher after a few
spilled drinks.

"He called me one night and said he was in the emergency room at
Brotman Hospital waiting for treatment," said Brad Elterman, a legendary
photographer who'd captured the Hollywood party-crash and rock 'n'
roll scenes in the 1970s and had known Burt for more than forty years.
"I asked if I could help, and he said, 'Could you just go check out this
art opening in Santa Monica and get back to me with the details?' He
was just relentless.'"

Once at an event, Burt never had a problem gaining entry—he
seemed to know every doorman and clipboard minder and most of
the people inside the party. I never once saw him get molested by
security—he was like a mini-celebrity in this bizarre subculture.

Darren Skoda was another New York transplant and OC with a daily collection of L.A. party details that was astonishing. Though in his seventies, he seemed to be everywhere, tirelessly working the phone, downloading info, and sending out real-time reports to his tight crew. Bespectacled and wax-apple bald, we called him the "Slither Dome" for his skill at effortlessly slipping in and out of events. He got in everywhere and knew every detail of every shindig of note— from an intimate birthday party for John Travolta in Beverly Hills, to a rapper yacht shindig in Marina del Rey, to the opening of a new trampoline gym in Malibu.

I once mentioned I was about to vacation in South Africa with my girlfriend.

"Huge party in Durban on Friday night," he said. "Let me know if you're interested and I'll send you the details."

And of course, in later years there was my main man, Avi Fisher, who had the fearsome look of an Israeli warrior—a muscular six-footer, his physique came with a shaved head, wraparound shades, and Doc Martin boots. He was blunt, impatient, and brilliant. During our documentary work together, a producer told me that no editor could squeeze more frames out of raw video than Avi. Time after time, we'd be stuck trying to bridge a point in our narrative when Avi would pull out a solution from the ether.

We both had matching chips on each shoulder and reflexively reacted against all forms of supervision. Each of us recognized an energy, curiosity, and sense of adventure in the other that could never be leashed by the typical workday.

Avi regaled me with stories in his gravelly Israeli baritone about his arrival in New York City in his late twenties, having no connections and speaking no English. He lived at the YMCA and got work as a barback in the East Village. As his language skills improved, he became a bartender. With an interest in movies, he took editing classes during the day. After a year, he moved to Los Angeles and was soon working as an assistant editor on television documentaries.

I noticed that whenever I tried introducing him to other Israelis in L.A., he showed no interest. Maybe the offer brought too many unwelcome memories. Avi had been a lead sniper in the Israeli army and operated on the front lines during the invasion of Lebanon in 1982. He'd had to shoot more than a few adversaries in close quarters. He'd also worked for the intelligence arm of the Israeli army's special operations forces on innumerable antiterrorism assignments.

At his first special services training exercise on a street corner in downtown Tel Aviv, his commander pointed out a distant balcony on the fifteenth story of a residential high-rise building.

"I need to see you on that private balcony within eight minutes, using any means necessary," barked his instructor. Avi was soon waving from the porch.

After the war, Avi spent five years lying on a beach in Greece trying to clear his head of all the carnage he'd witnessed. Upon hearing many of his brutal war stories, I found it remarkable that Avi could function at all, much less at such a high professional level. Socially, I noticed that Avi had also crashed a few movie premieres in L.A. without too much trouble.

Soon, after we began working together during the straitlaced day, Avi and I would metamorphose at night, exploring a variety of L.A. events as a supercharged crasher team—nocturnal caped crusaders. From my days as a reporter, I'd read about war correspondents always going out in the field in teams of two, the best number to deal with dangerous environments. If just one, you were on your own with no witnesses and an increased vulnerability to a snuffing. If three or more, your movements were slowed and you brought more attention from adversaries.

Avi's crasher skills were superlative. I'd never seen anyone so creative when approaching a tight venue, so attuned to atmosphere and party themes, so able to read people and sense approaching danger. As stress increased in a given situation, he'd grow correspondingly calmer and more clear-sighted. And when we were both caught in a security confrontation, he always had an ingenious answer that lowered tensions and provided an escape route. The Israeli intelligence services brought to bear on the ripe L.A. party circuit.

Though I'd grown up on L.A.'s Westside and had my own youthful fascination and encounters with the Tinseltown party scene, I'd never come across such a posse as the crasher community. They were all straight out of a Federico Fellini film. I became fascinated by this reappearing group of red-carpet rascals that seemed to pierce security at high-end Hollywood shindigs with ease, and who were ubiquitous at even the most trifling of events. Soon I began exchanging phone and e-mail coordinates with them, surreptitiously swapping party information.

Avi Fisher dancing through security. *Courtesy of Nur Nur Cummings*

Some of these social trespassers were in it for free gift bags and libations, industry networking, celebrity encounters, or a puffed-up feeling of exclusivity. Others were itinerant mooches, kleptomaniacs, liars, and poseurs who were greedy, petty, overly competitive, self-hating, and needy. But there were also quite a few outsiders and risk-takers who were physically courageous, curious, and adventuresome. They lived boldly, took creative chances, and pursued their own dreams.

I felt an attraction to their tight network—their daily, exclusive "party" e-mail list, their cell phone updates, and their aggressive search for the next sight and scene. On slow nights, they cruised Mulholland Drive and Melrose and Rodeo Avenues looking for any and all signs of a shindig—balloons, valet parkers, catering trucks, equipment rental vans, check-in signs, red carpets, rubberneckers, searchlights, helicopters, and paparazzi.

"There's a giant white tent going up just north of the Santa Monica Pier—I don't know what it is yet, but someone over there needs to check it out," was a typical cell phone exclamation from a crasher passing on a potential extravaganza.

"I just saw a bunch of white shuttle buses going up Sunset Plaza Drive in West Hollywood," was another breathless voice message. "This thing could be big."

Or, "There's a line of security outside a house on the Pacific Coast Highway in Malibu—it might be David Geffen's party," was one more urgent missive.

I believed I had the makings of a big feature story about a subterranean culture in Hollywood that hadn't been covered. I'd also made some wacky new friends. Strange adventures beckoned. New goals clarified. Perhaps not quite Pulitzer-worthy, yet I saw my career edging up a notch with the telling of this tale.

But as I look back, I realize my life was already unraveling.

———

It was the Clinton-era economic boom in the 1990s and I was on a roll. I lived in Santa Monica with a beautiful woman, Jodi, and I was thriving as a full-time reporter at the *L.A. Times*. I had a super network of friends and close family members living nearby. I brimmed with good health and vitality. But in the wheel of life, when all is going smoothly, a reckoning beckons.

At the *L.A. Times*, I realized something was up. For weeks I'd heard rumors that the paper was planning on downsizing. I worked in the Santa Monica bureau as a general assignment reporter covering a variety of issues in west Los Angeles County: city government, corrupt dog-training schools, environmental pollution, the O. J. Simpson case, gangs, fires, mudslides, and other forms of impromptu mayhem.

I loved the job. Working as a reporter put me in the central nervous system of one of the globe's busiest megalopolises. I had a knack for finding offbeat and bizarre stories, such as a group of midnight wave riders at Malibu who surfed by the full moon, a character study of a probation officer trying to broker peace amid a Westside gang war, and a group of elderly swingers. Like my journalistic brethren, I was insatiably curious about all topics and lived to track down any and all leads to sculpt them into succinct and compelling stories.

One morning our bureau chief strode into the middle of the newsroom and announced a meeting for the following week of all suburban reporters at the New Otani Hotel in downtown Los Angeles. Taking all of us off-site for a group confab was not a good sign.

My editor, George Hatch, was a Harvard-educated, Massachusetts transplant who understood that covering Los Angeles was a horizontal venture. Many East Coast editors brought a downtown sensibility from their past journalistic experiences when sizing up Southern California. They believed all stories should be focused on city hall, the courts, and local jails—venues that invariably were across the street from the typical central Boston or Philadelphia newsroom.

But L.A. County is spread far and wide, consisting of eighty-eight cities (and many unincorporated areas) across an urbanized region of more than four thousand square miles—larger than Delaware and Rhode Island combined.

The *Los Angeles Times* had numerous suburban editions as part of the main newspaper; these came out in supplements twice a week. The understanding was that its reporters needed to be geographically dispersed to keep up with such far-flung municipalities as Cudahy, Hawaiian Gardens, and even Malibu.

As the Westside bureau chief, no one was more cognizant of such responsibilities for the *Times*'s most important metropolitan outpost than Hatch. He relentlessly launched us out of our Santa Monica newsroom to cover such obscure communities as a group of pagan witches in Topanga Canyon, warring tribes of surfers in Palos Verdes, or gay-rights issues in West Hollywood.

As writer Dorothy Parker once (reportedly) said: "Los Angeles is seventy-two suburbs in search of a city." The only institution binding all that obscure concrete, remote asphalt, diverse peoples, and removed cities was the *Los Angeles Times*.

All twelve reporters and the two editors in our bureau approached the upcoming meeting with dread. On the morning of the meeting, we arrived at the hotel lobby and were offered batches of stale donuts and kegs of acidic coffee. We tittered nervously and milled about like jackrabbits marked for slaughter.

Carol Stogsdill, the downtown editor of the *L.A. Times*'s suburban editions, soon brought our caucus to order. She got to the point: all six suburban editions would close, and roughly two hundred editorial employees would be laid off, including me. It was the first of many waves of contraction for the *Times* and also the industry at large.

On returning home, my live-in girlfriend, Jodi, was sympathetic but agitated. She was a hyper-striver and already soaring in her career as a manager of entertainment research at a Hollywood consulting firm. She had stuck with me through years of impoverished freelance reporting. Now, after two years of modest success at the *Times*, I was thrust back into a mosh pit of uncertainty.

After a period of soul-searching, I gamely returned to my earlier catch-as-catch-can lifestyle. I freelanced for *Newsweek*, the *L.A. Weekly*—and any publication that would have me. I tried my hand as an on-air television reporter working at the Orange County NewsChannel and on weekends as a hair-sprayed meat puppet for KGET-TV, a local NBC affiliate in Bakersfield. Within a year, I got hired as a national correspondent in Los Angeles for the Fox News Network, which was transforming itself into the Fox News Channel. But after six months I got entangled in office politics, right-wing havoc, and a contractual dispute and left the network.

I was always more of a print reporter anyway. I loved depth, digging, and details—elements not associated with broadcast journalism. And with my receding gums and hairline, the long-term prospects for an on-air career looked treacherous.

I decided to reignite my newspaper reporter career with a story I never got to complete at the *Los Angeles Times*. It was about a long-standing police chief, Ted Cooke, in the small municipality of Culver City in the middle of west L.A. County. Cooke was an old-school commander who had risen through the ranks of William Parker's brutal LAPD in the 1950s and '60s. In the 1970s Cooke brought his rough-rider techniques to the Culver City Police Department and began implementing a series of outrageous tactics and procedures. He started handing out hundreds of concealed gun permits to local politicians, civic donors, and out-of-town celebrities such as Johnny Carson, Sylvester Stallone, Jim Belushi, boxer Ken Norton, James Caan, and Robert Blake.

Cooke also ran his own private security operation, Cooke Protective Services in Culver City, using his off-duty police officers to guard local warehouses, sundry businesses, and nearby Sony Studios.

Other security enterprises in Culver City didn't have much of a chance competing.

His department still used the outdated hog-tying technique for unruly suspects and was accused of profiling minorities and fudging crime statistics. When I was at the *L.A. Times*, Chief Cooke used to fax our bureau press releases about crime in his jurisdiction still using the word "Negro" to describe suspects.

I pitched the story to the *L.A. Weekly* and spent the next year obsessively reporting it—most of the time in my underwear while at my desk in my dark, rent-controlled apartment in Santa Monica.

These efforts did wonders for my domestic situation. As I began slipping on my share of the monthly rent, Jodi was slipping out of the relationship.

Then my mother was diagnosed with pancreatic cancer. She'd never quite gotten over the premature death several years before of my father, who'd died playing tennis at fifty-seven. As British immigrants with four kids by the time they were thirty years old, the financial pressures and physical demands on them were intense. They'd had an extremely tight bond. His death was a tremendous blow to all of us but especially to her.

In the meantime, the *L.A. Weekly* (at my behest and on my behalf) sued the Culver City Police Department for the public records of their concealed gun permits. I was now involved in intense litigation, reporting, and following up on multiple stories that had broken Culver City and its police department wide open. As I attempted to care for my ailing mother and repair things with Jodi, I fielded prank calls (and a few death threats) at all hours from pissed-off cops.

After four horrifying months, my mother died. Soon after, Jodi left me. Several weeks later, my college sweetheart, after a long bout with depression, committed suicide using a pistol, two miles from my home.

"When sorrows come, they come not single spies. But in battalions!" wrote William Shakespeare. Indeed.

After one year of relentless toil, insomnia, migraine headaches, and ceaseless pressure, I finally finished my police series for the *L.A. Weekly*. My pay for the whole project was $5,000. I was thousands of dollars in debt, bloated, and depressed. The professional boost I anticipated never happened.

There's nothing more pitiful than a widower on hard times. On many levels I *had* been widowed—career, relationships, and finances. My head was in a vice. The string of tragedies, bad luck, and heartache was overwhelming. I felt underwater, unable to move freely or think clearly, each day passing in a haze.

My bat-cave apartment looked as if it had been hit by a drone strike—missing furniture, peeling paint, framed photos tossed asunder, a bathroom with no toilet paper, and a refrigerator filled with Gatorade and Ensure. Single men and their surroundings often don't age well.

I was sinking into a deep slough of despondency, unable to conjure any plan for recovery.

2

NAVIGATING CRASHER CODES

L.A.'S MOST ELOQUENT CHRONICLERS, such as John Fante, Raymond Chandler, Carey McWilliams, and Michael Connelly, have described the city as a hellish paradise. Despite the globe's best weather and a gorgeous nexus of mountains, deserts, and sea populated by impossibly beautiful people, its endless sun is routinely eclipsed by political corruption, riots, and disasters—mudslides, earthquakes, and fires.

Los Angeles is surely the most anonymous and loneliest city in the world—a sprawling gray circuit board where the only chance at spiritual communion is on the freeway. Its immeasurable distances can feel oppressive and intangible. The city emanates transience; many residents are transplants seeking reinvention, chasing fantasies of fame, or running from a series of bounced checks. Others end up fleeing from Tinseltown horrors or space industry layoffs or quickly pass through to perpetrate murder and mayhem.

The physical and mental alienation of living in La La Land permeates the place: the shallow discourse, glitzy materialism, spiritual emptiness, crushing traffic jams, lack of community, and social disconnection.

Its widespread anonymity fuels a fear of connecting with neighbors that is punctuated by lurid, local crime newscasts. Residents have their social defenses up, whether in a public park, theater, bar, or nightclub. Trying to connect with a stranger in Costco will most likely end in your arrest or theirs.

I'd lived in New York City, and everyone there is out in the streets. You can't help meeting people. But in Los Angeles, most social activity occurs behind closed walls, rope lines, and palace gates. You have to know where to go and have the connections to get in. If you don't have beauty, youth, or money, the city can get very lonely, very quickly.

The manifestations of depression take many forms in different people. Some try eating their way through their anxiety or begin online shopping binges. Others turn to alcohol and illicit drugs to alleviate their pain. Many lock themselves in darkened rooms and cut off all contact with the outside world.

Unemployment is a force multiplier of despondency. Work is the enemy of melancholy. Without a daily place to go and with debtor messages piling up on my voice mail, I felt myself turning inward.

After an initial flurry of applications to various reporter jobs that went nowhere, my pace began slowing. I began rising later and later in the day. I spent many afternoons walking around Santa Monica watching beautiful, happy people walking their dogs, picking kids up from school, or heading into a pedicure salon. Sometimes I'd end up in a run-down pool hall near the beach playing billiards with other lost souls. Other times I'd walk for hours along the seaside bluffs looking out to sea, the image of eternity, searching for an answer. I felt aimless and invisible, a numb outsider looking into a diorama pulsing with life.

I tried waxing up my surfboards again, volunteering, reaching out to former friends and foes, calling my ex-girlfriend to take me back. Nothing helped. I had absolutely no energy and dwindling interest in anything. The ceaseless sunshine just seemed to put my sorrows in bas-relief.

Then one day, as I lay on my bed looking up at my cottage-cheese stucco ceiling, I had an epiphany of reaching out to Barton Whitaker to escape my situation.

Barton always seemed upbeat. With a platter of food in one hand and a highball in the other, he'd work his cell phone like an air traffic controller, sorting and disseminating dozens of incoming tips about the latest event or extravaganza.

Why not reconnect with this master social navigator? It would get me out of the house, give me a daily adventure, and who knows, maybe I'd meet another lonely soul seeking romance.

I'd heard that Barton put out a comprehensive e-mail list of daily happenings in L.A. called the Master List. It was a compendium of public relations agency tips, studio announcements, celebrity fundraisers, and art, spa, restaurant, gym, and store openings, among other occasions. The list also came with media contacts and stealth entry tips for different venues. It was the Bible for all Hollywood self-inviters and was sometimes updated on an hourly basis. Membership cost thirty dollars per month.

I called Barton and offered to pony up dues to join his club of reprobates. He was leery at first (doesn't a reporter already know all this information?), but after I revealed my joblessness, he relented and I began receiving his treasured list.

It was a revelation. Here in two short, single-spaced pages was a daily summary of events all over the L.A. basin with addresses, times, PR contacts, celebrity guests, and even parking instructions. One day a yoga studio opening would catch my eye, and soon I'd be squatting amid a group of shaggy practitioners in pretzel poses. Or I'd end up at an art gallery in Malibu with psychedelic paintings and strange acoustic music. Sometimes I'd finish an evening at a small spa gathering in Beverly Hills to celebrate a new celebrity face-lift, Brazilian bikini-wax, or tummy tuck.

Many Tinseltown events are celebrity-driven and tied to annual charity events loaded with food, drink, and hundreds of fashionably attired attendees. They consequently have the most beefed-up security and most challenging points of entry.

But the Master List also tapped into an infinite number of disparate L.A. proceedings unmatched anywhere in the world—a lobster festival in Redondo Beach, a beer-tasting contest at a new gastropub, a chorus of drag queens singing at a theater in West Hollywood, a boxing exhibition at a downtown gym, or a cannabis-sponsored 5K race at a local track club.

I began seeing a whole new side of Los Angeles—a city of wondrous ethnic diversity, wide cultural offerings, and fringe characters with panoplies of never-ending, offbeat celebrations. The city was peppered with hidden happenings.

Soon I saw the close-knit crasher group and the celebrity party circuit, with its collection of public relations handlers, caterers, and assorted enablers, as a small and recognizable community. Each daily outing was a fount of adventure, exploration, and excitement. It was a bright spot amid L.A.'s social isolation, a tonic for boredom, and a wellspring of networking opportunities and adrenaline. Once inside an exclusive event I noticed that people finally let their guard down. The social hypervigilance so common in public places dramatically dissipated and allowed for more intimate and friendly connections.

After attending several parties as a newly minted crasher, it was the first time I felt alive in months. I felt full of hope and increasing self-confidence. The analytics of entry stirred my mind. The risks involved summoned the blood and pulsed my body. It was a four-dimensional daily game that was stimulating and joyous. The thrill of getting away with it topped an actual invitation.

As I began ingratiating myself to fellow crashers and cycling into the party network, my depression lifted. I started picking up a litany of crucial, unwritten rules to successfully penetrate multiple venues. Preparation is key—know your floor plans, and pick out several names on the guest list that have been revealed online beforehand. Once at the venue, be persistent and probe every possible entry. And if you make it in but get eighty-sixed from a party, never try to sneak back in—now you're officially trespassing.

In order to get party info, you've got to give party info—always have your cell phone on code three—ready to send and receive the latest details to your associate pariahs, who are often spread out all over Los Angeles. (The reciprocal "cell intel" will save you hours chasing false leads and avoiding hours in the city's pulverizing traffic jams.) Live reports from a location are highly coveted. Activating Facetime on your iPhone and roaming a party surreptitiously streaming live video of the proceedings is a big hit with other Side-Door Johnnies.

Never bring your "bag of tricks" (wristbands, badges, stamps, wigs, uniforms, fake noses and glasses) anywhere near a party—always keep them sealed in the trunk of your car. Never carry identification. Exude a breezy confidence, and never make direct eye contact with security—they often avoid hassling cocky Hollywood-looking notables. If you're playing with a posh British accent, stay in character the minute you leave your house—don't try to suddenly turn it on at the palace gates. It can make for a jerky presentation and perk up the ears of security.

Keep bottles of real medical prescriptions in your vehicle—a great excuse to escape security to deal with the sudden onset of your "irregular" heartbeat. To avoid suspicion, never steal gift bags, hoard food, or guzzle drinks. Don't be the first in the buffet line or belly up to the bar too quickly. Always dress appropriately: If crashing an art opening, wear a flashy hair shirt, colorful clogs, and loud eyewear—blend in. Long-sleeve shirts are mandatory, needed to partially cover an unmatched wristband or off-kilter ink stamp. Keep a sliver of Scotch tape on the back of your mobile phone—lanyards, wristbands, and name tags often need to be reattached. Try to avoid clumping with two or more other crashers at an event—some are known to security, and you'll be guilty by association and potentially snagged in a scalawag roundup.

Avoid arguments with other guests or any extended conversations with security, no matter how friendly. Never post pictures on social media of your exploits. Grinning selfies next to glum celebrities posted on Instagram are catnip to law enforcement, especially in real time.

Consider the cautionary tale of Terry Bryant, the forty-seven-year-old "producer" who was arrested at the Governors Ball after the 2018 Academy Awards for absconding with Frances McDormand's Best Actress Oscar statuette. Known for his prior crashing exploits at other awards shows and after-parties, Bryant posted a video of himself on Facebook hamming it up at the event while holding up the purloined statuary and bellowing, "Look at it, baby. My team got this tonight. This is mine. We got it tonight, baby. Who wants to tell me congratulations? This is mine! Where's the Jimmy Kimmel party at? I can't believe I got this. It's for music."

After his video posting, and the intervention of a suspicious show photographer, who pointed him out, Bryant was arrested for grand theft as he was leaving the venue and booked into L.A. County jail on $20,000 bail.

In the words of one veteran crasher: "Humility, civility, retreat from heat." Those are key mantras to avoid an epic interloper melt-down that has the potential to play out globally. Do you really want your cousins in Australia to watch you being frog-marched in shackles out of a mega-event on live television that is guaranteed to be your epitaph and/or the first line in your obituary?

I also noticed the exquisite attention crashers paid to their tools of the trade. Props provided critical cover to the most outlandish of capers. It wasn't just Barton who stashed an extensive "party" kit in his car. Besides the aforementioned wristbands, wine glasses, lanyards, tickets, badges, media passes, wigs, clipboards, eye patches, earpieces, ultraviolet light ink, hand stamps, and colored pens, I noticed lots of additional paraphernalia: parking stickers, UPS deliveryman outfits, FedEx boxes, doctor smocks, Google glasses, fake glasses, collapsible wheelchairs, and referee uniforms. I saw some scoundrels using fake fire marshal badges, disabled-parking placards, and food inspector lanyards.

A few crashers have laptops, 3-D printers, and laminating machines in their vehicles. They'll take a cell phone picture of a badge at an event perimeter, return to their parking spots, download the image onto their computers, insert and crop their own photo, print, laminate, and wear. Many keep hard-charging lawyers on retainer during specific "event" weekends in case of complications.

I was mesmerized by the resourceful techniques used to gain entry at even the most security-fortified events. Some social entrepreneurs created travel and entertainment event websites with dynamic lists of upcoming gatherings and reviews of past extravaganzas. Afterward they leveraged their growing media status into legitimate invitations and placement on guest lists.

Others paid off employees at event-catering companies such as Wolfgang Puck, Patina, or Très L.A. for locations, times, and backdoor tips for entry to big awards ceremonies. A few gave monthly stipends to knowledgeable, well-placed security guards. Several crashers spent whole days bird-dogging their public relations and press contacts for classified party information.

I saw ingenious tactics, like the finger-point at the door—boldly reaching out and tapping a name on the clipboard list (without being able to read it).

"Your name is Steve . . . Thornton?"

"Yup, that's me."

"OK, c'mon in."

One day I read a guest name off a clipboard list held by a door minder by peering over it and reading the names upside down. After multiple successful entries using my new technique, my crasher handle became TUDLR (The Upside Down List Reader) for my uncanny, raptor-like eyesight that could decipher names on an askew clipboard from twenty feet away at the door.

Another method was blurting out a generic last name like Cohen or Berg. Invariably there would be one at an entertainment industry event.

"Cohen . . . Ronald?"

"That'd be me."

"OK, head this way."

Sometimes I'd listen for people's names as they checked in and promptly move down the table to another check-in clerk with a duplicate list and give the same name.

I witnessed other social opportunists working in tandem. One would distract the doorman with an urgent matter, and the other would slip by. Or they'd engage security in a photo op with a celebrity while their brethren scooted in. Others would ride inside a swarm of people at the gate or snuggle up to a celebrity for casual familial chitchat. When a couple checked in at a front desk, some tricksters would creep up behind and thrust a hand between them to also get their hand stamped.

I learned to fake a gimpy knee and try to hitch a "Trojan horse" car ride a couple of blocks away from the entrance, useful when dozens of Escalades were backed up. Women crashers were especially good at this technique—me, not so much.

One tactic was foolproof: Wear your best tuxedo, pour yourself a shimmering flute of champagne in the parking lot, and then strut back and forth in front of the lines of hulking security.

"Excuse me, sir . . . Am I allowed to drink this out here?" say I, hoisting the brimming cup of liquid gold.

"No, no . . . you've got to come inside with that. No drinks outside!"

One of the greatest crasher feats, which I saw many times and even tried myself with varying levels of success, was the *crash date.* I'd meet an attractive woman and ask her on a date to a future V.I.P. event. Your potential partner might not be that impressed with you personally, but most people in Hollywood are on the make and fancy the sounds of the upcoming extravaganza. The goal is to crash both of you into the event without your date knowing. Once in, you can play big-shot and luxuriate in the exclusive surroundings. *Hey, this is just part of my daily schedule—welcome to my world!*

Until it isn't. No first crash date ever survives a rebuff at the door or a security comeuppance at the party perimeter. That's not the image you're trying to convey. Heaven help you if you receive a tap on the shoulder inside and subsequently get the heave-ho. When things go south, ouch! Hell hath no fury like a misled crash date. You've made an enemy for life. I'm still suffering blowback from a couple of paramours years after the offense.

Many times, I had to ask myself, why was this core crew—about two dozen miscreants—doing this? Why was *I* doing this?

I began considering the psychological makeup of my fellow scapegraces. They were a motley group of all shapes, sizes, ethnicities, professions, and personalities. Some were successful real estate entrepreneurs and others were unemployed lowlifes. Many had pronounced resentments and a profound sense of not belonging, always pressing their faces against the proverbial window. Others were adrenaline junkies visibly bored once gaining entry, constantly looking for the next shindig and epinephrine fix. Some, like me, were just plain lonely and starved for conversation. Most were curious, intelligent, cunning, and actually completely harmless.

However, there were a few outliers with deep unconscious feelings of shame and self-hatred manifested in periodic outbursts of snitching, viciousness, and competitive jockeying among themselves. (More on that later.)

One personality trait in particular coursed through the group: an endless capacity to deal with rejection and embarrassment. It's why there are so few crashers in this megalopolis of millions who could also be joining in the fun. Very few people can handle walking through strange kitchens, affecting odd personas, crawling through bushes, or having a ready quip when that poke in the back ribs inevitably comes.

I reflected on my own background, growing up in Los Angeles with a loving but disciplinarian British father. He'd attended harsh English boarding schools that lived by the ethos "spare the rod, spoil the child," and he enforced a similar regimen in our home. Proper dining table habits were strictly imposed, loose vernacular quickly countered, and dress codes ruthlessly required. His highbrow sensibilities, however, couldn't compete against my hang-loose Southern California surfer-dude culture, and I rebelled early. By age ten, I was giving away free film tickets to friends in exchange for the thrill of sneaking in the back door of the local movie theater. In high school I was already hunting for mansion parties in the Hollywood Hills that were figuratively and literally far from my household—places I didn't belong. I reflexively became a petty, thrill-seeking rule-breaker with an antiauthoritarian streak. It took me a few counseling sessions to realize that many of my adrenaline-fueled capers were an attempt to exorcise the challenges of my childhood. Or was I just trying to connect with other humanoids?

Again, as I looked around at my fellow rascals, I thought of Hollywood (and Los Angeles generally) as a place for people seeking a new identity and second lives. Many of them were domestic immigrants, ambitious and hardworking with something to prove. In L.A.

there is always a huge churn of itinerant characters seeking to "fake it until you make it," an apt civic motto for the place. Pervasive lying is a historical foundation of the entertainment industry. What better locale for a dysfunctional, socially ambitious group of career-striving gatecrashers than a city that thrives on fantasy and misrepresentation?

Sometimes I'd pointedly question my fellow charlatans about their subterranean activities. I always got a chuckle at their excuses, which hardly measured up to all the free booze and food consumed, but admittedly had a weird utility:

- "This party would have been a dud if we weren't here to light little social bonfires everywhere and get this place hopping."
- "The food at the end of the night usually ends up in the trash anyway—mother always used to say 'Waste not, want not.'"
- "The public relations people always compliment me when they see me. If I'm in attendance, they know it's a happening party and they've done a good job spreading the word."
- "We're definitely not any kind of security risk. We actually *enhance* security by knowing the ropes and quickly spotting those who don't look familiar and could actually be dangerous."
- "I'm trained in CPR, and believe me, I've helped revive many an older gentleman after a cardiac face-plant at these events. Do you think I ever get any thanks for that?"
- "Hey, I'm not hurting anyone. I've worked for years as a teacher helping kids for meager wages. I'm just getting a little payback down here before I visit that big classroom in the sky."
- "I'm just a social influencer—spreading the word on what's hot and what's not. I'm a barometer of good times, a bellwether of plenteousness, a weather vane for the gravy train."

And, of course, Dr. Al "Meat Hoarder" Barrios always had a canine-related excuse: "My ailing dog would be dead if I didn't nurse him with all this prime rib. I'm here to help *him!*"

3

EARLY DAYS—PITFALLS AND PRATFALLS

AS I SLOWLY worked myself into the Hollywood party-crash network, I became more acclimated to my surroundings and attuned to indicators of potential events.

A parking lot packed with black limousines and SUVs was always worth quickly pulling over my car and taking a gander. A cluster of L.A. County Sheriff deputies staking out intersections around a known party venue was as well. A bunch of catering trucks backing up to the dock of a building would always set off a Pavlovian response—I'd salivate and my stomach would begin to growl. Clumps of wannabes and rubberneckers clutching pens and others wearing trade-press credentials usually indicated a celebrity affair. A hovering helicopter was a sign of the same. (However, a circling helicopter with a roving searchlight usually indicated a hunt for a runaway felon, rogue crasher, or the beginning of a freeway car chase soon to be on live television.)

I quickly developed an "edifice complex." I couldn't look at a building without considering the exits and easements, the fire stairwells and back doors, the low-slung balconies and surrounding shrubbery. Was a janitor's door ajar? Were there any ramps down to the basement? Did a grate block access to the underground parking garage? Every building became a stimulating challenge, a Rubik's Cube of visual toggling for potential entry and escape.

By midday, in the midst of my sporadic freelance writing schedule, I'd usually start checking my incoming e-mail for the Master List. I'd roam the online event sites such as masterplanneronline.com, timeout. com, laguestlist.com, laartparty.com, or guestofaguest.com. By late afternoon I'd start making calls to other crashers to exchange initial findings and party info.

At this point, Barton Whitaker was a key locus of incoming details. We sometimes called him "the Master." He had press agents, event organizers, caterers, and even security feeding him information throughout the day. Barton also had his minions driving all over the Southland in the course of their daily routines, phoning in salient sightings.

For crashers, intel was the coin of the realm. Doing a little research and picking out a few nuggets of data allowed one to begin bartering with other crashers for their findings as day rolled into night.

At times I was flabbergasted by the scope and detail of the circulating information. Once I got an e-mail copy of an invitation for a sit-down dinner at a Hollywood executive's mansion in Bel Air. The item came with the host's name, an address, the time, the menu, expected attire, list of attendees, parking instructions, and the five-digit punch code at the thirty-foot-high hedge gate. A couple of crashers I knew followed the detailed directions up to the hilltop manor, dialed in the gate code, and drove up the corkscrew driveway. They parked, swept in through the foyer, and were greeted by penguin-suited butlers offering them Veuve Clicquot Brut. After making homespun conversation with other guests, they were led into the large dining room for a festive multicourse dinner with one hundred other seated Hollywood notables. They ended the night sharing cigars and cognac with the by-now-inebriated host.

Another tip sheet was for an education fundraiser on someone's Beverly Hills back lawn. Meryl Streep was advertised as providing the entertainment. Once in, I was treated to Streep singing in pitch-perfect harmony with singer Melissa Etheridge. She next regaled us with some hilarious political jokes and several impressions of other celebrities.

One e-mail missive gave detailed instructions for penetrating the Pacific Design Center, the host venue for HBO's Emmy Awards after-party in West Hollywood. The instructions said to enter Wolfgang Puck's latest restaurant Red Seven in the Green Building, find an adjoining freight tunnel to the Blue Building, and look for the fire stairwell up to the second-floor party.

Sometimes the directives were horrifically off, and more than a few times I ended up below ground stuck in an endless rabbit warren of tunnels, freight elevators, and smoke-filled security offices. Occasionally I'd duck into fire stairwells and be locked in—none of the doors back to civilization would open. Thank goodness for my mobile Batphone. I'd call my party brethren already in the event and start squawking for help while directing them to a specific door to push open. Amid the haze of noise, anxiety, and alcohol, the rescue attempts could take over an hour.

If only the L.A. Fire Department really knew how many buildings had locked exits. I pictured a future celebrity-packed event after a mega-earthquake, a North Korean nuke strike, or an accidental fire with a rush of penguin-attired attendees, wine glasses in hand, pinballing throughout a maze of blocked exits. It would make the Triangle Shirtwaist factory fire in New York City look like a picnic.

For safety purposes, I also soon sniffed out the crashers that trafficked in false info and celebrity hype and put them on my alarm-bell list.

"PEPPER" GRABINSKI was one crasher notorious for inflating his knowledge of impending events. In his midthirties, he was a burly, animated dude with tousled prematurely gray hair and a savant-like personality. Blessed with a supernatural memory, wildly imaginative trespassing tactics, and a repository of infinite details of parties past, he seemed to know everybody of note—invitees and the self-invited. He was a gregarious Mike Ditka look-alike from Chicago who talked in a rapid-fire Rodney Dangerfield patter and habitually approached every woman at events with bizarre, generic come-ons.

"Hey, hey, don't I know you from high school?" "Didn't I meet you at the beach one time?" and "Was that you rollerblading down in Venice the other day?" were just some of his special salutations.

I never knew if Pepper was his real name but assumed it came from his manic energy rather than his salt-and-pepper tresses. We never saw him with a date. He was always alone and at the next event would begin another cycle of bird-dogging.

It was rumored that he lived on Supplemental Security Income, stayed up all night, and slept all day. His phone calls usually began around 9 PM and commenced with a flurry of questions: "Where are you? What's the wristband? Any food? Easy entry? What's the security company? What's the hot women quotient?"

In my first few conversations with him, I'd pour out all my information, expertly culled over previous hours. Then I'd ask for reciprocal details. Pepper would respond with a list of "potentials" that he'd heard about. A trampoline party in the Hollywood Hills with loads of bouncing unemployed actresses, a mansion bash in Brentwood, actor Christian Slater's birthday blowout.

But Pepper rarely had any addresses. He'd know soon from his special "inside" sources and would quickly advise. I'd never hear from him again until the next day when he'd regale me with "outrageous, unbelievable, over-the-top" soirees that he'd attended the night before.

"Hey, I don't know what happened. I was up in a dead-cell area and couldn't call out," he'd yawp. "But you should have called me back earlier, when I was in the lowlands. I would have lit you up with all the info."

"But Pepper, I thought *you* were the one supposed to call me back once you had the info," I'd yell back. "I never heard from you."

"All right, all right, next time. Let's move on," Pepper would say. "What's on for tonight?"

Pepper was also an expert practitioner of the "crash-test dummy" technique, a rampant ploy among crafty crashers.

"Hey, I've got this amazing tip for a party up in the Malibu Hills," he'd say. "It's a fundraiser for a private middle school. Brad Pitt will be there. Sting will be playing acoustic guitar. It's on Valmere Drive just off Corral Canyon. Starts at 7 PM. But you better get up there soon. These Malibu family types are in bed by 10 PM and it's a school night. Just call me when you arrive."

The early nature of this call (late afternoon) should have set off my alarm bells. At this time, Pepper was usually in a deep state of horizontal slumber. But maybe he couldn't sleep, his phone was beeping, his alarm clock went off accidently, or he had an outbreak of diaper rash.

Being a novice crasher at the time, I'd lapped up the information like an eager puppy and began girding for a tumultuous night. I plotted out the coordinates, called a willing crash buddy, and off we went, northward from Santa Monica.

After an hour of stop-and-go traffic on the Pacific Coast Highway, we finally turned up Corral Canyon Road and after twenty minutes of squiggly routes turned into Valmere Drive, a dead-end cul-de-sac. There were no cars on the street, no valet parkers, and no sign of any party. I got out of the car and tried to listen for Sting's acoustic strumming. I looked for balloons, some disheveled paparazzi, or catering trucks. Nothing. Dead silence. A flock of seagulls swooped overhead and carpet-bombed my car with a few well-placed viscous payloads.

I finally realized that Pepper had turned me into a "crash-test dummy." He knew his tip came from a dubious source, but it was detailed enough to warrant a reconnaissance mission. He certainly wasn't going to do it himself. Better to find a rookie and launch him into the canyons of Malibu.

Other times he'd call from an ostensibly raging party with the actual address.

"Hey I'm up on Clear View Drive just off Benedict Canyon in Beverly Hills—you should get up here. It's a mind-blowing scene. You'd love it," he'd squawk.

I'd drop all duties and rush up there. The party was indeed huge, with cars lining the streets and valet parkers scurrying up and down the hillside. But security looked unbreachable and cops were everywhere. My phone would ring.

"Hey, what do you think of the party?" asked Pepper.

"I don't know, I can't get in," I'd say.

"Why can't you get in? What's the problem?"

More pointed questions would follow, and I'd realize Pepper wasn't even at the party. He'd launched me on yet another reconnaissance assignment.

After a couple of these dead-end moon shots I became wary of Pepper's far-flung propositions. Despite his antics, I continued taking his calls—and even grew to enjoy his company—because he was a singular and entertaining character, even when leading me astray.

Besides navigating a growing cadre of such oddball personalities on the crasher circuit, I'd also had my share of early party pratfalls.

Once I was driving in the early evening along fashionable Melrose Avenue in East Hollywood. I noticed a line of people outside what looked like a new and hip eatery. I took a quick turn on two wheels and ditched my car on a side street. I crept up an adjacent alley and found the back entrance. A steady stream of workers shuttled large trays of food in and out the kitchen's back door. I grabbed a spare tray and followed them. There was no security, and I waltzed in.

On entering the main dining area, I noticed the clientele seemed a bit downtrodden. The servers were stirring some incomprehensible goop in large metal buckets. The interior was dun-colored, filled with fold-up tables, and the dining utensils were plastic. I stood and surveyed the whole scene. It was a soup kitchen.

On another occasion, I got tipped off about a food festival with some local chefs around the pool and cabanas at the swank beachside Viceroy hotel in Santa Monica. The front entrance had a red carpet and crisscrossing searchlights, and various denizens were parading back and forth having their pictures taken. (I always marvel at the movie-themed backdrop of many L.A. events that have nothing to do with the film industry.) A phalanx of thick-necked security personnel lined the entryway, many with ear wires, talking into their shoulders.

I thought I'd take the path of least resistance and head for the Achilles heel of all buildings: the side-door kitchen entrance. As predicted, the door was ajar. I dove in and almost knocked over a young busboy carrying multiple trays of plates and glasses. I shot into a small hallway and ended up in the employee locker room. With rising panic I bolted back into the kitchen and, wild-eyed, tried to get my bearings. Conversation stopped, and I was met by dozens of raised eyebrows. I felt a hot gaze on my neck and turned around to face an officious-looking manager who had a stern "WTF?" look. Mercifully, I saw a waiter heading to the pool. I whipped out my cell phone and pretended that my daughter was urgently calling. (I have a niece but no daughter.) I put my head down and pushed ahead.

The event was a direct hit—multiple serving stations of savory delicacies, fully loaded bars, and clusters of attractive guests.

I rushed the nearest bartender and ordered a double Absolut vodka tonic to calm the jitters. As I began tippling, I looked around. I saw a couple of other crashers who gave me quick nods. Everything was in order. Nary a waiter or manager gave me a second look. Though much of the consumption is free, crashing always comes with a price in the form of massive surges of anxiety. I finally began to unwind and found a nice viewing spot poolside.

I got a tap on the shoulder and a quick nudge to my spine. I whirled and faced two burly bouncers. They fixed me with fierce but quizzical expressions.

"Why did you come through the kitchen, sir?" one asked.

I quickly answered that I was returning from a short smoke outside and it was the quickest way back in.

"Well, you didn't need to slither through there. You could have come through the front entrance. This is a promotional party, and it's open to the public."

Another time I'd heard about an opening night for the Hollywood Black Film Festival that often included motion pictures with African themes. I always loved attending movie premieres during opening night of film festivals, of which there were dozens in L.A. annually: the Israel Film Festival, the Scandinavian Film Festival, the Outfest Los Angeles LGBTQ Film Festival, the HollyShorts Film Festival, the Red Nation Film Festival, the Shriekfest Film Festival, the Asian Pacific Film Festival, etc., etc.

My brother-in-law, Sidibe, was from Ivory Coast in West Africa and had a dazzling wardrobe of dashiki attire complete with boxy head wraps. I convinced him to lend me a multicolored, intricately patterned, head-to-toe outfit that conferred regal splendor.

I went over to his apartment in Venice, and he helped button me up. It was a tight fit due to my middle-aged gut, thickening from the rich buffet gastronomy I'd been consuming at social functions.

(Sidibe was always in great physical shape.) I instantly popped a few buttons like hot kernels in a popcorn machine.

"I don't know if theeeeees is such a good idea—my mother used to say 'a pretty basket does not prevent worries,'" said Sidibe in his rich West African accent.

And this pretty basket was creating worries by the boatload. I looked like a basket case. But I loved costumes and always found an excuse to dress up for all occasions. If I had my druthers, Halloween would be every night.

I asked Sidibe to join me, but he demurred. I had previously brought him along on a few escapades, and the result was always the same. While my chubby white brethren gorged at the buffet tables, pounded free tequila shots, laughed uproariously, or stole gift bags, security personnel rarely confronted them. With Sidibe, whose blackness was equatorial, security *always* made a beeline for him. I noticed the same result with his son. It was a real eye opener. Anyone who argues that black males in America get the same attention as white folk from security and law enforcement is clueless. It's the main reason there are few black party crashers. A prison term because of a free dinner is just not worth the risk.

I sucked in my gut and held my breath as Sidibe finished lacing me up. I left his apartment shoehorned into the dashiki and barely able to move but felt undaunted as I plunged into the night's festivities.

I was supposed to meet Avi Fisher outside the theater where the opening movie was to be shown. But like virtually every night in L.A., I immediately ran into massive traffic on the 10 Freeway heading east and told Avi to head in without me.

I was thirty minutes late by the time I arrived and wondered if my outfit would look conspicuous as I strode through an empty lobby.

A super friendly Nigerian greeted me at the entrance. He was quite taken with my regalia, and without even asking for a ticket led me to a seat in the darkened theater.

It was a two-hour South African feature film called *Winnie Mandela* that starred Jennifer Hudson and chronicled the famous political activist's childhood through her marriage and her husband Nelson Mandela's incarceration.

It was an engrossing drama, and as the lights came up I looked around. I was virtually the only white person in the audience and one of the few attendees wearing dashiki. To my relief, both African Americans and Africans greeted me like a long-lost brother in the lobby.

"Hey man, you on it. Keep the energy going," said one attendee who might have been Jamie Foxx.

"A magnificent presentation," said a regal Senegalese gentleman, though I didn't know if he meant the movie or me.

Movie premieres and related after-parties are always tricky occasions. Once, after an independent feature screening at Hollywood's Cinerama Dome, I followed the crowd to a nearby club for the usual food and boozefest. Swag is always a big topic of interest at film after-parties, and as I walked into the club I noticed there wasn't the usual pile of gift bags near the entrance. A woman guest, anxious at the lack of bounty, peppered the organizers for the reasons why. She was told in confidence that the bags would shortly be delivered and to be patient.

The party turned out to be a desultory affair, and I wandered outside the venue on Sunset Boulevard to catch some air and plan my next move. Suddenly a large pickup truck arrived piled high with blue gift bags firmly secured by tethered ropes and a tarp. The tarp was peeled off, ropes unfastened, and two employees began shuttling the bags into the party. The bags formed a ten-foot-high pyramid in the back of the truck and looked packed with all kinds of goodies. The woman with the swag fetish appeared again and asked if I could reach up and nab a couple of bags from the top of the pyramid.

I stretched out my six-foot-three frame but couldn't grasp the top bounty. The clock was ticking, so I started pulling a couple of bags from the pyramid's midsection. I tugged and tugged and pulled them loose. There was an ominous pause, and suddenly the whole contraption collapsed, catapulting hundreds of swag bags into the middle of Sunset Boulevard. Scores of pink discs filled with skin cream pinwheeled down the street, visors flew through the air, lipstick cases clattered across the ground, and perfume bottles shattered on the pavement.

Cars swerved to avoid the mayhem. Honking, yelling, and finger-pointing ensued. I tried to pick up the contraband and chuck some of it into the back of the truck, but the dam had broken.

"You bonehead—what the hell did you just do?" screeched one of the returning bag men.

"I'm sorry, I just wanted to quickly grab a bag before leaving," I sputtered.

"Well don't just stand there, do something courageous, like block the intersection until we get some assistance," said my antagonist.

I cantered to the middle of the road and began directing traffic. Soon police arrived and took over the proceedings. A stern, badge- and baton-wielding Mustache Bob interrogated me. He was trying to nail me on a theft charge, but the woman whose request for my assistance started it all came to my aid and testified that I'd tried to help, hadn't run, and just made a stupid mistake.

The cop let me go, and as I was leaving, one of the organizers offered me an intact gift bag. I declined and have since lost (most) interest in swag.

4

REALITY TV INTERLUDE

———

DESPITE MY EARLY INTERLOPER MISHAPS, I began accumulating significant skills, tactics, and knowledge about all aspects of gatecrashing. I was making new friends and influencing people, taking names and numbers, even starting to date again.

I comfortably cycled into the crasher network with its steady schedule of events throughout the year—awards shows in the early months, wine and food festivals throughout the spring, environmental fundraisers in summer, and then the holiday season with its hundreds of corporate parties and private shindigs.

As my journalism career hit the skids, I transferred my skills— investigating, researching, writing, and storytelling—into another field. I got hired as a writer/director on a nonfiction crime series, *Anatomy of Crime*, for Court TV, a cable television network. I produced episodes on animal smuggling, illegal vs. legal prostitution, murder for hire, and chronic criminals.

Soon after, I started writing and directing television documentaries on a variety of subjects for different cable networks such as the History, Discovery, and Travel Channels. I bunked underwater in the

North Atlantic for a show on nuclear submarines, followed a group of fighters in Russia for a program on mixed-martial arts, and delved into the history of cryptography and the breaking of the German Enigma code in World War II.

Around the year 2000, the *Survivor* series hit the airwaves and significantly changed television. Many narrative scripted programs, typical fare for the broadcast networks, often cost upward of $4 million

Adrian with Curly Neal while directing a Harlem Globetrotters documentary.

per one-hour episode. Now a big broadcast channel could produce a nonfiction "reality" show with high ratings for as little as $300,000 per hour.

I had an idea to create a reality program called *Dead Ringers* that would follow a group of celebrity look-alikes in a race across America. With no money, identification, or means of transportation, they would use their appearance and ostensible celebrity to rely on the help of star-struck strangers to cross the country. The finale would involve crashing a huge awards show in Hollywood.

I thought the perfect partner to help produce the show was Avi Fisher. With our storytelling and event-crasher skills, we'd be the perfect muses for a group of celebrity look-alikes performing multiple stunts of subterfuge. The program would reveal the essence of America's obsession with celebrity and illustrate the twisted, magnetic, mass adoration it elicits from millions of people.

To achieve our goal, *Dead Ringers* would employ six near-perfect celebrity look-alikes of such stars as Billy Bob Thornton, Tiger Woods, Tom Cruise, Beyoncé, Martha Stewart, and Whoopi Goldberg. We'd pair each of them with a talented but little-known comedian. Then we'd launch these dynamic duos on a race over a cross-country competitive obstacle course—think *Amazing Race* with celebrity impersonators—each with a comic "handler."

Dead Ringers would illustrate how superstars live separate lives from you and me. How they receive special treatment at restaurants, car dealerships, and sports arenas. How they can pick and choose lovers with the flick of a finger. How the public will do anything to accommodate their needs. How they are today's modern royalty.

We envisioned each twosome beginning their journey on the East Coast, then stopping at varied cultural hubs across the country where they'd complete several "celebrity-driven" tasks, obstacles, and capers for points before they moved on to the next destination.

At various venues, the teams might convince a group of local construction workers to watch a ballet, persuade a group of red-state conservatives to henna-tattoo "Hillary Clinton for President" on their foreheads, get a group of Nebraska beef farmers to join a vegetarian group, or get a pair of nuns in Louisiana to go hunting. Maybe a barefoot Tiger Woods doppelganger would approach a group of golfers at an Illinois country club and ask to borrow their spiked shoes for a shared round.

The two teams with the most points upon arrival in Hollywood would then compete to make the biggest crasher splash at an upcoming Hollywood movie premiere. Maybe that meant getting dropped off by helicopter. Or jumping out of a limousine with scores of Radio City Rockettes or walking up the red carpet with twenty friends in tow.

To pitch any television show in Hollywood, one first must produce a four- or five-minute sizzle reel showing the concept, characters, and a sample plotline.

I found a celebrity look-alike agency in L.A., called Mirror Images, run by an eccentric British expatriate woman with the Dickensian name of Dot Findlater. More than any other culture, the British have a fascination with all things celebrity. The assorted hijinks of even the most B-level actor in Hollywood are often splashed across the front page of the London tabloids, especially if it has anything to do with sex, the naughtier the better.

As a reporter for the *L.A. Times* I remember the scramble to cover the Hugh Grant fiasco when he was caught in flagrante delicto with paramour Divine Brown in his rental car off Sunset Boulevard. My sister was in London at the time and called nightly to report the latest tabloid headline. My favorite, after Grant was released from the pokey, was HUGH HURRIES HOME TO HURLEY. (His girlfriend at the time was supermodel Elizabeth Hurley.)

Dot had more than fifteen hundred famous look-alikes under her stewardship, ranging from politicians like Dick Cheney and Hillary Clinton to actors such as Brad Pitt and Angelina Jolie, to generals like Colin Powell and George Patton. She even had a "Live Ken Doll." Her Mirror Images agency booked the look-alikes for stints at business conventions, holiday parties, college graduations, and extra work in Hollywood productions.

She invited Avi and me up to her Hollywood abode to meet a few of her recruits to cast in our promo reel. As we approached her place, we saw "Tiger Woods" ducking in, wearing a red shirt and a black golf hat with the Nike swoosh. Dot greeted us at the door and led us into her living room. Seated around a table were duplicates of Justin Timberlake, George Clooney, Kenny Rogers, Julia Roberts, and of course, Tiger.

We did a quintuple take. It was surreal to have all these illustrious visages staring up at us, anxious to meet us, and hanging on our every word. We explained our idea for the show and outlined some potential plotlines for our sizzle reel. Maybe we'd film Julia Roberts walking into a high-end eatery and demand a back section be cleared out for her and a few friends. Or capture Kenny Rogers trying to collect tips at the Venice Beach Boardwalk before he even started singing. Or follow George Clooney asking a bystander on an L.A. street to help change the tire on his car. We left our "celebrity" meeting in a state of high excitement.

A few days later Dot called and said one of her best celebrity clones, a Steven Seagal dead ringer, was arriving in town from Texas for the weekend. The Golden Globe Awards were coming up that Sunday evening, and maybe we could hatch a caper where our Seagal twin attended the illustrious awards ceremony?

5

GOLDEN GLOBES PREP

THE GOLDEN GLOBE AWARDS kick off the Hollywood awards season in early January. The ceremony is one of Tinseltown's biggest marketing events, playing to millions of television viewers. The coveted awards are decided by only ninety-three members of the Hollywood Foreign Press Association, but they are often a reliable predictor of winners in subsequent entertainment awards shows like the Oscars.

The Golden Globes are held each year in the International Ballroom at the Beverly Hilton hotel, a Lego-looking structure with an L-shaped facade. The venue was founded by hotel magnate Conrad Hilton in 1955 and is located at the corner of Wilshire and Santa Monica Boulevards in Beverly Hills.

For party crashers, the Golden Globe Awards at the Beverly Hilton is the pinnacle event of the year. As the lead-up week to the ceremony unfolds, numerous high-fashion companies showcase their wares in amply stocked "gifting suites," where celebrities arrive to be showered with free goods and services. Klepto-crashers with sticky fingers aren't far behind.

I've seen many crasher scalawags kneeling in a massage chair in an enormous suite, their necks covered in peanut oil while getting a lubricious complimentary rubdown. Others walk the hallways with gift bags the size of truck tires stuffed with every conceivable cosmetic and fashion accessory hanging crisscross their chests like ammunition-wielding bandoleros.

Most of Hollywood's other big award shows, like the Grammys, Emmys, and Oscars, end with the invitees fleeing the host theaters for after-parties scattered all over town. But the Golden Globes is different. It's a laid-back affair with hundreds of movie and television celebrities feted at a sit-down dinner at tables spread over the International Ballroom. The food and wine flows freely, and after an orgy of self-congratulations lasting several hours, the attendees drunkenly spill out to innumerable after-parties right at the hotel. HBO usually hosts a rowdy affair by the pool. *InStyle* magazine takes over an adjoining ballroom. The Weinstein Company often set up a large circus tent just outside the hotel's western entrance. There is no need to go anywhere else.

From a party-crashing standpoint, the concentration of events in one venue is a big attraction. But we also planned to film our Steven Seagal look-alike crashing the Golden Globes for the sizzle reel. The whole operation became a movie within a movie—we not only had to crash the party ourselves but do so as a production crew filming our fake Seagal.

When Dot Findlater showed us her Steven Seagal clone in a series of formal headshots, we did a double take. This was our guy. The resemblance was astounding—the same jet-black hair complete with mini-pony tail; the furrowed brow and laconic scowl; the duplicate jawline and tough-guy smirk; his six-foot-three height and rangy frame. He was Damon Aper, a former Navy Seal who lived in Texas.

Damon Aper as Steven Seagal. *Courtesy of Damon Aper*

Dot told us Damon often got approached and plied for his autograph wherever he went. He was a big hit whenever he visited friends on military bases and was constantly asked for martial arts advice in the commissary. Damon realized he had something and began working on Seagal's speech and mannerisms. Maybe he'd find an interesting sideline in Hollywood as a look-alike or even body double.

He eventually found Dot's Mirror Images agency online, and she immediately signed him up. At one point, the real Seagal came calling, or at least his manager did. Damon was whisked up to a Beverly Hills mansion and kept waiting for several hours. Finally Seagal appeared with his manager in tow, greeted Damon gruffly and gave him the once-over. After a few pleasantries, some general questions, and a mention of possible extra work, Seagal looked at his manager and said, "Please inform the gentleman that he's excused."

Damon was led out, swearing he'd had it with Steven Seagal. But due to Dot's entreaties, Damon kept at it, performing a few comic gigs and appearing at several conventions. He eventually agreed to participate in our sizzle reel and partner in our Golden Globes caper with the lure of our *Dead Ringers* reality show.

We picked him up at Los Angeles International Airport on a Friday night, forty-eight hours before the big show. He was more thickly built in person than Seagal and talked with a heavy Texas twang. But when prompted he quickly transformed his voice and peppered us with his favorite Seagalisms:

"The jury presided. I decided."

"You've got five seconds . . . and three are up."

"I'm just gonna reach out and touch somebody."

"This is your captor speaking."

In our sizzle reel, we wanted to show the power of celebrity and the affect it has on even the most normal people. We got our camera crew and did a practice run the next night by bringing Damon to Grauman's Chinese Theater on Hollywood Boulevard. It was early evening, and the place was packed with Midwesterners and international tourists placing their hands in the famous celebrity hand and foot imprints outside the theater. We parked in a nearby alley behind a delicatessen. Then, with camera crew in tow, started trailing Damon, who wore a Zen monk meditation outfit.

"Oh my God, it's Steven Seagal!" screamed one hefty matron.

"It's him! It's him!" squawked another dazed fan. "He's handsomer in real life!"

"Can I just get a quick signature?" blurted out a John Wayne look-alike who temporarily forgot his own act.

Damon Aper as Steven Seagal in aikido mode. *Donna Eccleston*

At first, we moved easily through the circus-like throng filled with jugglers, panhandlers, and the growing group of rubbernecking tourists. Damon stopped and started signing autographs. Soon he was caught in a crush that pushed him back against the front of a retail store. Our furry boom mike snapped off, our cameraman got jostled and separated from our soundman, and we lost our backpack filled with batteries.

I looked up the street, and people were running toward us. Cars screeched to a halt. Our camera crew operations and use of bright lights enhanced the atmosphere of a visiting celebrity and escalated the pandemonium.

"OK, guys, we've got to stop this and get the hell out of here right now," said Damon to us as he switched to his Texas twang, temporarily befuddling some of his fans that were thrusting pens in his face.

"Hey, hey, it's not really Steven Seagal. We're filming an impersonator," I yelled to the growing mob as I took an impromptu perch on a fire hydrant. "Just give him some space and let him go."

"Yeah right," said a burly construction worker sarcastically. "I've watched all his movies, and I'm damn sure it's him. I *know* it's him!"

We all quickly regrouped, formed a wedge, and with Damon leading the way in Navy Seal mode, pushed our way out of the crowd. We flagged a taxi, jammed Damon and our broken equipment inside, and fled the havoc. I reached for my inhaler and noticed everyone was also frazzled.

After ten minutes of aimless driving, we did a stealth return to our parked car.

Despite the fracas (or because of it) we realized we had captured something real, about celebrity and fame and the insatiable needs of the madding crowd. It was fascinating but horrific. We were convinced we had a reality show.

We decided to start the big day by filming Damon at a West L.A. tuxedo shop getting outfitted for the nighttime awards. With our comic handler Brian Palermo leading the way and running interference for Damon, we followed the duo into the store.

The sight of a full camera crew with a burst of lights, sound, and action suddenly appearing in the establishment, along with the imposing visage of a lumbering Seagal, quickly stopped all conversation. It was a 10 AM alarm clock.

"Is there a manager here?" barked Brian. "We need to talk to a manager now!"

An unassuming and gracious middle-aged Filipino man stepped up and asked how he could help.

"Seagal, Steven here, needs a complimentary loaner outfit for the Golden Globe Awards tonight, and we're wondering if you can accommodate him?" asked Brian solicitously.

"We'd be honored to help out and get Mr. Seagal ready for the show tonight," said the manager.

"That's great, thank you," said Brian. "We're also wondering if you can clear everyone out from the back of the store just to give Mr. Seagal some privacy."

The manager assented, and several half-dressed clients began stumbling in a state of disarray as they were herded up to the front store window to finish dressing in bright sunshine.

About a half dozen store employees soon clustered around Damon and began tending to him like a crew of paramedics. Out came vests, jackets with satin facings, pants, shoes, bow ties, cummerbunds, pocket squares, and suspenders. One outfit was all silver and black and made Damon look like an avenging Oakland Raiders middle linebacker. Another had a pink theme with a purple bowtie that clashed with the Seagal scowl and made him look like an Oscar Wilde dandy. Eventually Damon decided to go all black, full ninja, with a shawl lapel and double-breasted jacket.

"If he wears simple black, people will instantly get his violent complexity," said Brian helpfully. Everyone in the group nodded vigorously.

We finally had our Seagal wardrobe. There were no requests for identification, a signature, collateral, or payment. There was a request for a picture of the store manager with Seagal in full regalia. We all walked out of the retailer with promises to return the formal garb within two or three days.

"Hey Steven, don't forget to wear those special socks," yelled the manager at the front door as our group headed up the sidewalk.

On our return to the crew van, we all whooped it up. We couldn't believe how easy it was for Damon, just because of his famous looks, to have his needs so instantly met. People bowed before him. With a nod of his head or an arched eyebrow, civilians instantly scattered to attend to his every want. We believed these reactions of normal people would give a deeper meaning to our show than just our series of silly stunts and capers.

Our next stop was a high-end car dealership, Online Motors, in midtown L.A. It had a huge lot filled with Porsche, Lexus, and Mercedes models. The Persian manager, Andre, hustled toward our crew as cameras rolled. He almost prostrated himself on the asphalt before Damon.

Seagal's comic body man led off with his typical pointed introduction. "Hi, I'm Brian. I work with Steven, and we're going to a big event tonight and we're looking for a car loaner," he said confidently, as Seagal absentmindedly perused the lot. "Steven won't drive a silver car, so all silver is out. It's got to be a mixture of black and white . . . goes with the ying and yang of Buddhism."

Andre ate up the verbal gobbledygook like catnip and scampered around the lot, breathlessly pointing out different models. After a few minutes, Brian indicated Steven wanted to check some luxury vehicles at another dealership, Dream Motorcars, next door.

Andre seemed crestfallen. One of us stopped to interview him after the celebrity crew left.

"When I first saw Seagal and showed him around I felt really good, but when I saw him go elsewhere, I realized I've got to do something really extravagant to bring him back here," said Andre, with growing determination.

Brian and Seagal soon had Amir, the manager at Dream Motorcars, offering them his best model on the lot: a Bentley Continental GT. All three took it out for a spin, with Amir hyping the car's attributes to Seagal while never looking at Brian, despite Brian's incessant questions about the auto.

"Is it environmentally friendly?" was Seagal's only query at the end of the ride.

"Without a doubt," said Amir.

On returning to the lot, Andre was blocking his rival's entrance, shifting from foot to foot in a state of excitement. He'd apparently made many phone calls and had a special $350,000 Lamborghini delivered to his dealership for Seagal's perusal. Could Seagal just come take a quick look? Amir gave Andre a baleful stare, and I thought the two might come to blows—a full-blown Persian catfight in the middle of La Cienega Boulevard.

"Normally we don't even let people sit in this car," said Andre as Seagal shifted his heft into the driver's seat and Brian plopped down into the front passenger spot. "I'm a little worried, but because it's Steven Seagal, I can deal with that worry."

Brian and Seagal peeled out with tires shrieking, engine revving and rooftop down for a quick test run. They were back within minutes.

"This is the one I want for the Globes tonight," said Seagal, looking at Brian.

"This is the one Steven wants for the Globes tonight," said Brian to Andre.

Our duo soon drove off in an Italian sports car worth hundreds of thousands of dollars with no down payment other than a short wave from Seagal. Again, there was no paperwork, no driver's license, no signature, no photo identification—just a verbal promise from a counterfeit celebrity that the car would be returned the next day, after the awards show. It was astounding to think that this opulent convertible could be across the Mexican border within three hours, out of Andre's grasp, without a trace, forever.

6

THE GOLDEN GLOBE AWARDS

———

W E ALL RECONVENED at my ramshackle apartment in Santa Monica for a final tune-up before the awards show. With the Lamborghini purring in the alley behind my building, we brought Damon inside and got him dressed up in his all-black tuxedo.

I noticed Damon's apprehension as he entered my dingy flat. Could this be the home of a successful television producer? Due to our frenetic production schedule, I hadn't exactly primed my place. Newspapers were piled high. Dirty T-shirts were flung about. Yesterday's underwear hung from a lamp. My television was on the blink. The carpets were pockmarked with coffee stains and needed a vacuum.

As Damon took in the scene I could see him wondering if his potential arrest for a short television promotion reel was really worth it. Who were these "producers"? The Golden Globes Awards show was one of Hollywood's biggest nights with security like Fort Knox, and here he was about to change into his Armani tux in a bathroom with no toilet lid.

We tried giving Damon some quick instructions.

"You have to believe you're Steven Seagal. That's the only way this will work," said Avi grimly.

"Our cameras will follow you, which will enhance your aura of celebrity," I added helpfully. "Feel free to occasionally treat us with some irritation."

"If we get stopped and questioned by security, let us, your handlers do the talking," said Avi. "You're way too important to be bothered with such trifles."

After a few more directives, Damon went into my luxury bathroom to change and transform himself into Seagal.

"He looks poised and calm, but can we stay poised and calm?" I whispered to Avi.

"We're definitely pushing some boundaries here," said Avi. "We're not only crashing one of the highest security events in L.A. but trying to film a whole other plotline with separate moving parts at the same time."

Avi and I were really feeling the pressure. As a backup, I brought in one of my closest friends and colleagues, MARY MUIR, who sat next to me in the newsroom when we were both reporters at the *L.A. Times*. She was absolutely fearless and a rock-solid partner in our upcoming shenanigans.

We had once filmed an episode of *Lockup*, a television series on prisons for MSNBC. I was the director and she was the associate producer. We got caught in a five hundred–inmate riot on the main yard at Corcoran prison, one of the largest penal institutions in California. The guards fired warning shots out of their towers and I hit the ground, eating dirt with all the other inmates sprawled across the facility. When I looked up, I saw Mary, my cameraman, and my soundman, all still standing, dutifully filming the action. Their fearless leader, the director, was groveling on the ground. After that little incident, the guards nicknamed me "Belly Flop."

Mary arrived at my place just as Damon exited the bathroom as Seagal. She did a noticeable double take. With his all-black tux and menacing stare, Seagal was now standing in my living room.

Damon's astonishing superstar resemblance and charisma helped mitigate our collective anxiety at the approaching awards show, and we all dove into the logistics of our escapade in my living room. Damon would drive the Lamborghini to a holding area just outside the Beverly Hilton. Mary, Avi, and I would take my other car, an aging Mercedes 420SL, with all the camera equipment and park at a Starbucks across from the hotel.

I'd already made arrangements with another crasher, ROGER, to provide us with fake lanyards with the NBC logo (the network airing the show) with our pictures on the front. He had his own laminating machine and was a superb graphic artist and Photoshopper/cropper. Those lanyards would only allow us to pierce the multilayered rings of security in the blocks surrounding the hotel and gain access to the media scrum outside the hotel entrance—no farther.

We hopped into our respective vehicles in Santa Monica and drove east up Wilshire Boulevard toward the Beverly Hilton. As we approached, I was astonished at the vastness of the security operation. Snipers roamed the rooftop. The LAPD and L.A. County Sheriff Department were out in force. Since it was only sixteen months after 9/11, Homeland Security and FBI personnel were scattered throughout the venue, many talking into their lapels and wrist mikes. Helicopter propellers slapped overhead. Paramilitary vehicles with battering rams were parked nearby. Media vans and their satellite antennae lined the blocks. Walkie-talkies clattered with incomprehensible jargon. The area seemed under a state of siege.

I wondered how Damon was dealing with all the chaos and suffocating security. I caught his face driving his deluxe wheels in my rearview mirror and gave him a thumbs-up. He seemed superhumanly cool and looked crisp. For a quick moment I thought it might be the real Seagal. He returned my thumbs-up and soon after peeled off Wilshire Boulevard toward his holding area.

Mary, Avi, and I continued driving through the security mayhem, arrived at Starbucks, and quickly ducked into the parking lot. We found a tight spot amid a cluster of black Escalades and parked in front of a sign that proclaimed, DON'T EVEN THINK OF PARKING HERE. A tow service address and phone number was listed in blaring red.

We left Avi to watch our car and equipment, and Mary and I headed into Starbucks. We found Roger holding court at a table in a back corner. A few other frowsy-looking crashers were lined up to pay homage and receive their false credentials. For our group of reprobates, this was the real awards check-in station.

Roger looked harried as he surreptitiously exchanged cash for lanyards with the other infiltrators as they all jabbered furiously. A paramilitary officer walked by on the sidewalk just outside the chest-high window wearing a foliage helmet, oblivious to the haggling within.

"WTF, where have you numbskulls been?" Roger sputtered, shooting me a look of irritation while fiercely gripping his secret suitcase filled with goodies. "You're thirty minutes late. I was just about to sell off these passes for top dollar. Do you know how many crashers want in on this?"

I furtively glanced at my cell phone and noticed that Roger had called and texted me more than a dozen times in the past hour. My ringer was off and amid the chaos I hadn't even looked at my phone.

I quickly apologized and paid him $180 for the three passes, a significant increase from our initial agreement.

We returned to my trusty Benz, unloaded our video production equipment, put on our lanyards, and sallied forth into the first ring of security. Our credentials were closely inspected and we were waved through. We made it up to a check-in table outside the north side of the hotel on Wilshire Boulevard, jammed with invitees waving their tickets and identification.

Our group stood slightly back, and I called Damon with directions to pull up directly in front of us and hand over his prized vehicle to the army of valet parkers.

Avi and I triangulated the spot of his predicted arrival with our two cameras, and within minutes, our faux action hero slid up in the red Lamborghini. He exited the vehicle smoothly and walked up to the check-in line. Mary played handler and, with clipboard in hand, facilitated his entrance beautifully with a hearty "Hey Steven, we've been waiting for you."

Our cameras were all over him, bequeathing a solid mantle of celebrity.

"Hey, hey, you guys have to stop filming. You're being way too aggressive," said an officious, henpecking, public relations hack. "We can't have you hassling our celebrity guests."

"It's OK ma'am, I know these folks. They're solid," said Seagal with a slight nod in our direction. The publicity hack took a stutter step back but kept an eagle eye on us.

Mary went directly to the front of the line.

"I'm handling Mr. Seagal tonight, and we need to get him in now," said Mary to the lead check-in official as she pointed him out a few yards away. At this point, Damon was in full-Seagal mode, legs askance, arms behind his back, and pose relaxed as he looked confidently into the distance.

"Oh jeez, OK, bring him up here and we'll get him right on in," said the official, who abruptly stood up and, without even checking if Seagal was on the list, came around the table and escorted Seagal and Mary up to the metal detector.

"I loved *Above the Law*, Mr. Seagal. You were an animal in that movie," said the official. "Enjoy your night."

Mary and Seagal/Damon were in. But Avi and I needed access, and we'd already raised the hackles of security with our earlier video antics.

Luckily, I'd already arranged an alternative plan with Barton "the Master" Whitaker. Each year Barton and his girlfriend YASMIN rented out a room in the Beverly Hilton for the night of the Globes. They then charged other crashers $60 each to cover the cost of their $500-a-night lodging.

I called Barton and he sent Yasmin down with their two room keys to meet me at another nearby checkpoint. Yasmin gave me a key that I flashed to security, allowing me to walk right into the hotel lobby. Afterward I met Yasmin inside and grabbed her additional key and walked back outside again to give a key to Avi.

Both of us walked back in again using yet another entrance, carrying our camera gear. The lobby swarmed with tuxedoed celebrities, cocktails already in hand. Paramilitary units ran leashed German shepherds through the hallways as we ascended to Barton's room on the fourth floor.

As we opened the door, I encountered about a dozen crashers all stuffed into a medium-sized suite. Bradley Bleat lounged on a bed chomping on chocolate bon bons and reading a hotel brochure. Dr. Al Barrios nibbled on some meaty hors d'oeuvres. Miraculously, Clara Vestergaard was already inside the suite looking around wild-eyed. Pepper Grabinski worked the phone, trying to sweet-talk a woman to come over—he'd get her in!

It looked like a group of low-rent *Ocean's Eleven* conspirators or a bad episode from the television series *Entourage*.

The awards show hadn't started yet, but every few minutes another twosome would shuttle in and out, working the same set of keys that Avi and I had used to get in. Soon Barton's room was standing room only. Bags filled with thousands of multicolored wristbands were strewn all over the floor, along with a rainbow of Sharpie pens, ultraviolet ink stamps, badges, and wigs.

Some crashers worked the lobby for intel on entry points and wristbands for the viewing parties on the hotel's first floor and then called up to the crash room for others to bring down the correct entry items.

The *InStyle* party required a bright pink paper wristband. HBO's was wide neon-green plastic. A large blue ticket was needed to enter the Weinstein Company shindig. All venues were loaded up with alcohol and elaborate food stations.

Once the final details of specific entryways, security personnel deployment, and known public relations hacks hit our fourth-floor romper room, havoc ensued. Crashers frantically dove for the relevant items in their personal stashes and started bartering for others. Screeching sounds of Scotch tape rent the air. Two self-inviters I'd never seen before started a tug of war over a misplaced bag. I'd never seen a group of adults behave so badly. Soon I joined the fray, arguing with another crasher over some previously promised wristbands. If a security officer had opened the door, the drama of our parallel stage play would have topped any during the upcoming awards show. I looked out the window and thought I saw the L.A. County jail's paddy wagon percolating in the hotel's parking lot.

"OK, everybody, listen up. It's go time," shouted Barton, who stood up from his command desk, trying to restore some semblance of order. "The show has just started. Everybody needs to calm down. We can't leave here all at once. We need to head out in waves of two or three people at a time or we're all going to get nailed."

Barton's admonishment brought everyone to attention. The bickering quickly stopped, and people lined up in orderly pairs like a Marine reveille at dawn. About every three minutes a small group began to move out.

Avi and I were juggling our camera equipment and assorted crasher paraphernalia and texting Damon and Mary, who waited for us in the lobby. As we disembarked from the hotel room, I took a quick look back. It looked like a bomb had hit the place, spreading crasher detritus everywhere.

We took an elevator down, packed with Hollywood bigwigs, and connected with Mary and Damon. The *InStyle* viewing party was nearby, and I quickly noted our intel was off. The place was jammed, and the attendees were wearing purple wristbands, not pink. Shite! I puckered up and perspiration again began trickling down the back of my neck.

"Hey, I'll handle this," said Mary, with Seagal-like equipoise. "Just trail Damon and me, and we'll all make it in."

Avi and I flipped on our camera lights and followed Mary and our favorite Navy Seal. Damon and Mary walked right in. We were stopped.

"Sorry, you can't film inside the party," said a guard.

"OK, we'll turn off our cameras now. Sorry about that," I said, as we kept moving. The guard was so overwhelmed with the crush that we walked right in.

Large video screens were posted all around the ballroom airing the live show. Soft background lighting enhanced the diaphanous lavender curtains hanging from the ceiling around the perimeter of the room. Waiters ferried large trays of saffron paella, steelhead trout, and chorizo pappardelle to innumerable food stations. Mary started nibbling on a fist-sized piece of shrimp and quickly drained a glass of Chardonnay. I downed a couple of quick vodka sodas. Meryl Streep accepted an award for best supporting actress on a video screen behind us.

I noticed Damon was a bit hesitant to dive into all the food and drink.

"Are you guys OK with covering all this? It looks like quite an expensive spread," he said.

"No worries, Steven, it's on the house," I replied.

Damon soon had a pyramid of tri-tip on his plate and began wolfing it down like a starving Texas country boy. But he didn't have a drop of liquor. Like a good Navy Seal, he wanted to keep a clear eye on the mission.

"Hey Steven, how are you?" said a short, slightly manic middle-aged guy with spiky, lubed, inky-black hair and an outstretched hand. "I haven't seen you in ages."

For an instant, Damon looked like a space alien had approached him. But he quickly recovered and engaged in breezy banter with the stranger.

It was Brian Grazer, one of the biggest movie and television producers in Hollywood.

After a few more moments of Hollywood palaver, Grazer gave Damon a hug and expressed hope they could work together in the future.

"Who the fuck was that?" asked Damon.

"Just one of the biggest moguls in Hollywood," I replied.

"Damn, should I go back and get his card?" asked Damon.

"No, just focus on the lobster," said Avi.

For the next couple of hours we watched an endless parade of celebrities accept their awards on the big screens—Richard Gere as best actor in *Chicago*, Nicole Kidman as best actress in *The Hours*, Martin Scorsese for best director for *Gangs of New York*. Jack Nicholson ducked into the *InStyle* soiree for a quick refill, as did Michael Caine and Julianne Moore.

At one point, Mary and Damon sat down with some dessert at a diner-type table directly across from actor Tony Shalhoub and his wife. Shalhoub looked up at Damon and Mary and said nothing, remaining expressionless. We thought he might have hated Seagal, didn't care enough about Seagal to acknowledge him, or thought Damon was a shoddy replica of Seagal. They all ate together in silence.

After a while we all started getting a bit tipsy and bloated from the food and drink. I decided we should get back to the work of making our sizzle reel. We spurred Damon to head back out to the lobby, and we filmed him interacting with fans and other famous notables such as Salma Hayek and Adrien Brody.

I thought I'd give him the ultimate celebrity test by wheeling him out to the ravenous batch of paparazzi at the hotel entrance. At first Damon was enveloped in a burst of flashing cameras and high-pitched yells, like "Hey Steven, hey Steven, give us a look over here, over here!"

Almost as quickly, the cameras stopped flashing, as the mob scanned for the next celebrity.

A laconic French paparazzi ambled over to me, a cigarette dangling from his mouth.

"That eeeessss not him," said the Frenchman. "I know eeeessss not him."

"Oh, you mean Steven Seagal," I said nonchalantly as I still kept trying to film Damon's walkabout.

"Eeeesss too heavy and a bit shorter, I'm telling you, he eeeessssss not fooling anybody here," said the cynical Frenchman. An Italian photographer overheard our conversation and piped in, "Nice a try, but no cigar!"

Wow, we'd tricked everyone—security, law enforcement, public relations managers, celebrities, Hollywood moguls, Midwestern tourists, high-end car dealers, and tuxedo retailers—but we couldn't fool a bunch of hard-bitten, foreign-speaking, world-weary paparazzi who'd spent years hiding in bushes, assuming disguises, and participating in high-speed car chases and residential ambushes getting that one money shot of a compromised celebrity. Their lifestyle sounded familiar.

I realized there really was a limit to how far we could push the hustle of a faux Hollywood luminary. It was only a small group, but there they were, right in front of us laying down a well-defined line of authenticity in a land of total fantasy.

Soon, the awards show ended, and a flood of real celebrities engulfed us in the lobby all heading to their respective after-parties. Goldie Hawn glided by with Kurt Russell. Hugh Grant jabbered with Adam Sandler. Nicolas Cage emerged clutching his date.

For the first time, Damon looked a bit weary.

"I think I'm ready to head back," he said.

"To your hotel?" I asked.

"No, to Texas."

7

PLAYMATES AT PLAY

WHILE AT PALISADES HIGH SCHOOL in West L.A. in the mid-1970s, my small crew of fellow hormonal students and I developed an unhealthy fascination with the movie *Shampoo*. We ate up the gorgeous figures of Goldie Hawn and Julie Christie, the rollicking pool-party scenes, and the exclusive Hollywood Hills mansions with Olympus vistas of the city below.

We were captivated by Warren Beatty's hairstylist character as he shuttled between innumerable paramours on his motorcycle, while covered in turquoise, rings, and scarves. We were engrossed as he navigated the romantic and sexual demands of his beautiful clients. We were entranced as he wielded his blow dryer like a love-gun over their layered tresses and tended to their bottomless emotional needs.

I'd often meet my nerdy school buddies in the middle of the campus quad for lunch, where we'd stand around and strategize about accessing such a life. Should we also try to become hairstylists? Could we get a summer job at a salon? What if someone's mother showed interest? With our pubescent patchy lip and chin hair, pineapple facial skin, skinny frames, and braying donkey voices, we were quite a group. We looked and felt like virgins for life.

Round and round the conversation would go. Maybe we should all start pumping iron or take motorcycle lessons or start wearing ascots. We even took concerted action on weekends by driving up the main canyon roads in Beverly Hills and Hollywood looking for any signs of a party. We cruised Mulholland Highway from north to south hunting for the sounds of a house band, valet parkers, or the distant strobe lights of a disco extravaganza.

We pulled into many a mansion driveway, thinking we'd hit a happening, only to be barked at by security on the hedge gate squawk box to clear out immediately.

Our one Xanadu, our ultimate fantasy, was to attend a party at the Playboy Mansion, Hugh Hefner's fantastical playpen in Holmby Hills, between Bel Air and Beverly Hills. It was our greatest hope. The place hosted an endless series of epic shindigs—the Halloween party, the Midsummer Night's Dream party, and the New Year's Eve party. Every week there seemed to be fundraisers for legalizing marijuana or abortion rights or first amendment issues. And there were smaller, routine gatherings like movie nights, game nights, or impromptu pool parties.

We followed Hefner's sybaritic exploits and outrageous lifestyle through the entertainment trade press and the newspaper society pages, and by leafing through *Playboy* magazine itself. Pictures of the events seemed too good to be true. Hundreds of scantily clad, beautiful, friendly, cavorting women. Jazz concerts. Tennis tournaments. Disco nights. Celebrities. Bounteous quantities of food and drink.

Hefner was said to never leave the premises. Everyone came to him. All he did was don his red and purple-lined satin pajamas, pack his pipe, and stroll his Shangri-la, ministering to his denizens.

A friend's father worked in the *Playboy* publicity department, and I tried to cadge an invite to an upcoming soiree with no luck. I applied to a catering company that I knew worked closely with the

Mansion for a summer job. I even contemplated going to the dark side, offering to work for a security company that patrolled events there. It was all pretty pathetic—the raving, idiotic fantasies of a frustrated teen in a testosterone firestorm.

Once I began my party-crashing activities twenty years later, my social calendar was amply filled and I wasn't as obsessed with the Mansion as the ultimate destination.

Around 1998, after several years of domesticity with his young wife, Playmate Kimberley Conrad, I'd read that Hugh Hefner had separated from her. Over the next few years, there was a notable uptick in social events up on the hill. Word went out on the crasher circuit that "Hef's partying again: he's single, he's found the fountain of youth, he's on Viagra 24/7—the palace gates are open, and it's a whole new scene."

It was a whole new scene indeed. Hef started dating twin blondes in their early twenties, Sandy and Mandy Bentley, and soon increased his live-in roster to seven women.

Avi and I had a surge of renewed interest and decided to act. The Mansion's big Halloween party was coming up on a Saturday night, and we started making entry plans.

We recruited another party crasher, Duane Flanigan, a former roommate of mine at UC Berkeley. Flanigan was a true Celt, a character of the first order, and vaguely resembled Lou Reed. He received a bachelor's degree in rhetoric and completed two postgraduate teaching certificates, but his ensuing high school teaching career was tumultuous. He had an unfortunate affinity for absinthe that fueled endless fights with authority. After a decade, he burnt all his teaching bridges and began a long search for his next career.

Flanigan worked as a salmon fisherman in Alaska, a Hollywood extra, a restaurant waiter, telephone salesman, and private investigator in L.A. He could never find his place. But he was incredibly quick-witted and calm under pressure, crasher qualities that saved us many times in parlous situations.

Duane Flanigan. *Courtesy of Shane Kerch*

We heard on the grapevine that *Playboy* planned to send shuttle buses to pick up attendees for its Halloween bash starting at 7 PM at parking structure 4 at the eastern entrance to the UCLA campus on Sunset Boulevard. The Mansion was a few miles up Sunset, followed by a right turn and a half mile on Charing Cross Road to the top of the hill.

I knew the Mansion's Halloween party often went until dawn, and I figured we had loads of time to arrive and hop on the shuttle bus. Flanigan dressed as Lou Reed with a black leather jacket, slicked-back hair, and dark sunglasses. Avi was outfitted as a circus performer with a frilly white shirt, red pants, and his trademark Hula-Hoop. I wore my full-length surfer wetsuit, construction boots, and a headbanger, shoulder-length wig. When queried about my costume, I told people I was "a work in progress." We all jumped in my decrepit Toyota, nicknamed the "Beer Can" by my friends due to its rickety aluminum structure, and coolly slid into the parking structure around 9 PM.

As we entered the facility and descended to the lower parking level, I saw a long table with check-in clerks by the stairwell. Dozens of glowering security personnel, all clothed in black, paced the area.

In front of the table stood a long line of about forty to fifty women holding their driver's licenses and other assorted identification, waiting to check in. Virtually all of them were dressed as either schoolgirls or nurses. As mentioned, Halloween is my favorite night of the year, a chance to get creative and go sartorially wild. I've never understood why on this special evening so many women in L.A. choose to restrict themselves to the two same banal outfits.

I ditched my car in a spot at the end of the structure, and we all tumbled out. As we approached the check-in table, we noticed there weren't many men in line. Hef likes to have a preponderance of young women at his celebrations, and that was OK by us.

As our offbeat threesome looked highly conspicuous, I told Avi and Flanigan to hang back while I put my cell phone to my ear and edged up to the table. I leaned over and began frantically searching for male names on the list. I picked off a couple and retreated.

Now armed with two names, all three of us approached and engaged a young woman with a white-knuckled grip on the list.

"Your names please?" she asked.

"Tom Edgerton . . . David Feinstein," I said as I kept looking for a third name.

"OK, I see both names and who is your third?"

"Jonathan Riley," I blurted out just in time.

"OK, I've got that name too. Can I see your identification?"

"Oh crap . . . we've left our IDs in the car, which is parked on the other side of the structure on another level," I said. "Do we really have to walk all the way back up there?"

"I really can't give you wristbands to get on the shuttle without the corresponding identification," she said firmly.

I looked down at her elbow at a healthy pile of pink, glittery, plastic wristbands with the Playboy bunny logo stamped all over them. They were tantalizingly near but so very far. The extended dialogue, bad costumes, male gender, and my pleading tone attracted several security taskmasters.

"Hey goodfellas, we need your IDs," said an enormous goon. "If you don't have them, we need you to move along."

We were shooed off, to the snickers of the various bouncers who watched us with beady eyes. The check-in line was thinning, and some last stragglers were stumbling in for the final shuttle runs.

Our motley trio decided to go up to the ground level and watch the final invitees head off to what looked like one hell of a party. Avi tried to engage a few nurses with some Hula-Hoop moves, and Flanigan hummed "Sweet Jane" to no one in particular. After several moments of watching waves of revelers load up the departing buses, we buttoned up and disconsolately returned to my rusty vehicle.

Flanigan insisted on smoking a cigarette as we stood around and analyzed our failed attempt. We were all dressed up and stuck in a below-ground parking garage.

Suddenly three women—two nurses and a schoolgirl—walked toward us. They were all wearing the coveted wristbands.

"Excuse me, were you up at the Mansion and are you all leaving?" I asked.

"We are soooo done," said a tall redhead wearing white jackboots, a hospital smock, and a stethoscope. "Way too many sleazy old guys."

"Any chance you could lend your wristbands to some sleazy *young* guys?" said Avi, as he began gyrating toward them with his Hula-Hoop.

"By all means, have at it. They're all yours," said the redhead, laughing, as she ripped hers off with a violent swoop. "But you better get going. I think the outgoing shuttles are about to end."

The redhead's two friends saw our desperate plight, took pity, and also forked over their wristbands. We thanked them profusely and manically started bandaging the wristbands together with clear tape. Once fitted appropriately, we sprinted to the embarkation point up on the ground floor while taking a wide detour around the check-in area.

We arrived, panting, at an empty shuttle depot. There was no line. In the distance a bus was disappearing toward the Mansion. Coming toward us was another shuttle that pulled up and disgorged dozens of inebriated guests. It was 10 PM.

One woman had a spellbinding costume. She was Tippi Hedren's character in Hitchcock's *The Birds*. She was covered with ketchup, and on her back was a large wire apparatus with scores of attached model ravens and crows that pecked her every time she moved. Finally, someone not dressed as a nurse or schoolgirl.

"Wow, a creative outfit—a damsel in distress!" I said.

"We are all damsels in distress," said Tippi, as another friend dressed in a leopard outfit nodded. "That party got old, and I do mean old."

Despite the caveat, Avi, Flanigan, and I eagerly approached the now deserted shuttle bus and tried to hop on board with our shiny new wristbands.

"Sorry, we're not bringing any more guests up to the party. Those shuttles end at 10," said the bus driver. "We're only bringing people back from the Mansion to the parking structure now."

"But we're with Lou . . . Lou Reed here," I said pointing at Flanigan who wore his best East Village punk grimace.

The driver gave Flanigan a good look. He hesitated for a moment. We were on the cusp! All our pinballing and racing around was not in vain! Finally, after twenty years I was only seconds away from the ultimate green light!

Then I blundered. I began to wheedle and sweet-talk. "C'mon, it's only just after 10—give us a break. Help us out."

The shuttle driver took off his glasses and gave Flanigan another myopic look.

"Ha, you almost had me," he roared. "You do look like Lou Reed, but sorry, no go! Can't do it, guys!"

We filed off the bus and trundled back to my car. We'd been at this game for several hours, and we were all frustrated and exhausted.

Once we were all strapped into my trusty 1984 Toyota, Avi suggested we not give up. Why not drive up to the back gate of the Mansion itself and see if we could drive in? After all, we had our wristbands and costumes on, didn't we? What to lose?

We agreed, and I peeled out of the parking structure with renewed purpose. I drove up to the back side of the Mansion on South Mapleton Drive and pulled over a couple of blocks away from the gate for a reconnaissance mission by foot. Flashing lights, squealing laughter, and a thumping beat emanated from the property.

The back entrance had a security guard and only a small amount of foot traffic going in and out. No cars traversed the gate. I thought it best to turn back, but Avi was on a holy mission.

"I'm going to climb up that brick wall next to the property and take a peek over and see if there's any way in," he said in full Israeli intelligence mode. Flanigan and I held back and watched from behind some bushes as I held Avi's Hula-Hoop.

Avi methodically grabbed some gnarled vines and began a free solo climb up the twelve-foot wall. About halfway up he seemed to stop, unable to find the next toehold.

Suddenly an LAPD squad car cruised up out of nowhere. Officers flipped on the searchlight and captured Avi fully splayed out like Spider-Man against the wall.

"Come down and stand facing us with your hands up!" screamed one of the officers on the car speaker.

"He's done," whispered Flanigan to me.

"It looks that way, but you don't know Avi," I replied.

The cops got out of their car.

"Good evening officer. I was just leaving the party and I couldn't find the exit," said Avi to the approaching cop as his Israeli accent became heavier.

The officers looked a bit nonplussed and hesitated for a moment.

"All right buddy, just get the hell out of here," said the older cop.

"Shalom," said Avi as he backpedaled into the night.

I looked at Flanigan with an arched eyebrow.

"What did I tell you?" I said.

"Wow," said Flanigan.

"And if it was you up there, what would you have said?" I asked.

"Don't shoot, I'm white!' said Flanigan.

We all scampered back to my car, sweating profusely. I even forgot Avi's Hula-Hoop back in the bushes.

Flanigan and I had seen and felt enough and were ready to check our costumes back into our closets, but Avi was now in full warrior mode.

"Fuck it, we've come this far. Let's go around and drive right up to the front gate, right into the eye of the storm," Avi said. "I just feel it. We'll get in this time. Nothing to lose."

"What about our freedom?" asked Flanigan.

Despite my percolating anxiety, I drove us all back to Sunset Boulevard and then up Charing Cross Road behind a couple of stretch limos and a black Mercedes with tinted windows. A PLAYMATES AT PLAY traffic sign with a busty silhouette figure greeted us on a lamppost halfway up the winding road. We got to the top of the hill, and I idled my rusty auto behind the line of luxury vehicles at the twenty-five-foot-high entrance gates.

They were quickly waved in. Security guards soon surrounded my car, all but kicking the tires and playing with my radio antennae.

"We were already in, and got a call from a friend who is still inside," I said as all three of us waved our hands showing our pink *Playboy* wristbands. "We just need to zoom up and pick him up."

This gave the guards pause and one of them started an extensive conversation with his shoulder mic.

"All right, you can drive up to the courtyard, but none of you can leave your car," said the main guard. "You can call your buddy from there and pick him up. Another guard will meet you up there."

Miraculously, the large iron gate swung open, and we started climbing the steep incline as I nervously revved my car in first gear. We were in! My car was on the property!

We pulled into the huge circular courtyard driveway to an astounding scene. A thirty-foot-high inflatable *Tyrannosaurus rex* hovered above, routinely dipping its huge jaws down toward my car. Naked *Playboy* bunnies, covered in nothing but body paint, scampered in front of us. The costumes were significantly more diverse than back in the parking garage—some couples flaunted a bondage theme, complete with riding crops and masks, two gorgeous brunettes were connected at the hip as "sexual Siamese twins," a Wonder Woman jumped out from behind a fountain.

Pulsing music, lasers, and strobe lights overwhelmed our senses. Additional large dinosaurs and assorted monsters were distributed throughout the front of the property. Fog machines added to the pandemonium.

My first instinct was to ditch my car in the nearest nook and for all of us to make a run for it, preferably in different directions.

"Halt! Verboten! Achtung!" screamed a security guard at me who was wearing a headset, black shin guards, gloves, and a purple chest plate. "I'm told you're here to pick up a friend. You've got five minutes. If any of you leave the car, you'll be arrested."

"OK, no problem," I quickly assented. "But can one of us go and fetch him? We can't reach him on his cell. He's by the pool."

"All right, one of you can go in, but again, you've got five minutes, and then we have to move you out," said the guard. "And no tricks. We've already arrested a dozen trespassers tonight."

Avi was our unanimous choice to search for our "friend." He calmly exited the car and disappeared into the maelstrom. One of us was now in and only two to go.

I idled at the courtyard curb in the car with Flanigan and counted our remaining time. Sitting in my brightly colored Beer Can, we felt badly exposed. Our shoddy costumes added to our conspicuousness. The guards watched us like hungry raptors.

Suddenly a convoy of black SUVs with tinted windows, most likely carrying celebrity cargo, fronted up. The guards scrambled and cantered through a nearby gateway arch, escorting the illustrious group to a nearby parking area.

I looked around. One minute went by. Two minutes. Three minutes. The guards had vanished. I glanced at Flanigan. This was our one and only chance. I accelerated through the arched portico and popped out into a small, densely packed parking area. Miraculously there was a tiny spot between two Escalades. I parked, and Flanigan and I quickly ejected from my vehicle, leaving it to the mercy of Bunny security. We melted into the crowd.

Avi texted that he was by the main pool, and we soon met him there. Multiple buffet stations and bars peppered the area. Lobster, salmon, steak, elaborate salads, and assorted pastas were abundant. The bars were amply stocked with every type of hard liquor. Naked denizens romped under the waterfall at the pool. A super-hairy, naked fat guy, who I thought might be porn star Ron Jeremy, did a belly flop off the top ledge.

I had to see the infamous Grotto, the adjoining watery cave notorious for body-swapping spank play in decades past. I half expected to see regulars Gene Simmons or Bill Cosby pop up through the jizz mist but saw only a few other gawkers. The place wreaked of chlorine, probably overly pumped in to contain the periodic bacterial surges.

I walked over to a large circus tent where throngs of attendees gyrated to a series of cover bands belting out the latest hits. At different points I saw Hef pals Bill Maher, Scott Baio, and Kelsey Grammer working the dance floor. They represented the young males in attendance.

As we were previously alerted, many of the men were in their sixties and seventies and were vastly outnumbered by the potpourri of half-naked, surgically enhanced women in their late teens and early twenties. Rumor was that Hef didn't like too many young blades slicing up his parties.

At one moment I watched *Mission Impossible* actor Martin Landau grapple near the dance floor with a topless young beauty, who looked like his great-granddaughter. He was spooling her thimble nipples from behind—his tongue dangling and whole face completely askew.

I met a dazzling, vivacious woman with a distinct southern drawl while sipping another highball at one of the bars. Her name was Melody, she'd recently graduated from college, and she'd just arrived in Los Angeles from Baton Rouge, Louisiana. And how, pray tell, did she get invited to the Mansion's biggest annual party?

"I knew no one when I got here, and all I heard is that the Playboy Mansion is the place to party in L.A.," she said, brushing her black bangs out of her eyes. "I just sat me down and wrote a short letter asking if I could be put on the guest list and included a couple of bikini photos. I mailed it directly to the Mansion and heard back almost instantly, and here I am!"

I thought of all the gymnastics that my own trio had to perform to get near the place, much less inside. It took Melody forty-eight hours. It took me twenty years.

Melody and I continued chatting about a variety of harmless subjects—the food in New Orleans, hurricanes, her Mardi Gras costume. The alcohol began soaking in, and the fantasy started looking real. I was finally at the Mansion talking to a beautiful woman whose interest in me seemed to grow by the minute. My dormant high school dreams were flowering. I imagined Melody and me performing synchronized swimming moves together in the pool, then gyrating to Steve Miller's "Jungle Love" on the dance floor, and afterward nuzzling over some wine in one of the pinball rooms. Then maybe an on-site tryst away from all the noise and pyrotechnics, in a sheltered cranny at the perimeter of the property.

I abruptly snapped back to attention. Both of our glasses were empty and needed adult beverage refills. I gallantly offered to fetch more liquid. After twenty minutes of waiting in line, I returned to our spot, highballs jiggling in each hand. Melody was gone.

I was momentarily deflated but soon ran into Avi, and we headed to the Mansion's private zoo, which housed pink cranes, monkeys, cockatoos, peacocks, and pelicans. Cameron Diaz and Drew Barrymore sat nearby, taking in the untamed wildlife. Avi, as was his wont, told Diaz she looked familiar and got a withering "get lost" look from Barrymore.

"No, no, I really do know you from the El Royale Apartments on Rossmore Avenue," said Avi to Diaz.

"How did you know that?" asked Diaz, her eyes widening.

"From living in the hood."

Avi turned and looked at Drew Barrymore.

"I never forget a face," said Avi who then walked away.

I followed him close behind.

"How did you know where she lived?" I asked.

"My ex lived in her building, and I saw her there many times when she was dating Matt Dillon," said Avi.

"First Jennifer Aniston, now Cameron Diaz," I said. "What is it with you and celebrities?"

"So far, I haven't made it to their level, so I like bringing them down to mine," said Avi.

As we returned to the main party, all activity virtually stopped as Hef descended from the residence to a poolside cabana with his seven circulating blondes. He was dressed in his usual red silk and purple-lined pajamas with two little red devil horns sticking out of his forehead.

Throngs of attendees crowded around his tent, taking selfies and paying homage. At times he seemed oddly bored, staring absentmindedly into the distance and lollygagging in his chair.

To spark him up, one of his Sandy, Mandy, or Brande girlfriends stuck her tongue out and began nuzzling his ear, but he remained slack-jawed. After a moment, with a quick head movement, he flicked her away like an iguana does to a fly.

Years later, I remembered that sordid scene when I read about Hef's final years and the deteriorating setting at the Mansion. In 2006 Hef's former girlfriend Izabella St. James wrote in her memoir *Bunny Tales* that the estate badly needed renovation: "Everything in the Mansion felt old and stale, and Archie the house dog would regularly relieve himself on the hallway curtains, adding a powerful whiff of urine to the general scent of decay," "Each bedroom had mismatched, random pieces of furniture. It was as if someone had gone to a charity shop and bought the basics for each room," and "The mattresses on our beds were disgusting—old, worn, and stained. The sheets were past their best, too."

In February 2011, 123 people came down with a fever and other flu-like symptoms after a DomainFest Global conference event at the estate. Epidemiologists at the L.A. County Health Department launched an investigation and reported that the cause was *Legionella pneumophila* bacteria, the source for Legionnaires' disease that is a lethal form of pneumonia. The bacteria were traced to the watery recesses of the Mansion's infamous Grotto.

In 2015, Holly Madison, the *Girls Next Door* reality television star and another longtime Hefner girlfriend, wrote *Down the Rabbit Hole*, a brutal tell-all about life inside the sex castle. She described an aged, doddering satyr who enforced strict rules, demanded impersonal scheduled sex, and encouraged vicious infighting among his female courtiers. The estate was filled with junk, including "ceiling-high piles of videotapes, stuffed animals, arts and gifts. . . . It was like an episode of *Hoarders*. But perhaps in his case it would be more appropriately titled *Whore-ders*."

After hours of bouncing around Hef's signature party, I saw Melody across the way. She was sitting on the lap of a humpbacked senior citizen, stroking and picking at his hair transplants. Melody was a live wire compared to most of the women, many of whom seemed anesthetized with drugs and alcohol—"Xanny zombies" with faraway stares and cryptic giggles.

My cohorts and I all decided it was time to go. I'd seen enough silicone, lechery, drunkenness, and doddering Uncle Dirty types to last a lifetime. It was 5 AM.

I'd resigned myself to the towing of my car. I figured it was a worthy trade to witness a historic moment in the greater culture at large—the beginning of the last days of the *Playboy* empire.

As I slalomed through the jugglers, acrobats, monsters, lascivious grandpas, drug-addled Bunnies, dancers, security thugs, and B-list celebrities back to my parking spot, dawn broke. It gave a surreal glow to the general debauchery and grotesquely etched the whole scene. Even more surreal was that my car sat alone and untouched in its parking slot. Was this a security ambush?

All three of us quickly hopped in and headed for the back exit. Near the perimeter, I locked eyes with the faux German-speaking security guard. When he saw us, he gawked and hesitated. He didn't know whether to slam the gate, call in reinforcements and detain us, or just flush us out.

I hit the accelerator and didn't give him a chance. Soon we were back on South Mapleton Drive heading toward Sunset Boulevard, truly a long night's journey into day.

PART II

COMMUNITY

Adrian with masquerade ball courtiers.

8

THE DAILY INQUIRY AND MORE SELF-INVITERS

M ANY OF THE MOST ALLURING HOLLYWOOD bashes involve fundraisers and charitable events. Causes need fundraisers, which need celebrities to maximize media exposure and bring in more money. With innumerable celebrities in L.A., there are always charity events to attend, usually during the same time every evening.

It's sometimes argued by historians that the Japanese attack on Pearl Harbor was partially due to a bad misunderstanding of America's Protestant work ethic. The emperor and his admirals and generals thought the United States was weak due to a pleasure-seeking lifestyle that could never compete militarily with a disciplined samurai culture. Hollywood beamed images around the world of hedonists lounging around swimming pools with lots of sun, surf, and sex. What the Japanese didn't completely realize is that the United States is a workaholic nation. Work defines who you are in America. One's whole identity and status—where one lives, social relationships, spouses, hobbies, and income—are tied to profession.

This same misconception still lingers today, not about America, but about Hollywood. Many around the world, including even other Americans, believe Tinseltown is filled with rich, cigar-smoking, Botox-injecting, wine-swilling layabouts who live for fun and pleasure. What they don't realize is that La La Land has an up-before-dawn rooster culture in which the 6 AM working breakfast meeting is typical fare for the brainy and ambitious. Film and television production schedules are often twenty hours a day for months at a time with no days off. Producers and agents typically take scripts home most nights and pore over them all weekend. Budd Schulberg's novel *What Makes Sammy Run?* is the classic depiction of the dog-eat-dog, win-at-all costs, workaholic culture of Hollywood.

After laboring for two decades as a writer/director in documentary television production, I can attest that the pace and timetables are overwhelming.

The result is that most charitable events in Screenland usually start early in the evening, often at 6 PM with a firm ending at 9 PM. By then people are already contemplating the next morning's work duties. I've often thought that Los Angeles has the best 6-to-9 PM nightlife in the world. After 9 PM, the place turns into a ghost town. But in that three-hour time frame sits a bounty of social events.

Unfortunately, this time frame is an extreme inconvenience for crashers, as it coincides with some of the worst traffic jams in the world. With multiple festivities going on all over the far-flung L.A. basin, navigating the correct party to hit in such a compressed interval is a finely honed science.

Enter the widespread distribution of cell phones in the late 1990s. Without them, party crashers would be ricocheting aimlessly all over Lotus Land in hit-or-miss ventures. The ancillary innovations have allowed the self-inviter network to closely coordinate activities, share real-time intel, including live video, and pinpoint event targets. GPS, online maps, and social media have amplified the available information in subsequent decades.

All my life I've had an affinity for eccentric personalities. I recoil from the typical Barbie and Ken types who pursue linear lives with boring plotlines. I gravitate to outsized characters with bizarre habits, freakish interests, and comic sensibilities. My inner circle of friends in high school and college was filled with nervy outcasts, animated kooks, and oddball intellectuals.

In my early years of gatecrasher immersion, I found myself chatting on a regular basis with a host of offbeat characters that made my previous friends look like Mormon missionaries. I'd spend hours on the phone with them allocating tips, comparing tactics, and sharing crasher anecdotes.

Whenever I had spare time during the day I'd canvass event websites, hunting for potential fundraisers, art exhibitions, live talks, networking events, company socials, restaurant, spa, and yoga studio openings, wine tastings, and movie premieres and their after-parties. I'd check in with public relations agency contacts, reporter colleagues, and event caterers. By midafternoon, I'd peruse the Master List. As mentioned, my first crasher phone call usually went out to Barton "the Master" Whitaker, who'd spent many hours ransacking all his contacts and gleaning new information.

I usually had to offer him a nugget to get a reciprocal gem that wasn't on his Master List and was allocated parsimoniously. That's how he kept his acolytes and social feeders in check, panting for more.

My second call went to SAM BRODY, an embedded caterer who worked for big celebrity event food providers such as Lucques, Wolfgang Puck, Patina, and Citron Catering. I'd met him many times at a variety of extravaganzas. In his midforties, he was powerfully built with a thick mop of surf-tossed blond hair. He was always clothed in caterer regalia—black shirt and tie, black apron, black pants, and black shoes, even when I ran into him off duty at the Vons supermarket in my neighborhood. I often wondered if he slept in the outfit.

At work, he was all business, barking instructions to a bevy of unemployed actors working as his servers. He managed a large staff with complex operations and a demanding clientele. Hungry celebrities get irritable when food and drink aren't instantly served. Though some of the world's finest wines, stiffest gin, and smokiest whiskey flowed through his hands, he never wet his beak on duty. Off duty was another story.

Sam was always a wondrous source of information, offering precise dress codes, back entrances, specific security deployments, pictures of wristbands, and stamps and names of VIPs for name-dropping. He knew of upcoming events weeks before they happened, would provide updates on the day of, and real-time details as the party was in full flower. And what did Sam get out of his generosity?

Well, on his nights off, he got full access to all my information and would join in the merrymaking. He became a loyal and devoted friend and represented a typical gonzo character in my crasher retinue.

My daily check-in for salient info also included HENRY HIMMER-MAN, known as "Hinky Hank," a perpetually suspicious, mildly paranoid, diabolically cunning crasher who always rolled alone. He was a pudgy pixie in his late forties with a gray Brillo hairdo, small round glasses, and a genial demeanor. Henry didn't seem to have any particular profession. His kangaroo paunch was swollen from years of consuming Tinseltown's finest drink and richest food, and it jiggled uncontrollably when he laughed. But he was a ferocious gossip and agitator, always peddling information for ulterior purposes that pitted other self-inviters against each other.

Still, he was knowledgeable and resourceful, and his intel was always spot-on. When Hinky Hank revealed key coordinates or specific info about a Hollywood extravaganza, it was true as holy writ. He was always helpful and friendly to me, and I couldn't help liking him.

In my early crasher years, the Santa Monica Place, a new mall near the beach, opened up. The development was loaded with cutting-edge restaurants. In the week before the ribbon-cutting, there was a large effort to publicize the eateries, and many of them held nightly "rehearsal" dinners that were open to special guests and the media. The food was, of course, free and the service overly attentive.

I dropped in one night, and as I headed to restaurant row on the third floor, I saw an earnest public relations executive taking a VIP group of a dozen people (ostensibly reporters) around the premises and extolling the offerings. As I got closer, I saw Hinky Hank in the lead, listening intently with a pyramid of food on his plate as he moved from grill to grill. The whole group was made up of crashers. Professor Al Barrios was pregnant with prime rib. Burt Goldenberg's shirt front was already blotched with wine stains. Bradley Bleat juggled three plates of varying ethnic entrees. Lavanda Frantiglioni's mane of hair was flecked with humus, chips, and popcorn. She'd been chowing down heavily and still looked ravenous. It was a roving Halloween gallery. The publicity guide had no idea of the food monsters trailing her.

One of the most accomplished crash characters in my growing crew was NATE FROTSKY. As mentioned, many in the infiltrator network, though intelligent and shrewd, had dubious professions. It was difficult to pin down exactly what they did during daylight hours. But Nate was different. He was a successful graphic designer with many legitimate connections in the entertainment industry. I saw him at venues far and wide. It seemed he was out every night. (He probably thought the same of me.) Due to his professional status, he was invited to many events. But to those he wasn't, he still went. He got in everywhere.

One of his secret weapons was his fourteen-year-old daughter. He once took her to Elton John's Oscar night Academy Awards viewing party at the Pacific Design Center in West Hollywood. The event is notoriously difficult to enter. The L.A. County Sheriff Station is nearby, and rings of officers are spread out around the surrounding blocks. Once you make it to the check-in tables, dozens of officious clerks request your name and identification for cross-referencing on their digital iPad lists, making it impossible to stealth-read guest names.

Not a problem for Nate and his young charge. He pre-researched some of the more obscure child nominees online and, armed with a good name, blurted one out at the table.

"Can I please see your identification," said a clerk to Nate's daughter.

"She doesn't have any identification. She's fourteen years old," said Nate to the clerk.

"And who are you?" said the clerk to Nate.

"I'm her chaperone. She's on the list plus one guest," said Nate.

"*Hmmm, uuuggghhh, hmmmm* . . . OK," said the clerk. "Head on in."

Besides this ring of social notables, I found myself in increasing contact with my old college compadre Duane Flanigan. After our Playboy Mansion adventure, we became closer. Our bond was rekindled in the fire of that epic crash.

Flanigan was a devout malcontent and congenital rebel. Alcohol was the gasoline that lit him up. For years after he graduated from UC Berkeley I'd watched him forfeit his teaching license, hopscotch through different professions, and lose job after job.

As his employment prospects dimmed stateside, I saw him pursue harebrained schemes around the world. He got his ESL certificate and tried teaching in China. Promised an instructor stint at a military academy through an online broker, Flanigan ended up in a small town in the center of the country, teaching toddlers at a day care center. No one spoke English, and his minders didn't want him to leave after he expressed dissatisfaction with the job.

Duane Flanigan relaxing at charity dinner. *Courtesy of Shane Kerch*

I got frantic e-mail messages from him asking me to contact the US State Department. He'd been kidnapped, forced to labor in a day care gulag, and was under the control of a "Mr. Zhu." After much back and forth, working through consulates and with foreign officers, his family and I got him out. Soon after, he went to teach in Saudi Arabia, one of the most rigid antialcohol police states in the world. Within three weeks he was expelled from the country after hosting a party in his dormitory for his students. He'd mixed up a huge batch of *pruno*—a fruit-based alcohol brew—in his bathtub. Armed guards escorted him to the airport.

He returned to the States and bounced around some more. He engaged in petty monetary schemes—donating blood for cash, participating in paid focus groups, offering up his ravaged physique for clinical drug trials.

After decades of this, he finally achieved a nice run of sobriety. While analyzing his checkered past he got a bipolar diagnosis from a therapist. Flanigan asked that I fill out an ancillary testimonial for his application for Supplemental Security Income disability benefits. Under TOILET HABITS I wrote in, "Always misses." Flanigan thought that phrase did the trick. He subsequently received a monthly check, courtesy of the federal largesse.

With the new money stream, he could now afford to drink. An arrest for public drunkenness and assault on a police officer (he could never abide cops) led to a long stint in Twin Towers—the L.A. County jail downtown. I visited him several times, and he seemed calmer, relieved of any responsibilities to the outside world.

Once he got sprung from the Big House, Flanigan asked if Sam Brody could help him get a job at a big-event catering company. With the ample champers around, I didn't think it was a good idea. But Flanigan persisted and said he'd be a great source for party tips. That got me.

Soon he was working celebrity extravaganzas, and weeks passed without incident. One evening he called in with a spectacular festivity— the annual fundraiser at the Los Angeles County Museum of Art.

It was a full-penguin-dress affair, and with Flanigan's expert back-door instructions I was soon seated with some sophisticated elder benefactors at a prime table. From afar, I watched Flanigan shuttling in and out of the catering tent, serving up multiple courses to his section with aplomb.

At one point I ambled over to him, but he seemed stressed and couldn't talk. As the night progressed, Flanigan's face seemed to get redder. *Uh-oh.* He was probably dipping into the wine casks between servings.

After about thirty minutes, I saw several police officers enter the party and jog toward the catering tent. There was quite a ruckus. A small crowd had formed.

I walked over to investigate and saw a distinguished white-haired gentleman in a black catering outfit writhing on the floor.

"3 . . . 2 . . . 1!" screamed the police commander.

ZZZZZSSSSSSSSTTTTTTTTT!

Flanigan was receiving another Taser shot to the chest. He was soon incapacitated and zip-tied, then carried off the premises bucking and writhing as the electricity wore off.

Another job and profession down the garburator.

When I visited Flanigan again in the pokey, he said his manager caught him tippling backstage out of a near empty Veuve Clicquot Brut bottle.

"I told him it was a one-off, a quick sip to calm my nerves," said Flanigan through the thick glass. "But then he goes and calls the cops! Well, you know me and cops. I saw the badges and mustaches coming and I blacked out." Flanigan spent another week in an orange jumpsuit. After he got out, a mutual lawyer friend from our days at Berkeley got the "resisting arrest" charges dropped.

I didn't hear from Flanigan for a few weeks, figuring he was busy researching yet another new career.

Then one day I got a call out of the blue. "Hey, I'm at the L.A. airport and just wanted to say goodbye," he said.

"There's never such a thing as goodbye with you," I answered. "Where to now?"

"I'm headed back to China," he said. "I found another English teaching job through a better online broker. This time I'm in Beijing. I'm sticking to a big city. No more little unnamed wonton towns in the interior. It's permanent this time. I've had it with the U.S."

9

AUSTRIAN OAK

———

I T WAS A SLOW SATURDAY NIGHT in Santa Monica, and I was like a penned-up billy goat in my apartment, antsy for something to do. My options were playing mah-jongg with a neighbor, seeing a classic movie at the nearby Aero Theater, or settling in with a new Joseph Stalin biography.

My cell phone rang. It was Barton Whitaker.

"I just heard there are some white courtesy shuttle buses running up and down Mandeville Canyon in Brentwood," he said. "They're picking people up at the Paul Revere Junior High School parking lot at Sunset Boulevard at the bottom of the hill."

I knew the parking lot well. I'd attended Paul Revere Junior High for three years in the 1970s. After years of living on L.A.'s Westside, any sightings of shuttle buses heading up into the hills from the flatlands meant some kind of massive mansion party with restricted parking up top. I told Barton I would check it out and report.

I jumped into my cocktail attire—blazer, slacks, freshly steamed collared shirt—and gave my shoes a quick buffing.

When I arrived at the parking lot, it was packed with a regal crowd lining up for the shuttles. Each bus entrance was manned with a minder who demanded names and identification for boarding. I decided I'd just follow one of the shuttle buses up the canyon and see if I could park nearby and walk to the shindig. It seemed like an easier option.

A shuttle bus moved out and I fell in line, following close behind. I got a call from another crasher, and while I was distracted, the big transporter jammed on the brakes. I skidded to a halt mere feet from the rear bumper and almost rear-ended the glitzy guests. A dog had run across the road.

I continued stalking the shuttle (at a greater distance) for a couple of miles up Mandeville Canyon Road. The bus turned right, up Chalon Road, to the imposing entrance of the Brentwood Country Estates, a gated community. A guard at the entryway flicked up the barrier arm and waved the bus through.

Before the arm could come down, I glided tightly behind the shuttle, inhaling exhaust, and yelled at the guard that I was also with the event. The guard shrugged, and I rolled on through.

A few hundred yards up the street, the shuttle pulled up to an enormous Tudor-style mansion and began disgorging its passengers in front of a ritzy bash. There was a red carpet, but security was remarkably laid-back, probably due to the earlier guest vetting in the parking lot and the fortress-like gates surrounding the neighborhood. I ditched my car farther up the street and walked right in.

It was a multimillion-dollar fundraiser for the Chrysalis Foundation, a large nonprofit organization that finds jobs for homeless and low-income people—definitely a worthy cause. The night was celebrating the employment placement of more than fifty-eight thousand clients. Hundreds of guests sat in a large garden at ornate tables. It looked like the rubber salmon dinner was over when I arrived, but the wine was flowing as an auctioneer hawked expensive items in a staccato baritone from the front stage.

This was the kind of event I hated crashing: a great organization raising money for a worthy cause. Sit-down affairs were also extremely confining and queasy capers. One had to search for an open seat at a table and then fend off the innumerable questions from adjacent guests as to who you were, why you were there, your connection to the organization, what you planned to bid on at the auction, etc., etc.

I looked over and saw that Barton was already seated and had a waiter fetching him a late dinner. He always amazed me with his ability to cast out for information and get the jump on everyone.

After walking around with a glass of untouched Chenin Blanc, I decided to make a quick exit. While hoofing it back to my car, I saw another massive gala across the street that I hadn't noticed on my way in. There were two large iron gates swung open to an almost vertical driveway. Lots of pedestrian traffic ambled in and out.

A group of fit-looking people started ascending the incline, and I jumped in behind. At the top of the fifty-yard driveway was a well-fortified security hut with a glass dome that looked like the Popemobile. Inside on a high stool sat a fierce-looking guard with a 360-degree view of the proceedings. I smiled and gave a friendly wave but got a blank stare back.

The residence had a palace-like feel with a grand arch entryway, high windows, and well-tended, extensive landscaping. I entered the vestibule and saw the event was in full swing. Waiters scurried to and fro offering savory edibles and endless champagne. There was a wide mix of people—young, old, and racially diverse.

I was instantly struck by the impeccable taste of the interior—majestic drapes, lanterns, candelabra, soft ceiling lighting, paintings, sculptures, modernist tables and chairs. In the living room I saw large framed photos of the Kennedy clan, including Teddy, Bobby, and JFK with windswept hair, *T. rex* jaws, and Chiclets teeth. Framed letters hung on the walls. There was a variety of colorful impressionistic paintings and sketches, some of bodybuilders, throughout the enormous, high-ceilinged rooms. Outside were innumerable deck chairs and couches tastefully augmenting a large swimming pool.

I chatted with a guest and found out the affair was a fundraiser for LA's Best, a nonprofit organization that funds afterschool programs for inner-city kids. I had once written about its activities while reporting for *Newsweek* magazine in the 1990s.

As I looked around, my head began spinning from the majesty of the place. I didn't know where I was or who owned it, but this was the home of a serious and formidable personality. Just as I was about to inquire, I heard a booming, recognizable voice.

"Hey dare, I just vant to tank youuu for all zee increeedible work you've done, you've really been faaaaaantastic," said a muscular, approaching figure. "We really appreeeeciate all your support."

I whirled and there he was, the resident of this opulent domicile. The former governor of California, mega movie star, and greatest bodybuilder of all time—Ahhhhnold!

I was momentarily stunned and reflexively began backpedaling but managed to blurt out, "Thanks, Arnold, we're doing all we can!" with both my arms outstretched.

I remembered seeing Arnold for the first time in the late 1960s at Zucky's Deli in Santa Monica, where I watched him consume a steak with a half-dozen eggs on top for breakfast. He was always a fixture in the neighborhood when I was growing up—working out at Gold's Gym, bicycling along the beach, or smoking his cigar on the streets of Santa Monica. I remember his omnipresent tan and how freakishly muscular he was. The Australian writer Clive James once referred to Arnold's look as "a big brown condom stuffed with walnuts."

Arnold slapped me on the back and posed for a quick picture. Mercifully, someone else immediately jumped into the conversation and shifted his attention away. Multiple guests approached him with selfie requests. Others wanted bodybuilding advice. Some asked him to give us all a bicep flex. He did, and the muscle still popped.

Adrian's grip-and-grin with Arnold Schwarzenegger.

Now I realized why there were so many photos and paintings of the Kennedys on the walls. Arnold's wife at the time was Maria Shriver, daughter of Eunice Kennedy, the sister of the Kennedy brothers.

There were quite a few bodybuilders in attendance, and several soon surrounded Arnold for an impromptu group muscle competition, posing, pumping, and stretching.

Though Arnold had recently separated from his wife due to his fathering of an out-of-wedlock child with his maid, the Sperminator showed no lack of energy, charm, or fortitude. His charisma and vitality were intact. Though accused of groping and crude language with women in the past, he was ever the gracious host at the event.

I noticed his two daughters and a few Kennedy cousins were in attendance, bolstering the crowd and supporting the cause.

After a few hours of kibitzing with guests and admiring the art and palace grounds, I headed to the front entrance to take my leave.

"Make sure you get one of dose," said Ahnold, pointing me to a pile of gift bags being handed out at the entryway.

I picked one up and looked inside. The bag felt like it had a mini-Hummer inside—it must have weighed more than fifty pounds and was packed with cosmetics, massage vouchers, and vitamin juices. I looked around at all the paying attendees, briefly considered the night's worthy cause, and decided I'd taken enough from the evening and politely declined.

As I walked past the security shack in the dim light, I again gave the guard a wave and a smile and again got no response. Maybe the guard was a mannequin and placed there just for show? After all, this was Hollywood. Producer Ray Stark of the television police show *Adam-12* always kept an LAPD squad car on his front lawn to scare away criminals, crashers included.

I was admittedly a bit dizzy from the evening's events. I walked down the driveway and absentmindedly hopped on one of the Chrysalis shuttle buses for the ride back down the hill.

Once I disembarked from the bus in a near empty parking lot at my old junior high school, I realized I'd left my rusty auto outside Arnold's place back up the mountain.

I stood in the dark and looked across my old playing field to the gym where I used to pump iron, hoping to be the next "Austrian Oak." Obviously that never happened, an increasing realization as I unconsciously rubbed my cauldron belly and picked at my deep navel.

But overall, the night was a success. I'd done a grip-and-grin with my boyhood hero inside his palatial sanctum, hobnobbed with Kennedys, and avoided being pegged as a social imposter.

Maybe this was a good moment to commit to an image overhaul. I thought of abandoning my decrepit vehicle to the local towing services and upping my game with some new wheels. Cut back on the crasher lifestyle. Rededicate myself to finding a steady relationship. Hit the gym again to remold my avocado physique.

I started striding purposefully toward my home a couple of miles away. The walk would be a good start.

Soon a soft rain began to fall. My pace slowed. My brand-new blazer started getting soggy. I'd only made it about twenty-five yards across the parking lot when I made an abrupt turn and walked back to the idling bus.

"Driver, is your shuttle making another run up to the Brentwood Country Estates?" I asked. "I need to get my car."

10

CLOSE CALLS

SOMETIMES I'D GO for months crashing multiple events across the L.A. basin and emerge unscathed. Sure, there were minor altercations, incidents, and accidents, some loud commands and finger pointing. Security occasionally confronted me, requesting identification. Fundraising organizers grilled me about my involvement with said charity. A bigwig periodically took a disliking to me. Now and again, I'd get launched.

Every so often, these minor pratfalls would dent my confidence, inject some hesitancy into my gait, and halt my swagger. But these minor setbacks were a bonus. They kept me honest, if you can call it that. They constrained my wild antics. They made me calculate risks more deliberately.

When I'd really attract trouble was when I got overconfident. Going out night after night, penetrating security, gobbling gourmet food and downing drink, hobnobbing with celebrities—soon you think you're part of the elite, when you're actually a schmuck.

I'd seen it in the behavior of other crashers. They'd develop a breezy style, talk and consume too much, and start taking outrageous risks. It's called hubris—excessive pride, arrogance, and a feeling of being untouchable.

I've seen crashers Trojan-horse themselves into parties by hiding in catering trucks. I witnessed another climb a tree outside the back gate of a Beverly Hills mansion, edge out on a branch thirty feet off the ground, and drop onto the sloped ivy of the backyard. I've watched others push their fellow intruders through party entrances in wheelchairs. With each success, they feel more and more invulnerable.

Until they're not.

At the turn of the millennium, I was riding high. I'd gone months on end with nary a crasher stumble or setback. My skills were superlative. My social network was expanding. My knowledge and information about events was extensive.

Adrian taking an incoming phone tip at a Fox Studios party while Flanigan keeps an eye out for security.

One day I heard that Mikhail Gorbachev would be receiving an award from the environmental organization Global Green. The event was to be held at the five-star Ritz Carlton Hotel in Marina del Rey near Venice Beach.

Since the time Gorbachev was ousted in a coup in 1991, he'd started Green Cross International, a nonprofit organization that helped to dismantle thousands of nuclear warheads, deactivate dozens of nuclear-armed submarines, and liquidate more than forty-five thousand tons of lethal chemical agents in both Russia and the United States. Global Green was a US-based nonprofit that worked closely with Green Cross International, and the awards night saluting Gorbachev was to be attended by four hundred environmental luminaries.

I had always been fascinated by Russian history and almost majored in it during college. The chance to see one of the great historical figures of the twentieth century, the man who launched the perestroika campaign, dissolved the Warsaw Pact, and ended the Cold War, was too great an opportunity.

As I arrived at the Ritz Carlton lobby on this special evening, the event was already in full swing. It looked like a standing-room-only crowd, as attendees were spilling out of the main ballroom. I easily mingled in and stepped right into the ceremony.

A Global Green bigwig was giving a speech at the lectern. I scanned the room for Gorbachev but couldn't find him. There were lots of button-down lawyers in attendance but also many unshorn types with gray ponytails and young crunchy activists all sitting at dinner tables around the ballroom.

Soon enough, the speaker finished his monologue and introduced Gorbachev, who marched up and launched into an impassioned jeremiad in Russian (with his interpreter) about abolishing nuclear weapons, the importance of individual action, and the threat of global climate change. It was a thrilling moment.

After the speech, everyone settled in for a vegetarian dinner. I watched Gorbachev walk purposefully back to his table. Though in his early seventies, he still looked surprisingly vital, considering the stresses he'd undergone. The red hammer and sickle birthmark still showed on his pate. He was animated, focused, and charismatic. There was no denying the gravitas of the man. One could see how and why he had tamed the old bulls of the Soviet politburo as a younger leader.

A parade of admirers approached his table, including Tom Hayden, Ted Danson, and Woody Harrelson. Oliver Stone once remarked that Harrelson had the best white trash face in the business, and watching him with Gorbachev was a surreal moment. Visually, they were a most unlikely duo, though still committed to the same green goals.

Years later I journeyed to Russia to make a documentary about the country's martial arts. I was struck by the earthiness and phlegmatic toughness of the people. Rarely was there a whimsical or fake smile. The conversations were always blunt and direct, and everyone looked you right in the eye. That was Gorbachev, a true emblem of his people.

I continued wandering the ballroom and watched Gorbachev from multiple vantage points. I couldn't get over that I was so close to such a titanic figure. Soon I attracted the attention of Gorbachev's ubiquitous translator, Pavel Palazhchenko, who eyed me warily.

Palazhchenko was the Zelig of Gorbachev's time as premier of the Soviet Union. His was an unforgettable visage—a short, middle-aged, completely bald man with a large hedge of a dark mustache. He seemed to pop up in every photo of Gorbachev from the time.

I quickly retreated from Palazhchenko's penetrating gaze and fronted up to a nearby bar, where I appropriately chugged a Stoli double. Then I had another. After fifteen minutes, I was well buttressed and eager to introduce myself to Gorbachev.

Pavel Palazhchenko at Reagan-Gorbachev summit in Reykjavík in 1986.
Courtesy of David Hume Kennerly

As I began circling back to his table, I watched his continuous interactions with people, where he exhibited a mix of bluster, gruffness, and occasional eruptions of laughter. He seemed completely unimpressed with celebrities. He didn't have any security personnel around him. His only guard dog seemed to be Palazhchenko.

I mulled over in my mind what I wanted to say to the great man. I knew I'd probably have at most a sentence or two. I started muttering to myself.

"Hello, Mr. Gorbachev. Thanks for saving the world."

"Hi Premier Gorbachev. We are all committed to a healthy planet because of you."

"Greetings Mr. Gorbachev. None of us can ever forget what you've done and what you continue to do."

"*Privet* ["Hello" in Russian], Premier Gorbachev. Tear down this ballroom!"

Finally, I noticed a break in the action. Yet another supplicant had just finished pumping Gorbachev's hand and was moving away. I made a headlong rush and lurched in with my hand outstretched.

"Mr. Gorbachev, thanks for stopping the madness!"

Unfortunately, I only got to the word *stopping* before I was stopped.

Palazhchenko caught my manic movement out of the corner of his eye and probably already had me marked as a stalker freak when I was murmuring my practiced greetings nearby. He suddenly whirled and screamed "*Nyet! Nyet!*" blocked me, and locked my forearm in an arm bar. He was unbelievably strong. He quickly manhandled me aside and followed with a hard shove that almost sent me sprawling.

I gave him a plaintive look.

"*Nyet!*" he yelled again.

I tried to look around him and catch Gorbachev's eye, but I wasn't even enough to notice. He was already greeting another admirer.

July 4 is a big party day in Los Angeles. Large mansions hold celebrations up in the Hollywood Hills, while various Bel Air estates host massive cannabis-sponsored blowouts. Venice Beach is the scene for innumerable backyard barbecues, and patriotic parades rev up the city's neighborhoods from Pacific Palisades to Marina del Rey to downtown.

In rougher parts of town, residents cap off multiple gun rounds into the sky to compete with the blaze of fireworks. Inebriated buffoons duke it out on the ocean boardwalk. On this holiday, chaos seems rampant and grows by the hour as day explodes into night. Once the sun dips, L.A. County sheriffs set up DUI checkpoints at sundry intersections to nab rowdy, drunken wastrels.

To escape the impending havoc, I often journey up the coast to the Malibu Colony, a one-mile hyper-exclusive stretch of beach of about a hundred homes stocked with celebrities and reclusive billionaires. The area is heavily gated and guarded, but the sand is fine, the sea has a vodka-like clarity, and the surf is always up.

For decades, moguls and celebrities have converged on this spectacular oceanfront community of vacation homes, throwing dusk-to-dawn parties and seeking seclusion. The Colony has produced endless fodder for gossip magazines and at times is overwhelmed with mobs of paparazzi. Multiple celebrity shenanigans, capers, and peccadilloes are par for the course.

Starting about noon on a typical July 4, the Colony erupts with volleyball games, surfing action, Frisbee competitions, barbecues, and live bands. By 3 PM it's raining rum at beach parties spilling out of gorgeous homes onto the sand. Beautiful people scamper about in dental-floss thongs and board shorts. A whiff of marijuana permeates the proceedings. It's an adult playpen, and the kids are afterthoughts.

Over the years, I journeyed north from Santa Monica several times for this annual bacchanal and was never disappointed. One of the great features was a private barge for a thirty-minute display of fireworks, funded by residents, that was towed in by tugboats and anchored a few hundred feet offshore. One year, there was an electrical malfunction and rockets started firing horizontally in all directions. Silhouetted

figures (the barge engineers) could be seen abandoning ship and div-
ing into the water to escape the carnage.

For this July 4 (in 2003) I rounded up my two reliable riding
partners, Avi Fisher and Duane Flanigan, and invited my girlfriend,
Natalie, to join us.

The festivities began portentously. Flanigan arrived at my house
at midday already in his cups, and Avi chastised him. Natalie was a
risk-averse, sweet personality who was terrified of and hated crashing and crashers. She was an L.A.-based entertainment writer from
Alabama of Southern formality who was also half-Choctaw and active
in Native American affairs.

I met her the previous year at a sumptuous movie premiere at
the Academy of Motion Picture Arts and Sciences main theater in
Beverly Hills. We hit it off immediately, and it wasn't until two months
later that she found out I'd crashed the event. The rift healed, but it
hardened her aversion to my interloper lifestyle.

Still, I implored her to join us for some Colony fireworks, and
eventually she agreed. Our relationship was humming. I loved every
minute with her and badly wanted to show her the beauty of the
Colony beach and watch the offshore fireworks together.

But Natalie was a mere civilian in my group of rope-line ruffians.
We were all experienced in the game and used to climbing fences,
assuming foreign accents, operating with flexible identities, and dropping vague names.

"Are you sure you want to bring her?" asked Avi in a whisper
outside my apartment.

"It's stunning up there and I really want her to see it," I said.

"You're taking a woman of color into restricted white country,
and she loathes crashing," said Avi.

"She'll be fine," I said with a wave of my hand. "She's got some
savvy operators to watch out for her."

Flanigan promptly appeared and accidentally dropped his gin tumbler on the sidewalk, smashing it into a million pieces.

"Don't say you weren't warned," said Avi.

Avi agreed to drive all of us in his SUV. I was excited to have my girlfriend and my main men participating in a grand adventure together.

We mistakenly placed Flanigan in the front seat, with Natalie and me wedged together in the back. As we drove up the highway, Flanigan, who had a deep fear of cops and reeked of spirits, kept pointing his finger at every California Highway Patrol car and exclaiming, "THERE'S JOHNNY LAW!"

Avi exploded and told him to shut his cake hole, that by gesticulating at every cop we were sure to get pulled over.

When we arrived at Malibu Colony Road, the street that fronted all the beach mansions, we were all in a state of high agitation. We cruised up and down the street but couldn't find any parking. In front of every house were clusters of bouncers with shaved heads, checking IDs and matching names on their private party lists. Natalie became more and more vexed. The whole scene looked too intimidating.

Finally, we passed one house and I noticed several partygoers exiting with yellow paper wristbands, a mainstay in my private collection. Avi pulled over in front of a fire hydrant, and I unzipped my bag and wrist-collared everyone with the appropriate bands. We turned around and pulled up in front of said house. Valet parkers swarmed our car. We jammed my tote bag under the front seat, disembarked quickly, and handed over the vehicle. I pocketed the valet ticket, and with me in the lead, we walked the few steps to the front entrance.

Without missing a beat, I held up my hand, waving the wristband like a semaphore, and blurted out, "We've already been in."

At that moment, there was a throng of people entering, the security was outnumbered, and the lead bouncer waved us in.

The house was packed with a blue-blood crowd. Many of the women had pearl necklaces and wore dresses. Their Thurston Howell husbands sported crisp white shirts and blue blazers with elbow patches and looked straight out of a Brooks Brothers ad. I heard lots of elongated vowels. The bartender suggested a pink gin fizz; I ordered several and delivered them to our small group.

This was a beach party? It looked like a ball for debutantes and their parents with everyone ready to dance the quadrille.

Avi took me aside. "It looks like no one here has taken a shit in five years," he said.

"But there's great food, drink," I responded. "OK, people are a little tight. But let's just relax here for a few moments."

"Remember what we talked about?" said Avi. "Your girl doesn't look like she's having much fun."

While Flanigan and Natalie chatted, I walked out to the back porch and set my sights up the beach. Debauchery was in full flower. A glassy-eyed couple wrestled on the sand. A well-dressed drunk still wearing his cravat lay faceup, passed out, oblivious to the sun. Two houses away was a loud headbanger band playing an AC/DC song, "Back in Black." Several millennials were on their haunches smoking blunts watching from a nearby roof.

I'd gotten separated from Natalie and realized Avi was right. It was time to blow this place and get her up the beach where she'd feel more comfortable.

Soon Natalie approached me bug-eyed and anxious. For a Native American from the bayou, all this creamy skin and upper-lip formality was unnerving. It was a cliquey group flashing us lots of nasty looks. I assured her we'd only be a moment longer and went back in for a last sweet pour.

As the gin fizz hit my lips, I heard loud yelling on the porch. A highbrow harridan in her early sixties was screaming at Natalie.

Apparently, Natalie had been unable to reveal the party host's name or any mutual friends when queried.

"So is this what you do, crash parties for a living?" screeched the harridan as she ripped the champagne glass from Natalie's hands. "You just walk into a family gathering and start eating and drinking to your heart's delight? Shame on you! Shame on you!"

I ran out and grabbed Natalie by the elbow. She looked mortified to the point of physical paralysis.

"I'm sorry ma'am, we walked into the wrong house," I said to the harridan. "I believe there's another party with a yellow wristband, and we got crisscrossed."

"You're damn right you've got the wrong house, and it's me that's cross," she said. "Now get off my property!"

I scanned the now-hushed debutante soiree and saw Flanigan hiding behind the chimney. Avi had his hands in some apple pie in the kitchen and was calculating his next move.

I guided Natalie by the arm and a sea of pearls and Sperry loafers parted, with lots of shaking heads and tut-tutting.

"Good God, how did this crowd even get in?" said one elderly gent.

"Where's Buffy?" asked a matron.

"She's out on the beach," said an older, glue-haired attendee. "Thank heavens she doesn't have to witness this."

I tried to console Natalie, but she was a mess. Little did I know, even after multiple mea culpas and prostrate apologies, that our relationship would never recover.

We made it out the front entrance and I whipped out the valet parking ticket while shielding Natalie from all the arched eyebrows, verbal darts, and death stares.

Avi was also in evacuation mode and gave fifty dollars to the valet. "Make this quick," he said. A blue-vested worker bee grabbed the money and the ticket and sprinted to fetch the SUV. Flanigan joined us, and we all huddled glumly on the sidewalk waiting for the return of our car.

Suddenly, another shriek rent the air. It was the harridan standing in the doorway behind us.

"OH MY GOD, THEY'RE USING OUR VALET—CALL THE POLICE!"

As I spent more years on the party crasher circuit and my close calls accumulated, that perpetual risk-taking began bleeding into my daily life. One especially harrowing incident involved a longtime party accomplice named ROLF GUNTHER. I grew up with Rolf in West L.A. in the 1970s. He was born in the United States to German immigrant parents and was both academically brilliant and ferociously ambitious. After attending UC Berkeley together, we lost touch for several years as he moved to New York City and roamed the world as an investment banker. By the twenty-first century, he was back in L.A. working for a hedge fund and we reconnected.

Both of us had broken up with our longtime girlfriends, and we were anxious to hit the social circuit and procreate. I was in the midst of my self-inviting activities and eager for a wingman. There were several advantages: Rolf was incredibly quick-witted, bold, charismatic, curious, spontaneous, and adventurous. And there were some wild-card characteristics: he'd gained significant weight and lost most of his hair. His verbosity, rotundity, and offbeat antics gave him a comic air, and at five foot ten he was often mistaken for actor Jason Alexander.

Like the *Seinfeld* character George Costanza, Rolf could be pushy, unrepentant, and socially oblivious. He had an unbelievable knack for pissing people off, getting in scrapes and scuffles, and ending up in bizarre situations. He'd walk into a room and within minutes there'd be a fracas.

I once visited Rolf at the UCLA Medical Center in Santa Monica, six days into a long stay where he was undergoing treatment for some serious blood clots. He was sitting upright in bed with his feet up, a jumble of intravenous drips plugged into his arms and wires hanging from his body. He looked like a pincushion.

Knowing my stealth skills, he had an oddball request. Could I help him crash out of a building instead of in?

"Can you get me out of here?" he asked looking up at me imploringly. "I can't take this anymore. I need a break."

"Uh . . . and where would David Blaine like to go?" I asked.

"Just sneak me out for a couple of hours," he said. "I'm sick of this hospital food. Maybe we can go to Sushi Roku. It's only a few blocks away."

"Are you out of your mind?" I said. "You could die and I would be an accomplice to murder. Not a chance!"

Within ten minutes I was helping Rolf unplug the restraints tethering him to his bed. He stood up but was still firmly attached to the complex medical apparatuses keeping him alive. Large IV bags filled with blood-thinning warfarin hung from a metal rack, connected to the tubes inserted in his arms. A tangle of blood pressure, EKG, and air saturation wires crisscrossed his body and fed into a computer console that monitored his vital signs atop a pushcart. All parts were connected and on wheels. He was mobile.

Rolf was wearing a green smock showing his bare back and tighty-whities. His arms and chest were flecked with tape holding the whole jerry-rigged thingamajig together. His shins were exposed, and he wore flip-flops.

With the coast clear, we walked out onto the fourth floor of the Internal Medicine wing, hopped on an elevator, and were soon in the lobby and out on the street.

I grabbed my car and turned back into the horseshoe entrance of the hospital. I shifted the front seat way back and stuffed in Rolf and all his attachments. The console kept beeping at a steady rate. The adhesive tape, drips, wires, and the bags all held. We drove off. I couldn't believe it. I smuggled out this Frankenstein-looking monster still attached to his medical equipment in intensive care from one of the most reputable (and highly surveilled) hospitals in the country—a singular accomplishment.

Within minutes we pulled up to Sushi Roku. As I helped Rolf and his medical paraphernalia out of the car, the valet parkers gawked. They didn't know whether to run, call the police, or just park the car. I threw them the keys and walked Rolf into the restaurant.

All conversation stopped. Several customers rose from their tables to get a better look. A couple of kids stood on chairs. The bartender halted service. The young maître d' dropped her menus.

"He's terminal and I'm just giving him a last dinner outside the hospital," I blurted out to an approaching restaurant manager. "We'd appreciate your best seat in the house."

"Of course, of course, right this way," he sputtered, sitting us next to a large window with ample foot space. "Just let us know if you need anything or want anything special."

Soon we were ordering up platters of the best yellowfish, tuna, eel, and salmon sushi in the house. Rolf's medical leashes kept him constrained, but he gobbled down everything within reach.

Rolf continually checked the computer console to make sure he wasn't flatlining or starting to.

In the midst of the mayhem, two familiar-looking dudes approached our table. "Sorry to bother you guys, but we're just curious as to what is going on here," said one of them. "Is this all real? Did you just get out of the hospital or something?"

"Just giving him the last supper," I said.

"Before I'm crucified next week," said Rolf.

We soon explained the real situation—the blood clots, the blood-thinning IVs, the monitoring equipment, and our breakout from the hospital.

The duo couldn't stop laughing and introduced themselves as Bobby and Peter Farrelly, the famed Farrelly brothers who had written, directed, and produced such huge film hits as *There's Something About Mary*, *Dumb and Dumber*, and *Shallow Hal*.

We invited them to eat with us, and they offered to pay for the whole meal while continually plying Rolf and me with innumerable questions about our antics. They were obviously sussing out plot points and characters for future films and insisted on getting our e-mail and cell phone coordinates.

In the middle of our confab, Rolf's computer console began beeping wildly and loudly, indicating an emergency.

"Oh scheisse, the battery's going out, and that's going to freeze up my IVs," yelped Rolf. "It's also going to alert the nurses I need help, and when they show up to my room I won't be there—I've got to get out of here *now!*"

The beeping was at a shrill pitch and assuming an increasing frequency. I ran out to the valet, threw them my ticket, and rushed back in to extract Rolf. The place was in an uproar. Everybody was now involved in the proceedings. Waiters and managers clustered around us trying to help. One said he was calling an ambulance.

"No, no, do NOT call an ambulance or medical help . . . I've got this," yelled Rolf, whose medical smock was now drenched in sweat and revealing plumber butt.

I struggled to untangle wires from Rolf's chair, keep the IV bags levitated, and make sure the intravenous lines stayed inserted in his arms. The Farrelly brothers started taking smartphone pics. They couldn't seem to get enough of the whole scene, which could've been a montage in one of their movies.

We made a mad scramble for the door, knocking over tables and chairs and running over several feet. One of Rolf's wires snagged a lady's purse. I reached down and flung it back. My rusty and trusty car was waiting, and we jammed Rolf and his contraption inside.

I looked up and saw the faces of customers pressed against the restaurant windows, pedestrians gathering, and the loyal Farrelly brothers beside us on the sidewalk.

"Hey buddy, we'll be in touch next week and look forward to talking with you then, if you're still alive!" said Peter Farrelly to Rolf, who nodded gamely.

The ear-splitting console continued frantically beeping, heightening the sense of clamor, confusion, and medical emergency. I peeled out, swerving toward the hospital. In the car, Rolf urgently tried turning off the beeping gizmo to no avail. I soon pulled into the horseshoe driveway of the emergency entrance to the hospital with tires skidding. Attendants were at first nonplussed at the delivery of such bizarre cargo but recognized the familiar sounds and began jogging in our direction.

"NO . . . NO, we can't go in this way!" screamed Rolf. "We've got to enter the other side of the hospital! I'll get nailed here. GO! GO!"

As medical aides began grabbing my door handles, I lurched forward out into the street. I might have dislocated a few shoulders. I sped away, and as I looked in the rearview mirror I saw looks of total confusion and concern. Thoughts of a police chase on live television crossed my mind.

We quickly circled the block, and I pulled up at the medical center's back entrance. Right then, Rolf pulled a cord and disconnected the screaming console. I ditched the car at the far end of the driveway and extracted Rolf and his rig.

I found a far doorway and injected him back into the hospital. Rolf remembered there was an equipment storage area on the third floor with extra wires, plugs, and electrician tape. We took a freight elevator up, miraculously found the correct room, and reattached all Rolf's equipment.

Soon I was escorting Rolf back to his original room on the fourth floor. Several nurses gave him glowering looks but didn't say anything.

"Oh crap," muttered Rolf as he found a note from the head nurse under his pillow on the bed.

"We urgently need to talk with you in the morning about your actions this evening," said the note.

"I'm screwed," said Rolf disconsolately.

"Get a good sleep, and things will all look better in the morning," I said as I backed out the door, thinking it best to make myself scarce. "May flights of angels sing thee to thy rest."

At 7 AM the next day, the head nurse arrived at Rolf's room with a contingent of security guards. It was now a jail cell.

"You broke every regulation at this hospital by leaving the premises without permission last evening," she scolded. "You put yourself and many others in danger by your actions. From now on, we're posting a full-time guard outside your door to ensure you don't leave again. You're now on lockdown."

I checked in with Rolf by phone the next day, and he seemed to take the punishment in stride. But I noticed flashes of impatience and his "rules don't apply" philosophy beginning to surface in our short conversation.

Within forty-eight hours, Rolf's restlessness was back at full throttle. My phone rang.

"I need out again, this time just a quick Starbucks," said Rolf as he implored me for help again.

"No way, Houdini. Way too risky for all involved," I countered. "You're going to end up in County or shackled to your bed." He hung up on me.

Shortly thereafter, Rolf performed another hospital breakout, this time walking several blocks to a local Starbucks in his regalia. As he walked along the sidewalk with his IV bags, console, and welter of wires, passing cars beeped and gave him the thumbs-up sign.

An elderly lady graciously opened the door for him at Starbucks, and he wedged himself and his equipment inside the café.

The place went silent, but that didn't stop Rolf from ordering up a double espresso. He sat at a nearby table and waited for his favorite concoction.

He heard an approaching siren but didn't give it much thought until a squad car pulled up in front. Out jumped an officer who entered and began spraying Rolf with questions. *Why are you dressed in a medical smock and attached to medical equipment? Are you a current patient at a local hospital? Do you have permission to leave and walk around the area?*

Soon the officer marched Rolf outside and tried stuffing him inside his patrol car with all his medical machinery. It didn't fit, and the console went off again.

The officer turned on his rooftop swirling lights and insisted Rolf walk back to the hospital in front of him. For the next twenty minutes, Rolf retreaded his path, ambling along and breathing heavily in the sunshine with the officer tailing him silently with lights flashing. It was the closest thing to a presidential escort that Rolf had ever received or ever would.

I got a phone call from a mutual friend: "I just saw Rolf walking along Wilshire Boulevard being tailed by a police car. He was in his hospital skivvies and draped with IV bags and wires. What's he done now?"

When Rolf reached the hospital, he was met with a full security squad who escorted him back to his room. The head nurse was apoplectic. The medical center released him the next day, figuring they were less liable than trying to hold him.

"I just don't get it," said Rolf when I talked with him soon after. "I found out this damn chick at Starbucks called the police on me. Why the hell would someone do that?"

11

PAUL McCARTNEY
AT MUSICARES

WHEN I HEARD PAUL McCARTNEY was to be honored as the 2012 MusiCares Person of the Year at its annual gala, I wanted in. The affair is hosted by the Recording Academy, the organizers of the Grammy Awards, and the night's proceeds provide resources to musicians and members of the recording industry needing financial and medical assistance.

As usual, the $1,500 ticket price was way out of my league, but I had to pay my respects. The chance to see an iconic Beatle perform, live and up close, with a host of other legendary musicians covering his songs, promised to be an epic occasion.

John Lennon was always my favorite Beatle. I loved his dark iconoclasm, his nasal voice, the morbid undercurrents to his music, his edgy personality, and his political activism. But McCartney's catchy melodies, so integral to the Beatles' success, were ingrained in my brain. And the hits from his solo career, such as "Jet" and "Band on the Run" were unforgettable and echoed my youth.

The McCartney extravaganza was to be held at the Los Angeles Convention Center's main ballroom and would host roughly three thousand industry heavyweights with a vegetarian menu chosen by McCartney himself. I'd always found the downtown convention center a penetrable venue due to its large size and numerous loading docks, underground garages, side doors, and back entrances. I'd glided into many an event there—from yoga workshops to fashion industry trade shows to post–Emmy Awards parties.

But the McCartney tribute promised to be an otherworldly affair with a cross section of global celebrities such as Smokey Robinson, Carole King, Richard Branson, Brian Wilson, and Jack Nicholson. With such a celebrity-dense gathering, there promised to be suffocating layers of security, guaranteed to induce stomach-flipping levels of anxiety in potential crashers.

I decided to partner up with my fellow rule-breaker and music aficionado SHANE KERCH, who was a virtuoso in such high-stakes situations. He was in his midfifties, stood about five foot eight, and had wild black hair that came with a rock 'n' roll attitude. Shane was always a stalwart wingman. A biochemist turned real estate magnate, he was a brilliant businessman by day and a savvy gatecrasher at night. He was also an expert photographer and, with his pocket vest, multiple cameras, and faux press lanyards, would blend perfectly into the media scrum.

On the night of the fundraiser, we decided to show up in the middle of the pre-event cocktail reception, when arrivals would be at their peak. I researched several names of employees of the Recording Academy who were sure to attend, and Shane and I committed them to memory. As we drove east on Interstate 10 from Santa Monica toward downtown, we ran into the usual hellacious traffic and spent our time in the car barking out our chosen names and their spellings over and over. Each of us assigned ourselves three names each, as backup.

On arrival, we parked in the convention center's underground parking garage and clambered up the fire exit to the lobby. At the entrance, we saw a familiar line of massive black Escalades with tinted windows dropping off an endless stream of luminaries.

The security presence looked like Guantanamo Bay, and the atmosphere felt kinetic. Flattops with wrist radios, earpieces, and wrap-around shades stood every few feet. All of them seemed in constant conversation with one another.

Shane and I tried looking self-assured, despite our tightening sphincters, soggy armpits, and labored breathing. After slaloming through a gauntlet of rhino-necked guards, we made it into the registration area. Hundreds of attendees lined up in front of dozens of long tables to check in and receive their lanyards for the evening. After waiting a few minutes, our turn came, and Shane and I blurted out our chosen names as breezily as possible, considering the circumstances. A middle-aged, eagle-eyed minder quickly found them on his iPad and I began reaching for a lanyard.

"Hold it, Tonto, we need to see your identification," he said sharply, rapping my extended hand.

"Damn, we left our wallets back in our driver's car," I responded, going into my usual spiel. "Who knows where they're parked at this point. I can try giving them a call." I made a show of dialing (my sister's phone number) but couldn't get through.

"We can't reach our driver," said Shane. "The event starts soon. Can you give us a break?"

"I've been given strict instructions that no one gets a lanyard without ID," he said. "*Next!*"

An intense security guard, alerted by our protracted conversation, came over, stood behind the minder, and leveled us with heavy stink eye.

Time to go. Shane and I cantered back through the security mine-field and headed for our car. We grabbed some lanyards from the trunk and flipped them back to front on our chests, just showing the black, opaque underside. Then we headed to the catering trucks at the side entrance and waltzed past hundreds of plates filled with McCartney's vegetarian feast into the main ballroom.

Hundreds of attendees were now beginning to flood in and take their assigned seats at elaborate tables filled with flowers, cutlery, and wine. The ballroom lighting was dimmed and the roof stippled with hundreds of sparkling lights, which gave the place a planetarium feel. This was no rowdy concert crowd ready to flip open their Zippos and ignite a joint. It was a sophisticated, button-down, black-tie congregation. The Woodstock generation had definitely assumed a new look.

We hovered on the perimeter of the attendees, careful not to linger for more than a few seconds while looking for some spare seats. Crashers are like white sharks—you've got to keep moving or you're dead.

The tables filled up quickly. This was a massive tribute to a live Beatle, and it looked like 100 percent of ticket holders were attending. It was going to be tight as a tick. The mood was electric as spectators fidgeted with their silverware and talked in hushed anticipation.

Suddenly the show started with the acrobats of Cirque du Soleil's LOVE performing a piece from their Las Vegas show. After a few moments, McCartney and his band briskly and unexpectedly took the stage and launched into the Beatles' "Magical Mystery Tour."

It was an unprecedented move for the gala, as the Person of the Year usually doesn't perform until the very end of the show—and sometimes not at all. The song stunned the audience into rapt silence. Here was the cofounder of the Beatles and his band singing one of his legendary hits without warning or delay.

Security was unimpressed, many of them walking from table to table for a close gander at everyone's lanyard. Shane and I continued walking the perimeter, hoping for a pair of spare seats.

Paul McCartney performing at the 2012 MusiCares gala. *Courtesy of Shane Kerch*

The emcee, British comedian Eddie Izzard, took the mic after McCartney's initial set, made a few jokes, and reminded everyone that "for Paul McCartney, words are not needed. The music speaks for itself."

An array of famous musicians began their tribute sets, putting their twist on McCartney's legendary songs. The Foo Fighters pounded out "Jet," getting a standing ovation from McCartney, and Alicia Keys performed "Blackbird" on the piano. Alison Krauss followed with "No More Lonely Nights." The songs were so good, anybody could sing them and elicit strong reactions. The crowd sang along word for word and erupted with prolonged applause.

As the musicians bore in, the tribute songs poured forth, and the night wore on, the security began standing back, finally giving Shane and me some badly needed relief. We'd been circling the immense ballroom scanning for a life raft—anyplace to sit—for more than forty-five minutes. Finally, between sets, audience members began moving around, getting out of their seats and fraternizing with each other at adjacent tables.

I spotted two open seats at a near center table about a hundred feet from the front stage. I motioned to Shane and we made a move. As we got closer, one of the two spare seats filled. Norah Jones then began singing "Oh! Darling" on a new rotating stage behind us that, in our seat-seeking frenzy, we hadn't even noticed. We were caught standing in the crossfire of the shifting operations of the MusiCares show. A giant light beam meant for Norah Jones lit me up like a pinball machine.

We had no choice but to try to hunker down at our target table. I sat at the one open seat, and Shane crouched beside me, popping up and down continually like a whack-a-mole, reeling off pictures in his photographer role.

The other members of the table were all stiff white music executives with their spouses. They kept flitting their attention between the moving performance of Norah Jones and their two new irritating interlopers. Finally, the song ended.

"Excuse me, but who are you guys?" said one double-chinned, gray-pomaded Humpty Dumpty.

"I'm Elvis Presley and this is Screamin' Jay Hawkins," I said in my best Elvis impersonation while pointing at Shane.

My joke elicited frosty stares.

"Actually, we're just taking some pictures for Getty Images," said Shane.

"And what's he doing?" asked Humpty Dumpty, pointing at me sitting at the table.

"I'm carrying some spare batteries and bird-dogging some key visuals for our chief photographer," I answered.

Humpty Dumpty grunted and gave us a skeptical smirk. Several of the attendees at the table had looks of permanent surprise—stretched faces and raised eyebrows—the result of bad cut jobs. On the party circuit they were known as "rabbits screaming through cellophane" or "Frankenbunnies." And it wasn't just women. Some of the men had off-kilter Kirk Douglas chin clefts and cheek implants. The flickering lights bathed all this facial scaffolding in a prismatic Halloween glow.

Katy Perry appeared on the rotating stage and began belting out "Hey Jude." She wore a sleeveless gown and a large pink petal head-piece that rose a foot above her head. Her stirring voice and *Alice in Wonderland* attire mercifully diverted the attention of the attendees at our table. Tony Bennett followed with a jazzy version of "Here, There and Everywhere," and Sérgio Mendes performed his famous bossa nova hit version of "The Fool on the Hill."

I soon noticed another table nearby that had several seats open. Humpty Dumpty resumed his pointed questioning after the Mendes set, and I whispered to Shane that I'd reconnoiter a new table and signal back.

My new target table was close to the main stage, centrally located, and seemed half empty. By now, between music sets, there was ceaseless foot traffic up front, as many of the event's key executives moved around to hobnob, network, and slap each other on the back. Sweating profusely, I waded through the crowd, bumping elbows with Tom Hanks, Stevie Van Zandt, and a few coked-out musicians I didn't recognize.

I got to the table and sat my quivering ass down trying to catch my breath. A pudgy-looking fellow in his late thirties with a distant stare sat two seats to my left. I gazed at his profile, and the longer I stared, the more familiar he looked. He vaguely resembled Paul McCartney. Then I realized it was Paul McCartney's son, James.

Uh-oh. If Paul McCartney's son is sitting at this table, it's probably a very important table. As the penny began to drop, I turned to my right and confronted a gut-wrenching sight: an enormous pair of bug-like sunglasses was directly monitoring me from six feet away. She was wearing a feathery white hat and an opaque expression.

"Who you?" she enquired in a vaguely familiar accent.

I began to speak, then stutter, then sputter something incomprehensible.

It was Yoko Ono.

"I'm me," I finally blurted out, shooting out of my chair and standing stiffly.

I then realized I'd been sitting in Paul McCartney's chair. He was obviously backstage preparing for another set or kibitzing with the organizers. George Harrison's widow, Olivia, was also at the table, looking at me with an alarmed expression.

I bowed deeply to one and all and fled.

I ducked and weaved back through the crowd, jostling several attendees, stepping on some waiters' toes, and tripping over several chairs toward Shane at Humpty Dumpty's table. "We've got to get out of here," hissed Shane. "Your buddy [Humpty Dumpty] is over there talking with security."

I looked around and was overcome with paranoia. We seemed in the center of a giant security dragnet closing in by the second.

Our best hope was to rush toward the front stage and embed in the large media scrum—to hide in plain sight. Shane agreed, and we soon found ourselves kneeling among hundreds of other photographers in front of the enormous speakers. We kept our heads down and I helped Shane polish his lenses, swap out his digital cards, and reinstall his batteries. The key was to look busy, very busy. I stayed crouched for what seemed an eternity waiting for that fatal tap on the shoulder.

The savior, God bless him, was Neil Young and Crazy Horse, his longtime band. They came out and launched into an outrageous rendition of "I Saw Her Standing There" with squealing guitars, improvised riffs, and Young's howling, high-pitched voice: "*She was just seventeen, and you know what I mean . . .*"

Neil Young performs "I Saw Her Standing There" at 2012 MusiCares gala. *Courtesy of Shane Kerch*

Soon the whole crowd was on its feet, stamping and singing along. Even security got into the act, moving and swaying. Young's appearance and his take on the early Beatles classic has become legendary, viewed millions of times on YouTube. Even after Young finished, the entire crowd stayed on its feet for a lengthy ovation. McCartney, back at his table at my former seat, stood beaming and clapped wildly.

As the evening drew to a close, James Taylor and Diana Krall coperformed intimate and affecting takes of "Yesterday" and "For No One."

McCartney hopped back onstage to perform a new song, "My Valentine," for his bride, Nancy Shevell, and the Wings song "Nineteen Hundred and Eighty-Five." He finished with "Carry That Weight" and appropriately "The End."

"Thank you so much everybody," McCartney told the audience. "That's it—go home! Thank you for caring and thank you for coming."

As the crowd began dispersing I noticed attendees still shaking their heads in wonderment. It was an exhilarating and spectacular evening. I was emotionally worn out from all the memories stirred by the music and my constant dodging of hostile guests and probing security.

While walking out I locked eyes with Humpty Dumpty, who was putting a coat on his wife's shoulders. Across the expanse of several tables I shrugged and gave him a thumbs-up. He flipped me the bird.

The only other downside was that my ears were ringing for days afterward. In crasher world, you always pay a price in the end.

12

KING WORLD KNOCKOUT

MICHAEL KING WAS A MARKETING WHIZ who, along with his brother Roger, built King World Productions into one of the most successful television syndication companies in America. The duo distributed such television bonanzas as *Wheel of Fortune, Jeopardy!*, and *The Oprah Winfrey Show*. When CBS purchased King World for roughly $2.5 billion in 1999, the company was also syndicating other hits such as *Inside Edition* and *Dr. Phil*.

While continuing to work as a consultant for CBS in his post–King World career, Michael King also pursued his passion for the boxing industry. He started a top-notch prizefighting gym in the city of Carson, about thirteen miles south of downtown Los Angeles, and launched a boxing promotion company, King Sports Worldwide, based in Brentwood, California.

With hundreds of millions of dollars in personal wealth, King hoped to rekindle America's passion for boxing by seeking out and training promising amateurs who could later become professional stars. By 2012, boxing's popularity in America was eroding due to competition from mixed-martial arts and the failure of its amateur program to produce iconic names. After several years of fledgling success and many millions spent, King decided to ramp up his promotional efforts by starting a series of professional boxing events, with four planned a year, at a converted airplane hangar in Santa Monica.

I knew the venue well. Barker Hangar is an enormous structure that housed and built large aircraft in World War II and is situated on the south side of the Santa Monica Airport, one of the busiest single-runway general aviation airports in the nation. In its postwar years, the giant aero shed was converted into one of Southern California's top venues for charity, corporate, and private events, as well as video and film shoots. Over the years I'd attended many an extravaganza there—concerts, awards shows, discount clothing sales, trade shows, and gala dinners.

Barker Hangar is a crasher Disneyland. It's not only three miles from where I live in Santa Monica but also regularly hosts spectacular events that are heavily publicized. "Anything happening tonight at Barker?" is a typical salutation during my daily crasher phone calls.

The hangar's interior is thirty-five thousand square feet, surrounded by another sixty thousand square feet of adjacent exterior areas for tenting, parking, catering, mobile bathrooms, and other support facilities. On big nights, the area transforms into an enormous warren of trucks, thronging crowds, searchlights, signs, parking personnel, and shipping containers—providing lots of entry opportunities and cover for conniving crashers. The sieve-like perimeter is almost impossible to secure. The shrieking aircraft landing every few minutes on an adjacent runway enhances a feeling of almost wartime havoc. "In chaos lies opportunity" sums up the party-crashing ethos at Barker on a typical night.

Indeed, some evenings feel like the Blitz, the bombardment of British cities by the German Luftwaffe in World War II. A long line of Cessnas, Pipers, Long-EZs, and corporate jets rain down from the skies, enveloping the area with the smell of aviation fuel. On more than a few occasions I've lounged, hot toddy in hand, on a high stool and flinched as a screaming jet appeared, headed for the party hangar.

A boxing event is notable for its volatility and high-stakes drama. When I heard Michael King was going to launch his new boxing promotion business with an opening exhibition at Barker Hangar, "Boxing at Barker," I couldn't think of a better locale.

I called one of my usual crash partners, Shane Kerch, and we made plans for a night of pugilistic pandemonium. Upon arrival, we encountered the usual commotion and parked our car in a nearby lot on Airport Avenue. We were tipped off that a hand-sized hanging lanyard was needed for entry, and I had a few generics in my black tote bag. We put them around our necks and did our usual flip trick, showing the back opaque side on the front of our chests.

In the parking lot, we ran into Gary Trejo, a middle-aged, former professional welterweight boxer and a friend of Shane's. Trejo didn't have a $200 ticket and was hoping he could ride in on our wake. We gave him a faux lanyard. Unfortunately, he insisted, despite our entreaties, on bringing his dog, Ozzie, a rambunctious Labrador retriever.

We entered an open gate on the east side of the hangar property and walked toward security guarding one of the side doors. Shane and I waltzed right in with our lanyards, but Trejo was stopped on account of the dog. He tried arguing his case, but security was adamant: no dogs allowed at the boxing match.

Trejo returned to his car to lock up Ozzie. He then came through another entrance and made it in. Soon, he was high-fiving and jiving with other ex-boxers and guests he knew. One of them gave him two valid VIP lanyards. Trejo then went back out to his car and put one of the VIP lanyards around Ozzie's neck. This time, he confidently walked the red carpet, holding his leashed dog.

A canine-averse guard gave them an extended look, and Trejo and his dog faced another ban. But Trejo reached down, grabbed

Ozzie's VIP pass, and held it up for the guard, who bent down and gave it serious scrutiny.

"Oh, a VIP. OK, no problem," said the guard. Then they scampered in.

I had never attended a live boxing match. Over the years I nursed a cursory interest in the sport following big televised fights.

My feelings about the "sweet science" were agnostic. Admittedly, there was something primal about witnessing two athletes stripped to the waist trying to pound each other into unconsciousness. Watching a pair of solitary individuals throw every resource into a battle that involves elements of pain, will, endurance, skill, strategy, wits, and fear could be thrilling. But knockouts that left fighters crawling to find their mouthpieces on the canvas while their eyes rolled into the back of their heads were unnerving.

In high school, a group of friends and I, filled with brio after watching a recent Muhammad Ali fight, staged a roving exhibition in my parents' backyard. It was an improvised, ignorant, and messy affair that involved a bunch of pimply, trash-talking kids trying to take each other's heads off with oversized gloves and no training. A couple of us had our bells rung, and one duo ended up taking off the gloves and resorting to a pathetic, scratching, biting, groin-punching wrestling match. There were moments of incoherence, some blood, and some bruised egos but luckily no serious injuries considering the idiocy of the contestants. Consequently, I've always had great respect for the mental and physical willpower of boxers after my boneheaded backyard experience.

As I entered Barker Hangar on Michael King's big opening night, the electricity in the air was overwhelming. It seemed like all the panoply of a Vegas bout was transported into the unlikely venue of an airport shed in small seaside Santa Monica. There were roped-off, ultra-VIP ringside suites with white leather sofas and close-to-the-action seating. Waitresses with chest-high legs served hard liquor and fussed over bubble-bellied patrons clamoring for gourmet burgers. A concentrated contingent of goodfellas and goombahs draped in gold chains and silver pinkie rings gesticulated wildly in conversation. I heard lots of "*dems*" and "*doooes*" and "*doonts.*" There was a whirlwind of chest bumps, high-fives, grip-and-grins, and flashing selfies.

Heralding trumpeters wearing ostentatious orange capes and white plumed helmets circled the ring, blaring fight songs. Advertisers walked the perimeter handing out tchotchkes. Ring girls held up countdown minute signs to fight time. Groupies and models worked the floor.

The Hollywood contingent was there in force. Comic actor Kevin Pollack was the emcee. Arnold Schwarzenegger took a ringside seat with his entourage. Actors Scott Caan and Jason Patric fist-bumped friends and eagerly awaited the action.

I saw lots of mashed faces and cauliflower ears, former boxers who looked familiar. Large parts of the audience stood up as Tommy "Hitman" Hearns arrived and embraced former rival Sugar Ray Leonard. I watched Hitman interviewed ringside and was struck by his earnest, slurred speech. He looked like all the trials and tribulations of the world had coursed through his head and body. What a warrior. What a price to pay.

I waited until the last possible moment before the first bout commenced and quickly angled toward a VIP seat. Shane had cloaked himself in his Vietnam pocket vest and camera gear and embedded in the media section. I saw a couple of open ringside spots in a small group of people who didn't seem to know each other—a perfect slot for the uninvited to blend in.

"Hey, hey you wid Bobby?" said a middle-aged, Lords of Flatbush type with an inkjet-dyed pomade.

"Yeah, yeah, I'm with Bobby. Great guy, super guy," I said, sounding like Donald Trump.

"Well, there's no Bobby in our group here," said my new acquaintance. "I think I gotcha."

Yes, he had nailed my forehead to the center of the ring. Now, how to get up and off the canvas? "All right, you tapped me," I admitted quickly. "But I've never been to a live professional boxing match in my life and I just want to get a quick, close look. I'd like to see and smell a little blood. Can I just sit my hairy rump here for a few minutes?"

Flatbush laughed and, with a wave of his pinkie hand, assented.

Soon, Kevin Pollack was onstage cracking jokes and making introductions. The crowd of about twelve hundred began to settle in. The fist and head bumps, the faux stare-down salutations, and peacock posturing of the audience members dwindled. A tense quiet cloaked the makeshift arena.

There were to be five fights of ten rounds each in multiple weight classes, including nationals from Ireland, the United States, South Africa, Cuba, and Georgia. Louis Rose, a middleweight from Compton, California, opened the slugfest by high-stepping into the ring with his opponent, Emanuel Ledezma from San Antonio, Texas. After introductions, a reading of the rules, and the zombie stare-down between the two foes, famed announcer Michael Buffer took the microphone in mid-ring and bellowed his trademark call to arms: "LET'S GET REEEEAAAADDDDYYY TO RUUUMMMMMBBBBBBBLLLLE!!"

I couldn't believe the intensity. Boxing was a rough trade, but watching it on television looked one-dimensional compared to the thwumps, grimaces, grunting, blood, sweat, and tears of a live match.

The jabs were crisp, sharp, and filled with electric baton–like shocks. I could practically feel the body shots as fighters clenched through the pain. During hard head hits, I witnessed momentary suspensions of consciousness and a glassy-eyed scramble to get one's bearing. At times the sweat and saliva (and sometimes blood) exploded off noggins and sprayed nearby bystanders.

The sounds rattled—involuntary burps, shrieks, yelps, and the deadening thumps of leather and bone compressing flesh. I kept thinking of Norman Mailer's description of the sounds of one boxer endlessly pummeling the head of another as that of a baseball bat pounding a watermelon.

A professional fighter friend, Lee Tonks, once described the elasticity of time when in the ring. When things were going well and you

Announcing round 6. *Courtesy of Shane Kerch*

were fighting with a perfect orchestration of power, quickness, and accuracy and your opponent was on the ropes, each round seemed to last seconds. But when it was your head bouncing off the canvas or your body contorting from endless blows, time seemed to inexorably slow—each round felt like forever.

By the eighth round, Rose had Ledezma staggering after trapping him in a corner and blasting him with a couple of brutal strikes to the skull. Ledezma looked unsteady and badly hurt. The referee stepped in and stopped the fight.

At the break between bouts, as the music picked up and Pollack kept up his comic patter, Shane came over looking wild-eyed. I'd always considered him a boxing aficionado, but the experience of witnessing so much brutality with a close lens shook him up. I had the same feelings of enthrallment and repulsion. This was life at its most elemental.

Soon after, a contingent of Flatbush flunkies showed up and I was flushed out of my VIP hot seat. That's the tough thing about crashing—you're always on the run or waiting for a poke in the ribs or a grip on the shoulder. You can never just sit and relax.

I retreated to the next class of seats about twenty yards away and found another perfect vantage point. Though I wasn't ringside, the venue still felt intimate, and the intensity of the next several fights was barely diminished. Next to me sat a mug-faced porterhouse with the habit of calling the action in a hyped-up baritone. This would-be color analyst kept up his rat-a-tat chatter throughout all the bouts. At first I found this expert intensely irritating, but I eventually warmed to his primitive insights.

"It's a right, now a left hook, there's an uppercut, he's killing the body so the head dies, cutting off the ring, that stomach punch collapsed his ankles, he just took a six-pack to the chin, there's no plan in his game plan." Then he'd explode with exhortations like "TAKE THIS MOFO OUT!" and "THAT'S IT! RIP 'EM! KILL 'EM!"

Behind me was a throng of additional screamers howling for blood. "Put the lights out!" "Mix it up!" "Do it now!" "That's the way, carve 'em up!" "It's bedtime, put 'em to sleep!"

As the decibel level increased, I turned around and watched a wannabe yuppie boxer in slacks and a blue blazer two rows back shadow punching in synchronization with the action onstage. The embedded bloodlust was at a fever pitch.

The final bout of the night, the main card, was a matchup between undefeated heavyweights from Southern California, Charles Martin and Alexander Flores. There's something about a heavyweight contest that exponentially ratchets up the tension. With both fighters listed as six-foot-five and weighing in at 250 pounds, each punch has the power to end a life.

Martin was a southpaw with a huge helmet of dreadlocks and an unorthodox and clunky style. Flores was a more polished boxer but seemed a bit chubby around the midsection. Compared to the earlier matches, their punches seemed like bombs, detonating off their midsections and exploding off their heads. I found myself wincing and cowering behind a couple of wiseguys.

By the third round, Martin started pummeling Flores and dropped him to the canvas with a right to the body. At the beginning of the fourth round Martin trapped Flores near the ropes and leveled a brutal combination that left Flores kneeled over on the canvas, grimacing in pain. The referee began administering the count and quickly ended the fight. Martin earned the North American Boxing Association heavyweight title with his victory and celebrated with his wife and infant son in the ring.

Heavyweight boxer Floyd Patterson once described the "confused hurt" and the deep embarrassment and shame of getting knocked out in front of so many people, friends and supporters. Once in a fight against Swedish boxer Ingemar Johansson, he found himself crawling around the ring trying to collect his wits after multiple knockdowns.

As he stared through the ropes, his vision returned and he locked eyes with John Wayne, only a few feet away. All he wanted at that moment was to hide.

I could see Flores struggling to escape grogginess, which morphed into self-reproach and chagrin as he approached Martin for an embrace after the fight. As the great writer Gay Talese once observed: "Only in boxing do you have that ritual, of two men, nearly naked, exhausted, the smell and taste of each other, after such serious battle, the strange intimacy of that. . . ."

It's indeed an odd formality to observe. Two giant men, after beating the bejesus out of each other, one imposing his will on the other, finally coming together for a hug and bouncing the rest of us back to civilization.

After the event, Shane and I stuck around, downed a few vitamin Vs (vodka, not Viagra) and chatted up a few of the card models, boxing groupies, and sundry goombahs that still lingered. It was an invigorating night that only reinforced my conflicted feelings about the sport.

I ended up attending another King Sports "Barker Boxing" spectacular several months later that exhibited the same glitzy promotion, energy, and gore. But the series was not to last.

Michael King died suddenly the next year, in May 2015, putting an end to the boxing experiment at Barker. There hasn't been another bout there since.

13

BACKYARD WHO?

I WAS SITTING IN THE STUDY of my rent-controlled apartment trying to write an outline for a television documentary series, and it wasn't going well.

As I sat at my desk, pulling out tufts of hair, my cell phone lit up.

"Massive party up in Pacific Palisades, roadblocks are going up, and flatbed trucks are bringing in dozens of port-a-potties and lining them on the street," said my crasher friend Nate Frotsky, who also provided the coordinates. "Rumor has it there'll be some big-name bands, food, drink, dancing bears, lion tamers, the works!"

I knew the area well. Having grown up in Pacific Palisades, I'd attended many a social affair in this part of town. It was an exclusive grid of residential blocks just north of Sunset Boulevard near the tony Riviera Country Club, featuring enormous mansions with sunken tennis courts, Olympic-size swimming pools, well-tended lawns, and helipads.

I grew up in a more modest part of the community in an area near the village square with one-thousand-square-foot houses built in the 1940s. My British parents referred to it with typical understated British humor as the "ghetto section" of the Palisades. We were brought up with no television (banned by my mother) and no shower. All six of us shared one bathtub for decades.

"We're British. We don't shower, we bathe," said my father to repeated entreaties to put a nozzle in the bathroom wall. "How can one possibly get clean with water just bouncing off you? One must soak to release the dirt and toxins."

When I heard about the party, I called my crony Shane Kerch, and by early evening we were leaving my crumbling apartment in Santa Monica for the Riviera Country Club neighborhood a couple of miles away. As we turned off Sunset Boulevard and headed up San Remo Drive toward the extravaganza, we faced a phalanx of LAPD badges, guns, and squad cars. Yoicks, this was some grand-poobah event. We made a hasty U-turn and retreated to a parking spot I knew, several blocks away. Better to hoof it in than get trapped in confrontational banter in our car with the men in blue.

As we parked, I saw crasher Pepper Grabinski walking hurriedly by. He wore a fake lanyard that said SECURITY. His eyes flitted from side to side. His neck was drenched. I wanted to yell at him to turn around. He was beyond conspicuous and could take us all out.

I, too, felt an overwhelming anxiety at the crushing security preparations. Was this the president of the United States or some visiting foreign dignitary? A Russian oligarch? A celebrities-only summit?

I tried calling fellow interloper Nate Frotsky, who was usually the first person in at every party. I got him on the phone, but my cell had spotty coverage and all I could hear was "Backyard . . . Who . . . Backyard . . . Who!"

"But WHO?" I kept screaming. "Who are you talking about? How do we get in?" I finally gave up plying him for information.

When in doubt, wear all black—you can pass as a fashionable guest, a member of security, a caterer, or even a passing shadow.

On this evening Shane and I looked like respectable morticians; our shoes were buffed, buttons intact, and our blazers freshly pressed and dry-cleaned.

We avoided the main check-in entrance and took an indirect route to the proceedings. We ran into our first roadblock several blocks out from the mansion. Miraculously, two security guards were giving directions to some wrong-way guests in a Maserati. We strolled by and soon were at a side entrance to the mansion grounds that was clotted with glaring guards. I panicked and motioned to Shane to head for the Andy Gump portable toilets that were set in the middle of the street.

Shane and I spent the next twenty minutes hiding side by side in adjoining lean-tos hissing at each other through the vents and engaging in cupped conversation on our cell phones. We were desperately trying to come up with an entrance strategy as more and more guests arrived and security battened down the hatches.

"Goddamn it, is anyone in here?" yelled one drunken guest as he violently shook my door handle. "You've been in there for hours! I've got to take a major dump!"

I peeked through a slit and saw a bloviated, red-faced, stockbroker-type stooge used to getting an instant response. There was by now a big line outside waiting to expel all the food and drink consumed inside the party.

"Hold on man, I'm dropping off a payload myself! Gimme a break," I yelled back.

There was a thirty-second pause. Then the pinch-deprived idiot began rocking my Gump, causing the malodorous mess in the toilet to slosh over the lid.

"You need to get out now, buddy! I'm ready to explode," barked the stooge. "If you don't, I'm coming in there."

"It's Willy Wonka's chocolate factory in here. I highly suggest you don't," I yelled back.

I finally burst out. I wish I'd had a big pail of Gump goop to dump all over him. I started to say something but held off. The last thing I needed was a shit-flinging fight with a drunken financial analyst in the middle of the street. I blew by him and reconnected with Shane up the block. We collected ourselves, and I soon noticed a large truck had pulled up by the side hedge gate. Dozens of burly roadies were unloading amplifiers, synthesizers, keyboards, and other rock 'n' roll paraphernalia and carrying them into the party.

I motioned to Shane, and we went over to the back of the truck.

"Hey, you guys need a hand?" I asked innocently.

"Sure, if you don't mind dirtying yourself up a bit," said one dude skeptically.

"Dirty is my middle name," I said.

I picked up part of a drum set and Shane lifted up a black sandbag, and we followed the efficient train of stagehands right into the party. The guards barely gave us a gander.

The mansion grounds were immense. Birch, eucalyptus, and pine trees dotted the roughly two-acre property of park-like grounds. Meandering pathways cut through elaborate ponds filled with Japanese koi, bass, and bluegill. On one end of the expansive lawn was a huge stage with overhead steel beams, a panoply of lights, and electrical grids. Off to the side loomed an outdoor kitchen with a wood-burning oven and behind it a multilevel, multi-winged estate fit for a king.

We reached the stage alongside the bearded roadies and dumped our goods on the platform. I looked around and saw multiple buffet stations and bars spread throughout the property. A fleet of servers glided through the well-heeled crowd unloading West African peanut stew, chicken liver pâté, roast pork buns, and other delicacies.

Shane and I quickly forgot our roadie duties, hopped off the stage and blended in with the crowd. I ran into Nate Frotsky, who said I'd just missed an explosive rock 'n' roll set from Joan Jett and the

Blackhearts. He mentioned that Eddie Vedder would soon play, followed by the mega rock group the Who.

The Who in someone's backyard? WTF? It was hard to believe.

We soon found out that the event was a joint effort by real estate mogul Jordan Kaplan (at his home) and the rock band's Who Cares About the Next Generation charity to help raise awareness and funds for autism treatment and teens with cancer.

David Spade did a stand-up routine onstage. He then handed off the mic to comedian Howie Mandel, who hosted a live auction for such items as a Bally Wizard pinball machine (vintage 1975), a replica of the Who drummer Keith Moon's sparkle red drum kit, and a framed print of producer George Martin's string quartet of the Beatles' song "Yesterday" signed by Paul McCartney and George Harrison. Later Mandel offered a rehearsal day with the rock band Kiss, which also included two guitars, a bass, and a snare drum donated by lead singer Paul Stanley. Then there was a Fender Stratocaster guitar signed by Pete Townshend, Joan Jett, Eddie Vedder, Rick Nielsen, and Joe Walsh.

Boxer Sugar Ray Leonard got a few laughs and grimaces when he offered to hit someone for $10,000 so they could "see how it feels"— and he closed the sale!

Pearl Jam front man Eddie Vedder popped onstage and sang some of his trademark hits, "Can't Keep Up," "Rise," and "Last Will and Testament," using his acoustic ukulele.

As I roamed the grounds I saw Dustin Hoffman, Cindy Crawford, Adam Sandler, and Judd Apatow bopping to the music and scarfing down the gourmet offerings. Other members of the Westside moneyed class attended, and at times it looked like a commercial real estate festival. Tickets were $3,000 a pop.

In the middle of it all was Pepper Grabinski, who looked relieved and ecstatic. He'd ditched his security badge and was in his usual modus operandi trying to chat up every married woman at the party.

I searched the crowd and realized the only people in attendance were either the super-rich or a handful of jumpy-looking crashers.

As the skies darkened, the crowd began humming with anticipation at seeing one of the world's greatest rock bands in such close quarters. The roadies seemed to pick up the pace, loading every conceivable piece of equipment up on to the stage. Then a quick announcement, flashing purple lights, and out walked the Who. They lit into their opening number, "Bargain."

Here, fifteen feet in front of me, was one of the most influential rock bands of all time, with sales of more than one hundred million records and performances at the Monterey Pop Festival, Woodstock, and Live Aid in a career spanning half a century. As Roger Daltrey and Pete Townshend walked onstage, I expected to see two decrepit, stooped, ashen-faced rockers warbling their last ditties. Instead they were vital titans still at the top of their game in their early seventies. Neither had an ounce of fat on them. Daltrey still had a lion mane of hair, his trademark strut, his piercing scream *"YEEEEAAAAAAAAHHHHHHH"* (during "Won't Get Fooled Again"), and still windmilled his microphone cable onstage. Townshend played guitar using his fast arm-windup motion, performed concise downstrokes, and plucked and fingerpicked his instrument expertly. His voice was still strong and resonant.

As they played "Baba O'Riley" I found myself howling in attempted unison with the phrase "Out here in the fields, I fight for my meals." I misted up at the *Tommy* song "See Me, Feel Me." Sentimental memories washed over me during "I Can See for Miles." I remembered walking on a beach in the south of England with my since-departed parents as a child listening to the song on a portable radio. The band played for little more than an hour but packed their set with multiple hits and pounding energy that never let up. It was mesmerizing, deep, and meaningful.

Some in the audience, whose greatest lack of restraint is overfilling their coffee thermos before a morning conference, seemed to go haywire—doing jumping jacks, splits, and smashing into each other in mosh pit hysterics. I saw ripped pants, missing shoes, snapped necklaces, and other rock 'n' roll lacerations. It was a baby boomer white riot.

Afterward I shook the hand of Zak Starkey (the son of Richard Starkey, also known as Ringo Starr), the Who's drummer since 1996, and wished him well from everyone in L.A.'s crasher community. He tilted his head and gave me a wordless cockeyed look.

As the crowd dispersed after the event, I hung around, soaking in the epic dimensions of the evening. As a former cynical reporter and ink-stained wretch, I'm not easily floored, and I'm especially skeptical about the special talents and status of celebrities. I've always found most of them wanting in person and much smaller than their public images. But the performance of the Who in this Pacific Palisades backyard, singing the songs of my childhood in the town I grew up in, well that was special.

Eventually, Shane and I wandered back to our car. It was around midnight and the streets were deserted, as they so often are in exclusive communities. As kids we used to call them "neutron-bomb neighborhoods"—all the mansions are still standing but the humans are extinct. To our surprise, around the corner came an older gentleman walking his dog.

"Excuse me, were you guys at that big party a few blocks away?" he asked. "I'm just wondering why they kept playing all those Who rock 'n' roll songs so loudly on the speakers. Don't they realize we're all trying to sleep?"

14

PUMPED UP
WITH PALTROW

USUALLY FIND EVENTS BY NETWORKING WITH OTHER CRASHERS, perusing the party tip sheet the Master List, and scouring the web. But sometimes, I'll notice a happening during a simple drive-by. Behind the wheel of my car, usually on the Westside of Los Angeles, I'm always scanning the urban topography for the telltale signs of a festive occasion.

One early evening I was navigating the dense traffic on San Vicente Boulevard in Brentwood, a hyper-rich retail thoroughfare packed with high-end eateries, spas, and fashion boutiques. Up ahead, I noticed a throng of people gathered outside a storefront in a state of exaltation, sipping drinks and nibbling from trays of food. There was the typical red carpet, balloons, and a bevy of photographers. I figured it was a retail opening of some sort, probably a celebrity vanity project.

I peeled into the parking lot of a local bank, ditched my jalopy, and strolled up the street to investigate. As the visuals came into focus, I noticed dozens of impossibly beautiful middle-aged women with enhanced musculature milling about. There weren't many men, and with my potbellied silhouette, I immediately felt conspicuous. But with nothing to lose (except a few dozen pounds), I sauntered into the middle of the scrum.

It was the grand opening of the Tracy Anderson Studio, a multidimensional, state-of-the-art gym for bored wealthy housewives, Malibu moms, and other tanned and toned varietals. Anderson, a celebrity fitness guru, had partnered with Gwyneth Paltrow to bring her signature method of dance cardio and high-repetition, low-weight strength workouts to her new eighty-five-hundred-square-foot venue on L.A.'s Westside.

When it comes to health and fitness, celebrities have an especially strong sway over the rest of us—by following their regimens, we think our lives will drastically improve. I've also noticed that many of the rich and famous have a strong interest in health and life extension. Larry Page and Sergey Brin, the founders of Google, have poured tens of millions into such research. After all, it's highly unlikely all that wealth can be transported to the big party upstairs. Better to stretch out life spans and exploit all those billions of dollars on tangible things while down here on terra firma.

I thought about all this as I slalomed through a gauntlet of celery shakes, mushroom-chocolate hors d'oeuvres, and granular bran muffins to the check-in table. I used my trademark "finger-point" method by thrusting out my right index and affixing it to a name on the clipboard list.

"Richard Hetherington?" asked a young check-in clerk, looking down and up.

"Yes, I am the right honorable Richard Hetherington, and I badly need to get in shape," I responded with the slight hint of a British accent.

"You definitely do, and you've definitely come to the right place," she said, stamping my hand with a red ink star.

Soon I was hobnobbing with throngs of svelte women with ripped abs, popping biceps, flexed calves, and bulging veins in their necks. Some carried infants and were joyously employing them as free weights, routinely jerking them from the ground up to their mid-sections, holding them out and thrusting them over their heads.

I quickly sent out a DEFCON 3 text alert to my network of social imposters, hyping details and outlining coordinates for this last-minute jamboree.

There was a strong celebrity contingent, and I quickly noticed supermodels Stacy Keibler, Molly Sims, and the ubiquitous Kim Kardashian.

Soon Gwyneth Paltrow arrived with her husband, Coldplay lead singer Chris Martin. (At that point in time, they hadn't yet "consciously uncoupled.") She looked the paragon of California health—almost six feet tall with gleaming, tawny skin, lustrous blond hair, and an Olympian physique. She looked better in person than on screen.

Besides her abundant acting skills, I was always fascinated by the success of her health and wellness website—Goop.com—and the profusion of offbeat (and very expensive) products. Paltrow had taken lots of heat and scorn for the seeming frivolity of those items and the alleged pseudoscience behind their health claims.

Who could forget such heavily promoted goods and services as the monthly $103 camel milk delivery subscription, the $4,000 two-person cedar sauna, or the $66 jade eggs—small green oval stones for insertion into one's vagina for "spiritual detox" that can be recharged with the energy of a full moon? There were the odes to various cleanses, bee-sting skin treatments, and barefoot strolls. But nothing got more attention than Goop's recommendation that women partake in vaginal steaming also known as a Mugwort V Steam at the Tikkun Holistic Spa in downtown Santa Monica.

"You sit on what is essentially a mini-throne," wrote Paltrow, "and a combination of infrared and mugwort steam cleanses your uterus, et al. It is an energetic release—not just a steam douche—that balances female hormone levels. If you're in LA, you have to do it."

In September 2018, Goop settled a consumer protection lawsuit brought by California prosecutors for $145,000 that included the notorious $66 jade eggs. The suit challenged Goop's claims that sticking the stones up women's vaginas would help "increase sexual energy," develop "vaginal muscles," and improve hormone balance and bladder control. The lawsuit alleged that the lifestyle colossus made claims that were not scientifically valid. Goop agreed to refund customers and halt advertising for several of its products that touted their health benefits.

Despite heavy media coverage of the lawsuit and boatloads of ridicule, Paltrow seemed to be living her creed, demonstrated by her vitality and the opening of this new fitness studio.

Soon enough, guides began giving tours of the spaceship facilities. There were five VIP training rooms, including a main multi-mirrored workout room featuring extensive marble paneling and humidifiers that blew rivers of steam. In the primary room, I bounced on the Super G Floor, a wood flooring supported by hundreds of hidden spring coils that lessened the impact on deteriorating hips and splintered knees during high-intensity exercise sessions. From the ceiling hung the Tracy Anderson patented Iso-Kinetic Band System—a rainbow of large colored rubber bands, the better to stretch, torque, and twist one's flabby physique into shape during tortuous cardio workouts. Our guide pointed out the extensive sound system, heat and humidity controls, and the profusion of ankle and arm weights, thick towels, and antiseptic spray bottles.

We peeked in on the his-and-her locker rooms outfitted with fire-hose showers and bath oils by the British company Ila Spa. There was some high-intensity training equipment—"hit" machines that resembled torture tools used by the Spanish Inquisition. The studio had a fully outfitted salon with a blow-dry bar stuffed with products by celebrity stylist David Babaii. Besides free valet parking, members were guaranteed one free "blow-out" per month. With my receding hairline, I figured I'd skip that benefit. On the other hand, maybe my hirsute silverback could use a frisky blow-dry?

Membership costs were staggered, with the platinum version listed at $1,500 per month. A $500 mandatory initial consultation—a "Body Blueprint"—included blood paneling, body mass index analysis, and nutrition advice. Paisanos like me were given a token nod and allowed to drop in on select fifty-minute classes for $45. Anderson was also promising a food delivery service for $49.95 per day and a Liquid Program boasting 100 percent raw and organic juices and smoothies to sandblast your colon and clear up your bloodshot eyeballs.

There were endless pitches about body assessment, resistance, and mat-based training, instructional DVDs, spinach smoothies, pushing fat to the surface, and firing the accessory muscles.

At the end of the tour, I wandered back out to the party. The few men in attendance seemed overly plucked and perfumed. Some had face peels, chin tweaks, and puffy platypus lips. But all the women radiated health, and many tested the workout equipment while continuing to hoist their infants.

In the midst of this sea of vitality, I caught the prow of a listing ship. Duane Flanigan's inescapable visage appeared above all the body plumage. His purple, John Barleycorn face stood out like a blood moon. Alerted by my group text, he'd somehow staggered in and managed to stay.

"I can't believe this place," said Flanigan, peering around. "These women look like they're from another planet. Maybe it's time I got back in shape."

"That could actually take a *lot* of time," I said. "And lots and lots of money."

Flanigan gave a harrumph. But I did notice the environment was having an effect. He walked over to the veggie juice bar and ordered an enormous kale shake. He took a step back and studied the frothing beaker as if an alien had just landed. After a few hesitant sips, he whipped out his omnipresent flask from his blazer's inseam pocket and spiked the leafy concoction with a stealth shot of bourbon. He drained it and gave me a wide green smile.

After an hour of imbibing more colon-stripping shakes, stuffing ourselves with additional roughage, and trying to engage several fitness titans and supermodels in conversation, we decided we'd had enough. We both carried burgeoning stomachaches from the fresh, spongy intake and left feeling hopelessly pudgy and inadequate.

At the time of this writing several years later, I decided to revisit the Anderson Studio for the "Iso-Kinetic Band" class that promised "maximum calorie burning through band-based cardio that softens impact and minimizes bounce." Maybe there was hope for a lump like me and I could finally shock-shift myself into shape.

I arrived in the sparkling lobby, dutifully paid my $45, and was led into the main workout room. I met Teal, a spectacularly robust fitness trainer who seemed apprehensive. She gave me a quick once-over and I could tell she was wondering if I'd survive the class.

"On a scale of one to five, one best, five being worst, what kind of shape are you in?" she inquired.

"I'd say I'm about a four," I responded nervously. "I walk regularly, play beach volleyball, and swim naked on weekends."

She half laughed, half gulped, and half coughed. "OK, I just want to keep an eye on you, as this is a very high-intensity class," she said. "If you feel stressed, slow down. Don't push yourself too much."

I nodded mutely and looked around for any spare medevac paddles. All I saw were mounds of mats, hundreds of freshly folded towels, and some ankle weights that I was told to put on.

Six other stunning middle-aged women with sculpted buttocks joined the class. I nodded at them and tried to make small talk, but they refused to engage and kept their eyes on the enormous front mirror.

The climate-controlled heat in the room was set at 95 degrees and the humidity at 75 percent—the better to loosen muscles and flex spines. Within minutes of merely standing I was feverish and dripping like a sweat hog.

As a couple of my classmates stretched and moved about, I noticed that some surgically enhanced parts of them weren't moving. On the Westside of L.A. we call the type "frozen yoga."

Teal flicked on the enormous sound system and started blaring her hip-hop playlist, the signal that our crucifixion session was commencing.

We were told to reach up and grab fistfuls of the multicolored bands hanging from the ceiling and bring them down to waist level. Teal led us through a slowly escalating series of flapping arm and sliding foot movements. Soon we were doing jumping jacks while I tightly held on to the taut bands. I was ever grateful for the bouncy floor that absorbed my ample poundage and spared my gout-ridden knees.

Next we were incorporating struts, chest pops, box steps, and hip swivels in four-count repetitions as rapper Drake screeched over the pounding speakers.

> Keep it right there, no moving
> Make my way around the bases

I tried my best to keep up with each of Teal's gymnastic moves that were tightly synchronized to the deafening lyrics.

> I like best when you're fresh faced and no foundation
> Willing and ready for the taking

Adrian shredding limbs in Iso-Kinetic Band class at Tracy
Anderson Studio.

It was an odd juxtaposition to watch all these formal, white,
wealthy women gyrate to the violent, misogynistic lyrics of black rap.
Oh well, whatever burns calories.

Finally we were on our knees, bent over, and flicking out our legs
in frantic repetition. I had a white-knuckled grip on a fistful of bands,
my thighs felt like rubber, and my head started spinning. Suddenly
something snapped. I thought it might be a ligament or my Achilles

tendon or maybe my mind. But in a split second I realized one of the bands got loose and ricocheted into my forehead, sending me sprawling. I felt like I'd been shot.

An assistant scurried over, checked me out, and righted me. I looked over to the far corner of the room and noticed another woman (in a separate workout?) jumping up and down methodically on a small portable trampoline while clutching the notorious ceiling bands. None of the other trainees bothered to acknowledge me, although Teal looked ready to speed dial 911.

After another fifteen minutes, my face was blue from lack of oxygen, my teakettle belly had slipped the surly bonds of my waistband, and I was overcome with nausea. This time, I let the bands go gingerly and fled to the air-conditioned lobby.

Sam, the front desk clerk, gave me a concerned look and fetched me some water and a fresh towel.

"The workout in there is absolutely insane," I panted, as I looked up at shelves of Goop products.

"Yes, it is. That's why Brentwood's buffest come here," said Sam, with a slightly sadistic grin.

I was absolutely soaked. After a few minutes of rehydrating and walking in circles, I returned to Teal's torture chamber and tried to regain my dignity. She came over and suggested I hold only one band in each hand and employ the ones in the middle that had less torque and tension.

I gallantly finished the final fifteen minutes and staggered out. I felt like Mel Gibson in the last scene of *Braveheart* where's he's hung, drawn, and quartered and his remains are fed to the dogs. Every muscle in my body felt electrocuted. Every joint zapped. All vertebrae dislodged and realigned. Tracy Anderson (and those Paltrow pulleys), you have my respect.

I sat on a bench outside the studio, tried to catch my breath, and watched as another cluster of energetic dervishes arrived for the next class. The profusion of ripped torsos left me feeling oddly claustrophobic and unconsciously rebellious.

After what seemed like an hour of paralysis, I rose with a crackling spine, walked gingerly to my car, and drove to an In-N-Out Burger, where I ordered a double cheeseburger, "animal style"—that's one with *all* the trimmings.

PART III

ON THE ROAD

Adrian percolating in an Esalen hot springs tub.

15

SIDE-DOOR SUNDANCE

"LET'S TAKE THE HUSTLE TO ANOTHER LEVEL," said the gravelly baritone on the other end of the phone.

It was 10 AM and I was dealing with a paint-stripping hangover from a well-stocked food and wine event from the night before.

"Waaaaaa? Say waaaa?" I responded, fumbling for my bearings in the cluttered playpen called my bedroom.

"Let's ramp things up, get out of town, move some scenery around," said Avi, as his staccato Israeli accent came into auditory focus. "L.A.'s seen enough of us. Let's hit Sundance next week."

It was mid-January 2004, and the thought of schlepping into the mountains of Utah, at that moment, seemed Himalayan.

"Sorry bud, you're going to have to find another Sherpa," I said. "We have no passes, no tickets, no travel reservations, no place to stay. I hear that film festival can be a nightmare if you're left out in a blizzard."

"What's wrong with you, man?" shouted Avi. "Where's the risk-taker I've always known and loved? My mother always says, 'When in doubt, do!' And it's time to do, do, do!"

"OK, OK, let me hydrate and get back to you," I said, as the veins on my forehead throbbed.

About twenty minutes later there was a loud thumping on my door. Avi appeared, waving the International Creative Management (ICM) Agency's treasured "Sundance Party List," which he'd gotten from a lawyer friend. He shoved it in front of my face, and my vision narrowed. It was an Excel spreadsheet with the elaborate details of a Prussian military plan. Every thirty minutes, from 6 AM to 2 AM, were notations for every conceivable social gathering, post-film party, post-Q&A tea, snow lodge barbecue, and celebrity lounge. Every event came with a specific address, the public relations contact, and a sprinkling of famous attendee names.

Wow. This was a scale tipper. How could I pass up such a well-paved road with all signs and directions laid out before me? In five pages were ten straight days of fun and frolic, some skiing, and the ultimate networking opportunity. Here was a chance to attend the greatest film festival in the world, only a ninety-minute flight from L.A.

The annual gathering in Park City, Utah, is *the* place for dedicated cineastes. For two weeks, roughly thirty thousand attendees view the most mesmerizing new independent feature and documentary films from all over the world. There are filmmaker panel discussions, fundraising seminars, midnight screenings, and get-acquainted sessions.

Besides the latest films, the place was a crasher paradise, with porous celebrity brunches, industry dinners, and late-night mountaintop parties packed with creative, fascinating people and unlimited food, drink, and swag. Not to mention midnight skiing, wine tasting forays, snowball fights, and stunning scenery.

Once the decision was made, Avi and I leapt into action. Avi researched and collected our press applications. I had freelanced for one of America's first "daily digital" newspapers—*The American*

Reporter—and was able to get a legitimate assignment from my editor. Avi made good use of some letterhead from *Yedioth Ahronoth*, an Israeli newspaper, and typed up a letter of roving commission. We'd both heard that press credentials significantly changed one's status at the festival and lubricated all entry points.

Unfortunately, we had no luck finding a room in town. We'd heard horror stories of people wandering Park City's Main Street in 10-degree weather at 3 AM, begging passersby for a swatch of carpet on a condo floor. But we felt fortified with our press passes, a couple of key contacts working for the festival, and our wolfish crasher instincts.

Soon enough, we were landing in Salt Lake City and riding a shuttle bus into the snow-bedecked peaks of the Wasatch mountains. We disembarked with our backpacks on Main Street and began scrambling for lodging as the sun was setting and feathery snowflakes began falling.

I ducked into a local restaurant and asked the host if she knew any resting place for two unruly, disheveled film enthusiasts. She gave me a knowing look and immediately proffered the Chateau Apres Lodge, a large hostelry with dozens of small rooms, a few blocks away.

"I think the private rooms are completely booked, but I know they often open their big shared dormitory spaces to handle the overflow," she said, flicking her mouth with a toothpick. "And the charge is usually about twenty dollars per person per night."

The price and location sounded right, and Avi and I hoofed it over. The place looked like a cartoonish version of a Swiss ski chalet, with alpine wood paneling, a row of pyramid-shaped cabins on the roof, and a line of Christmas-shaped pine trees lining the front. Inside were more timber paneling and a roaring fire in a red brick kiln, situated in the middle of the lobby. I half expected to be met by a group of yodelers in knee-high socks and Birkenstocks.

The restaurant host was correct. All the private rooms were booked. Dave, the manager, suggested the male dormitory area, just off the lobby. Soon we were led into a cavernous room with about fifty bunk beds filling rapidly with the belongings of dozens of young, starving, aspiring filmmakers. The place was a hot concrete bunker that reeked of bad body odor. It felt like Cell Block H in the local county jail. The adjacent toilets were streaked with bung skids and overflowing with beer piss. I heard the women's dorm section was a palace in comparison.

Avi and I were led to a couple of bunks near the bathroom, and we plopped down our gear. Avi looked like he was having flashbacks of his time in the Israeli army. But this would have to do.

We were hungry, and I pulled out my ICM party list and found a big HBO shindig that was about to commence at a local restaurant. We put on our ski hats and ventured forth. Outside the eatery on Main Street was a large crush of photographers and film types, wearing black leather bomber jackets and dark turtlenecks. The twenty-one-year-old clipboard maven at the door seemed overwhelmed as numerous wannabes screamed out names on the list or names of people they thought were on the list. Several beefy locals backed her up. Entry didn't look promising.

We thought of trying the back, but the snowdrifts looked high and we wanted a quick solution. I noticed a large garbage bin in a nearby alley and walked over to find a bunch of discarded FedEx boxes that were in relatively good shape. We stuffed them with some newspaper, taped them up (good crashers always carry tape), and put them in presentable form.

"FedEx, FedEx, we've got a delivery for HBO!" I shouted, as the crowd parted and both of us walked in single file with separate boxes held over our heads.

"Who is the delivery for?" asked the clipboard maven.

I brought the box down to my chest and pretended to study it closely.

"It's for a Mr. Chris Albrecht [the CEO of HBO], and I believe they're a bunch of DVDs. . . . It looks high priority," I said nonchalantly.

"Oh, it's for Mr. Albrecht, OK," said the maven, glad to quickly solve just one of many problems at the door. Avi and I were waved in.

A friend of mine who witnessed the whole encounter said he heard one of the bouncers mutter, "Don't FedEx delivery guys work alone and wear uniforms?" But by then it was too late. We'd already scampered up the stairs and dispersed into the party. I quickly found a back room and shoved my corroded FedEx box out a window and watched it bounce off the snow.

When I returned, Avi had also ditched his box and had a rum runner in hand. We marveled at the auspicious start to the proceedings. Soon we were at a sumptuous buffet of skirt steak pinwheels, caramelized pork rinds, buttery tilapia, and an assortment of farm-to-table salads.

I began making the rounds, chatting amiably with industry folk and handing out my newly minted business card: MAHER PRODUCTIONS—WRITER/DIRECTOR. I also slotted in some investigative work for the *American Reporter.* I bumped into *Capturing the Friedmans* documentary film director Andrew Jarecki and saluted his new film, which was premiering at Sundance the next day.

Across the room I spotted actor Scott Glenn of *Training Day, Urban Cowboy,* and *Absolute Power.* I gave him way too many compliments about his acting skills, and he took it all in stride. Nice guy. Modest. Intense.

Eventually, I met Jessica, an attractive woman who looked like a younger Suzy Chapstick, the famous ski bunny from the 1970s. Crashers are always looking for the next bigger, better party, and Jessica tipped me off about a wild event at a mountaintop estate that was about to begin.

My tummy was already bulging with rich, gourmet food, I'd drained a few mojitos, and I'd hit everyone of note at the HBO function. It was time to head for higher altitudes.

I nabbed Avi, and with Jessica we hopped in a taxi and began the winding switchback ride up into the Deer Valley ski resort. Up ahead atop a mountain peak was a ginormous multistoried mansion that was pulsating with party action. The top floor had floor-to-ceiling windows and throbbed with strobe lights and a giant disco ball. On the other levels, attendees hung from balconies. At the entrance, one lone bouncer holding a guest list tried to cope with a surging throng of arrivals. We had no idea who owned the place or who was hosting.

There was a sled leaning against the side of the lodge, and I motioned to Avi and Jessica to help me pick it up. We carried it through the front door, as I gave the bouncer a quick nod.

Once inside, we noticed the usual hodgepodge of Hollywood agents, starving filmmakers, fledgling actors, big-shot producers, and local lumberjacks. The place overflowed with food and drink. Scarves, ski vests, and hats were piled in corners. Music pumped from the upper floors. We placed the sled near the fireplace.

A box girl came by offering enormous Dominican cigars. I grabbed one and puffed contentedly on an adjacent balcony, while sipping a Stoli and taking in the glittering lights of the valley below.

We soon heard the third floor had an indoor basketball court. After draining our drinks, we hopped in the property's private elevator. When the door opened, we saw an astounding sight. More than sixty people in various states of inebriation were playing a full-court game of hoops. It looked like a combination of rugby and American football. Basket-brawl might be the right phrase. No referee and hard fouls, including the occasional tackle, were par. Guests seemed to jump in and out of the game haphazardly, depending on their need for rum refills.

Avi, Jessica, and I hopped into the scrimmage. A tall lanky guy on the other team definitely had game. He looked like he'd just finished an agency power lunch at a Beverly Hills eatery with his black mock turtleneck and Johnston & Murphy shoes. He effortlessly bombed in thirty-footers from behind his impenetrable Maui Jim sunglasses, permanently stuck on the bridge of his nose.

No one was wearing proper athletic shoes, and soon, black scuffs from all the formal heel-ware peppered the gym floor.

Though there were a few overly competitive drunken thugs, the biggest danger was some of the women. Every time one of us touched the ball, a bevy of eager damsels mobbed the dribbler with Edward Scissorhands fingernails. I saw the unfolding game as a metaphor for Hollywood's desperation and excess: too many people on too small a court for too few positions, and lots of collateral damage.

I was just about to make one of my signature moves, a crossover dribble with a spin to the rim, when a cluster of female basketball bees swarmed me. I felt the flicks of dozens of talons shredding my frame, until one caught me just below my right eye. Blood spurted out and I thought I'd been maimed—a Cyclops for life.

Now I realized why the agile agent-baller never took off his sunglasses.

I stopped the bleeding with some ice, found a bandage, and returned to the fray. I looked out the panoramic windows and noticed it was now snowing. It was an unforgettable sight I was glad not to lose.

After hours of revelry, Avi and I returned to our flophouse in the early morning hours. By now, the place was jammed. Every bunk was filled and overflowing with personal effects—computers, notepads, hiking boots, backpacks, and even sleds and snowshoes. Some guests were already passed out, snoring loudly. But others, amped up from all the film action, talked loudly over the bodies of their inert bunkmates.

There was glamour all day and then squalor at the end of the night—a contrast that dogged us throughout the festival.

I climbed into a top bunk that soon became a sagging hammock. My shins hung limply over the end of the bed. The toilets flushed incessantly and the sweat, piss, and poop stench mix was overwhelming. Groups of young, hormonal men living together can quickly devolve into a Neanderthal-like state. Neither Avi nor I got a wink.

We rallied the next morning by attending an 8 AM producers breakfast at the Filmmaker Lodge downtown. After fortifying ourselves with triple espressos, salmon, eggs, and toast, we sat down for a talk on funding for public television given by the female head of PBS, Pat Mitchell.

"This is my first Sundance, and I must say, I'm astounded by all the energy and knowledge and skill of the attendees," she said at one point. "This place is just bursting with ideas and ambition and dedication. Why just last night I had a guy follow me into the women's bathroom waving a script that he insisted I just had to read!"

There was a delayed pause as Mitchell shifted her notes at the podium.

"Sorry about that," I blurted out raising my hand.

The whole place erupted with laughter. It was a bald falsehood but, as my first girlfriend once observed, I'll die (or kill) for a chuckle.

After the PBS brunch, we hastened to a documentary showing of *The Fight*, an account of the epic boxing bout between the American Joe Louis and the German Max Schmeling at Yankee Stadium in 1938. Despite the long line, our press passes got us in, although we were carpet-bombed with publicity materials by the film's public relations agent. After the film, I wrote a quick review in a local café and headed to a lunch hosted by Kodak Films at a nearby eatery.

The event was wide open. Skyy Vodka tumblers lined the inner entrance, and after some quaffing, I ambled inside. At a far table I spied one of my all-time favorite people: Jane Fonda, Vietnam protester, seminal feminist, workout guru, sex symbol, and Academy Award-winning actress. I kibitzed with new acquaintances, picked at the buffet, and casually began circling her table, where she was engaged in earnest conversation with some young female filmmakers.

My lack of sleep, alcohol intake, unshaven visage, and nervousness made me look like a slightly addled Vietnam veteran—not a good way to approach Jane Fonda. I caught her eye and leaned in to her table abruptly.

"I uh, love all your, uh, films," I stammered. "*Barbarella* was uh, so underrated."

"Sure, sure, I'm glad you liked it," said Fonda, through a taut smile with a hint of terror. She looked ready to flee back to Hanoi.

Avi saw the unfolding disaster, quickly grabbed me by the shoulders, pulled me off the table, and marched me outside.

"C'mon man, *Barbarella*, seriously?" said Avi.

"You don't realize this about me, but it's one of my favorites—between that and *The Godfather*," I said.

"I think Skyy really is the limit for you," said Avi.

We decided to watch *Born into Brothels*, a searing documentary about children who grow up in the prostitution houses of Calcutta, India. My good catering friend Sam was now working as chief usher at the cinema, and he facilitated our entry.

The movie was devastating. One of the directors, Zana Briski, gave the children their own cameras to document their lives inside the brothels. Despite their sordid surroundings, their photos reflected undying hope, fortitude, and mesmerizing details. I left the theater choked up and floored.

This was the thing about Sundance—a constant whipsawing between the superficial glamour of Hollywood party life versus deep, emotional journeys into some of the planet's most powerful films and documentaries.

To clear our heads we walked around town, clomping through the snow. Off Main Street was a ski lift ferrying film attendees up into the mountains for a few downhill rides between screenings. The Hollywood cell phone chatter was unceasing in the pristine mountain air. Locals called these types "Men in Black"—conspicuous figures in the bright white landscape.

The big event that evening was a celebration for Miramax, the independent film company owned by Harvey and Bob Weinstein. It was to be held at Riverhorse on Main, Park City's most prestigious restaurant. The Weinsteins were notorious for their paranoia, and we knew security would be severe.

The event hadn't even started but a throng was already out front, spilling into the street. We ran into Avi's ex-girlfriend, who was now an actress of increasing fame, having recently been nominated for an Emmy on a television series.

During her relationship with Avi, she was a dedicated crasher, and with her beauty and quick wit, she had facilitated their attendance at many an awards show. Now, her swelling fame was denting her access. She couldn't afford to crash a swanky bash and get caught. Her ejection might hit the media and hurt her career. But neither was she famous enough to get invited to all the big events.

We encouraged her to join us, but she was blunt. "I'm in party purgatory right now," she said glumly. "The Weinsteins may know of me. Getting kicked out by Harvey? That's not a gorilla encounter I want."

A large black Escalade abruptly pulled up. Out stepped Nicole Kidman with her entourage. Avi gave me a quick signal and rode the celebrity wake in. I was momentarily distracted trying to sweet-talk an actress, late to react, and got rebuffed by a couple of big beards.

Cell phone reception was spotty, and I was unable to reach Avi inside. Damn, these entry opportunities often open and close in seconds and I'd gotten sidetracked. I decided my only hope was the back of the restaurant. I walked a half block up Main Street and doubled back behind the row of restaurants.

Huge snowdrifts hugged each building up to their second-floor windows. My heart sank, but my increasing desperation at missing out drove me on. I traipsed along the snow ridge, half crawling, half jumping, and sometimes plunging in up to my chest. Finally, I got to the back side of the Riverhorse.

There was a break in the snowpack and the back door was visible but surely locked. I slid down the embankment and hit the door with a thud. I grabbed the door handle, pulled, and it popped open! I climbed halfway up the semi-dark stairwell and sat down, plotting my next move.

The party was now going full throttle. I heard thumping background music, glasses clinking, and loud conversation. But I was dripping wet from my snow tramping and somewhat paralyzed. I sat for what seemed an eternity.

Suddenly the back door flung open.

"We need you to stand back!" said an enormous bouncer, looking up at me. "We've got a VIP coming in."

He entered hand in hand with Britney Spears, who was followed with another enormous personage who gripped her other hand. I stood up and pressed myself flat against the wall, and all three quickly barreled by and disappeared up into the second-floor mayhem.

WTF? How the hell did they get to the back door? Did Britney ride one of them down the snow bank like a giant toboggan? Were they all wearing snowshoes? Did Harvey's security provide sleds? It remains one of my great, unsolved mysteries.

Now shot through with adrenaline, I clambered up the stairwell and came to two adjacent doors. The party seemed right on the other side of door #1. My central entry might be too conspicuous. Way too risky. Door #2 seemed quieter and I hoped would provide more circuitous cover. I opened it, lurched in, and shut the door behind me.

I was in complete darkness. About a hundred feet away, I made out a seam of light. I started stumbling toward it, tripping over unseen boxes, stubbing my toe on some gym weights, and face-planting a couple of times on the sticky hardwood floor.

I stood up and got caught in a dense batch of goose jackets, mink pelts, and ski parkas hanging on a coat rack. I felt myself falling again and, flailing wildly, grabbed an ankle-length fox-fur coat and took the whole rack down. I lay stunned and still for at least a minute, waiting for Harvey's goons to bust down the door, administer a thorough stomping, and haul me away.

Though I was buried in mounds of deluxe, perfumed (and most likely illegal) animal fur, I fought my way upright like a courageous Jeremiah Johnson.

I made it to the other side of the clothes closet, peeked through the door crack, and burst into the party . . . right into a small circle that included Nicole Kidman, Russell Crowe, and Sydney Pollack. "Hiya there!" I yelled out a bit too enthusiastically, and then darted to the bar, where I started downing cocktails like I was about to face a firing squad.

"Nice entry," said Avi, tapping me on the shoulder. "But slow down. You're in. There's nothing to worry about."

Avi drifted off and connected with an old producer friend. It was definitely a very exclusive, intimate crowd studded with celebrities and big-shot power brokers. Waiters scurried about with every form of gastronomic treat on endless platters.

"Can I buy you a drink?" I said to a very attractive woman who looked slightly bored. "It's on me, anything you want. Happy to cover your friends too."

"The drinks are free," she scoffed, not getting my attempt at a little humor.

I proceeded to pepper her with questions and offered a few of my own recent ribald Sundance tales. My come-on wasn't having much effect.

"Look, I'm really, really picky," she snapped impatiently.

"Well, that's where we differ," I said.

As I moved away, I noticed an attractive acquaintance, EMMA MCGUIRE, across the room. She was a budding film composer and a savvy industry player.

"Did you crash this party?" she asked with a knowing smile.

"You know I never go to parties I'm invited to," I said.

We parried for a while, and then an august presence entered the room. Things went quiet. Harvey was in da house.

I studied him closely. He was of Michelin Man girth with a thick, meaty, unshaven face. His right eye was perpetually half-closed. His shirt was untucked and mostly unbuttoned. A profusion of gray steel wire chest hairs sprouted forth. Supplicants swirled around him as he moved, catlike, from group to group while constantly scanning the room.

By this time, I was fairly buttered. My anxiety was blunted and my fearlessness buttressed with innumerable tequila shots. The food, the rarefied surroundings, and the altitude had all gone to my head. Emma looked ravishing and I madly wanted to impress her.

"Wow, is that Harvey Weinstein?" she asked.

"Sure is. Would you like to meet him?" I said.

She didn't get the chance to answer.

"HEY HARVEY, come over here!" I boomed across the room, as I waved him over in a commanding fashion.

He halted his conversation, arched an eyebrow, and gave me a squinty look. *Who the hell is this guy? He's in my party, looks vaguely familiar, and is standing with a tall, beautiful blonde. Maybe I should check him (actually her) out.*

Harvey ambled over with a slit smile and a darting, suspicious gaze.

"I just wanted you to meet Emma McGuire. She's an amazing composer and might help with some of your film scores," I said.

Harvey didn't bother to ask or catch my name. His eyes were unwrapping Emma's supple bodice.

He asked a few perfunctory questions and ended up taking her card. This was before #MeToo, and I didn't realize at the time that I was delivering Emma to one of Hollywood's biggest sex wolves. Luckily, he never called her—she managed to dodge 260 pounds of nitroglycerin.

The party continued for several hours, and Avi and I returned to the Swiss flophouse, fairly blotto, for another sleepless, smelly night. (I never did see Britney or her two chaperones again. Maybe they went to an adjacent party?) We were up again at dawn and began making the endless rounds of breakfasts, brunches, seminars, director forums, press Q&As, world cinema panels, and one-on-one pitch meetings.

There were other escapades. We attended a billiards competition, a Hula-Hoop party, some gin promotions, and a time-share sales talk hosted by a local condo association.

All the film industry social events were moving at warp speed. We'd crash a movie premiere after-party, and after five minutes we'd leave and compulsively crash another up the street. It would have the same people, the same Skyy Vodka, the same swag, the same caterers, the same vendors, and even the same crashers.

"Why the hell are we leaving this party?" asked Avi one day in a fit of exasperation. "We just got here! And weren't we at this party earlier in the evening?"

His observation stopped me in my tracks. We had made a full tour of the town's festivities that night and hadn't even realized we were back at ground zero.

"You're right. We're just chasing our own tails," I said. "Maybe it's time we forgot all the events and just focused on the films."

In later years there was a moment the festival's party atmosphere started overwhelming the movies. The zenith was when Paris Hilton rode up Main Street with her head sticking out of the sunroof of a white stretch limousine, taking selfies and waving to the crowd. Hilton "didn't have anything to do with the films," lamented Robert Redford. "What movie is she in?"

Avi and I rededicated our energies to the celluloid offerings and began reclaiming our sanity. But near the end of the festival, we felt a last urge to rejoin the party. We sat around the Chateau Apres lobby, where we noticed a somber group who hadn't been able to attend anything. I asked a woman who said she was a *Price Is Right* model if she was having a good time.

"This place sucks. I haven't seen one movie, haven't gotten into any big parties, and have spent most of my time waiting in the snow," she said bitterly. "I'm never coming back here again."

She began asking us about our plans for the evening. She mentioned she had a slight chance of getting into ICM's big final party where her friend was employed.

"That sounds great!" I said. "Let's hit it!"

The model smirked. "Good luck with that," she said. "There's like fourteen hundred people on the list and the fire marshal said only seven hundred are allowed in."

Avi laughed heartily.

"Perfect. That's just the way we like it. Let's go!"

16

ESALEN INTERLOPERS

I T WAS MY FIRST TIME visiting the Esalen Institute. For years while a student at UC Berkeley in the early 1980s, I'd heard about this New Age sanctuary perched on a spectacular bluff in the middle of the Big Sur on California's Central Coast, the most dazzling stretch of shoreline in the world.

Known as Esalen, the nonprofit retreat center played a key role in the Human Potential Movement that began in the early 1960s. Two Stanford graduates, Michael Murphy and Dick Price, founded the institute to explore human consciousness by offering a range of classes on international philosophies, religious disciplines, psychological techniques, and physical wellness. They created hundreds of workshops in areas including meditation, spirituality, psychology, yoga, ecology, alternative medicine, and organic food. They hosted inventive encounter groups and personal awareness exercises and brought in far-seeing thinkers such as Timothy Leary, Carlos Castaneda, Aldous Huxley, Joseph Campbell, Ansel Adams, Ken Kesey, and B. F. Skinner to conduct seminars.

Before Esalen was founded in 1962, the site was known as Slate's Hot Springs, a draw for tourists looking to soothe their physical ailments and gay men from San Francisco who spent their weekends in the baths. At one point, author Hunter S. Thompson, twenty-two years old at the time, worked as a groundskeeper and an armed security guard on the property. One Slate's veteran remembered there was nothing more terrifying than watching Thompson, the self-proclaimed "Minister of the Interior," coming down the dirt path toward the hot springs, wielding a bullwhip, a Doberman, and a truncheon to flush out trespassers.

After college while living in San Francisco, I decided to finally make the three-hour journey south to take a one-day massage therapy class at this magical sanctuary. Just south of Carmel, I jumped on Highway 1 and began the winding trip down the two-lane road that at times had been cut out of the side of vertical cliffs. Every turn afforded another mesmerizing vista. Nineteenth-century author and world traveler Robert Louis Stevenson once called Point Lobos, at the northern end of Big Sur, "the most beautiful meeting of land and sea on earth."

Esalen did not disappoint. The verdant grounds were dotted with rustic cabins, waterfalls, streams, gardens, yurts, and rocky coves along the shoreline below. The property hosted more than four acres of organic farms. The retreat was built on eighty-foot-high bluffs stretching more than a mile that overlooked a deep purple/blue sea studded with thick kelp beds.

And there were the geothermal hot springs that burbled year-round, filling the stone tubs at the edge of the cliffs with endless pulses of soothing water. I ate my fill of macrobiotic food, learned the intricacies of Swedish/Esalen massage, and watched from the "baths" as a train of spouting whales a hundred yards offshore headed south to Baja for their mating season. The whole place was rough, dramatic, and intoxicating.

My first trip to Esalen was the beginning of a long obsession, and I returned many times (invited and uninvited) over the ensuing decades. Until recently, Esalen offered as many as five hundred workshops, with more than fifteen thousand participants a year, outlined in detailed biannual catalogs. There were serious confabs on mythology, philosophy, and once in the 1990s a meeting of Soviet cosmonauts and American astronauts comparing their views on the cosmos.

But as the center of the Human Potential Movement, Esalen also had its share of flighty, shallow, and sometimes absurd classes and movements. Some critics felt the place was drenched in narcissism, self-obsession, and obliviousness to real-world problems like racism and poverty. There was an ethic that only by turning deeply inward could people realize their full potential. For these self-seekers, turning outward and helping others didn't seem part of the plan.

The result was such amorphous workshops as Ferocious Heart, Spinal Awareness (with Humor), The Posture Dance Connection, Gateway to Soul: Process Acupressure, Beyond Jogging, Treating the Unique Child, Singing Gestalt, and Listening Hands, to name a few.

Through the years, I witnessed some jaw-dropping moments of self-absorption. I once saw a pregnant woman, an aspiring godhead, rhythmically pounding out a tune using her tumescent belly as bongo drums while singing off-key on the main lawn. God knows what the fetus was thinking.

One time I sat in on a Paint Therapy class my brother was taking. A shaggy group of middle-aged would-be Van Goghs were having a go at multiple canvases with every color of oil imaginable. One woman in her late fifties was a symphony of sighs as she fitfully colored in an outline of what looked like a grazing water buffalo. Suddenly she threw down her quiver of brushes and sobbed wildly. The instructor ran over and with hand to elbow asked her what was wrong.

"I just can't . . . I just won't . . . I-I-I," she sputtered. "I just can't figure out what to do with purple!"

Another time while eating dinner on the outdoor patio, sitting at a crowded table, a group of a half dozen wild-looking mind voyagers approached us. They were covered in mud and food, and some looked as if they'd soiled themselves. A few were throwing tantrums, yelling nonsensically, jumping up and down, and hurling everything within reach. Soon they were flinging chunks of the evening's potato casserole dish at each other, back and forth above our heads, some while barking. They eventually moved off down the hill toward the hot springs.

"What the fuck was that?" I asked a young bearded local.

"Oh, pay no mind to them. They've been at it all week," he said. "They're in a Nine-Year-Old Regression class and they're just acting out their infantile demons."

After one yoga session, I complimented the teacher about her class, her energy, and her expert instruction.

"Thanks for all the beauty you see in me," she said with a thousand-yard inward stare.

Sometimes I'd sit in the hot springs and just listen to the fascinating and endless psychobabble about "being in deep process," "seeking inner chi," and "power gazing."

The baths were always a co-ed hotbed of sexual tension, and I'd watch aggressive males cloak their come-ons in the language of the spiritual poseur.

"I've been watching you these last few weeks, and the tension in your midsection looks unbearable," one instructor said to a beautiful female, who actually looked just fine percolating naked in the hot springs. "Maybe it would help if I internally realigned you."

"Big Sur has a climate all its own and a character all its own," author Henry Miller wrote in his 1957 memoir, *Big Sur and the Oranges of Hieronymus Bosch*. "It is a region where extremes meet, a region where one is always conscious of weather, of space, of grandeur, and of eloquent silence."

I always felt Esalen reflected that Big Sur nexus of extremes meeting—it was part holy church, physical health center, nature retreat, and psychology laboratory but also a depraved bordello, drug haven, political hothouse, and homogenous sanctuary. In 1990 a graffiti artist left his take in spray paint on the entrance to the property: "Jive shit for rich white folk."

One of the big challenges at Esalen is making a reservation. The place is always jammed, especially on weekends. Unfortunately (or fortunately) I'm the spontaneous type, and making reservations doesn't always jibe with my last-minute plans.

If I was considering a free jaunt, my main goal was making it to the hot tubs that I accessed through a secret back entrance. The palliative effects of the geothermal spring water infused you with a glow that stayed in your bones for days. On road trips between Los Angeles and San Francisco, I'd usually just stop in for an afternoon. I would soak for a few hours and be on my way. My problems always happened when I stayed longer.

One languorous afternoon an attractive spirit woman suggested I stick around for dinner. We sampled some wine at the bar and tucked into the macrobiotic offerings in the dining area. After an hour of fluid conversation, her boyfriend joined us and instantly took a savage disliking to me. Esalen's sexual politics can be fevered. He flooded me with questions about what class I was taking, why I was there, and who I knew. None of my answers seemed to impress him.

I parried his incessant queries and gibes with a friendly smile and eventually took leave for one last dip in the hot springs.

"So, you're going down to the baths?" he asked, a little too intensely.

"Yeah, I'm heading down there," I responded. "I hope both of you can join me."

"Yes, yes, we'll see you down there shortly," he said.

I loped down the path with a towel over my shoulders, disrobed in the clothing area, and settled into my favorite tub at the far end of the baths. It was a moonless night, black as pitch with stars in abundance. Two women slid in next to me, and we chatted for a while. Just as one of them asked my name, I heard a ruckus at the bath entrance. A bevy of large security dudes were moving from tub to tub.

"Adrian! Adrian! Is there an Adrian here? We have a message for Adrian!" they repeated over and over while leaning in and questioning each tub group.

I'd had a fair bit of wine and initially almost raised my hand and took ownership of my birth name. But I recovered my wits and held back.

The bouncers received a number of "Nays" from other bathers, and as they approached my tub, I yelled out, "No Adrians here!" and quickly ducked underwater.

The security detail retreated but hovered by the entrance, questioning those coming and going. I realized the "boyfriend" back up in the kitchen had loosed security upon me to control his damsel and take down her would-be suitor.

I felt completely naked and vulnerable. In fact, I *was* completely naked and vulnerable. All my clothes and belongings, including car keys, were on a rack by the entrance. My only option was to wait it out in the hot, roiling waters. But what if the boyfriend came down and pointed me out? I soon realized his initial snitching was gutless. He wasn't the type to show his face. So I waited and waited and waited.

Finally, after about an hour, the security group retreated. I emerged from the tub with wrinkled, shriveled skin. I felt like a boiled chicken. I dressed quickly, grabbed my stuff, and fled out a back route. Two hours later, while driving home on Highway 1, I was still hyperventilating.

As Avi was one of my chief fellow adventurers, I'd always wanted to show him the wonders of the place. We planned our trip for a busy weekend but couldn't book the sold-out lodging there. One way you could enter the property (at the time) was to reserve a ninety-minute massage. We figured we'd book some bodywork but couldn't get through the labyrinthian voice mail reservation system and decided to just go. We arrived midmorning on a Saturday, parked on the highway, and snuck in through my usual back entrance.

Esalen often has free general classes, separate from the paid workshops, that are open to all on the property. We walked up to the main lodge and saw a listing for a class on "Calming the Mind" to be held shortly in a nearby yurt. To prepare, we lit up a joint.

We arrived at the class a few minutes late, reeking of reefer, and took seats on a semicircle of pillows with about a dozen others. The attendees were giving their names and where they were from. The bearded instructor was not amused at our tardiness.

"Again, for those who are late, this is a class that will give you tools to find some brief calm and inner peace in a hectic world gone berserk," the teacher intoned softly.

Avi was a whirlwind of nervous energy, constantly rearranging his pillow, his socks, and his posture.

"And you, Mr. Jitterbug, what's your name?" asked the teacher looking pointedly at Avi.

"Jitterbug," said Avi.

The class laughed.

"Where are you from?" inquired the teacher.

"I live about an hour and a half south of Santa Barbara," said Avi.

"And what town is that, may I ask?" said the instructor with a touch of asperity.

"Los Angeles," said Avi.

Everyone in the class laughed again. The teacher responded with a mirthless smile.

"We often manifest the overwhelming pressure in our daily lives with incessant physical tics, flinching, and constant movement," said the teacher. "Many of us just can't sit still," looking again at Avi, "like this fellow before us over here."

The instructor was stirring the beast in Avi. I'd seen that look before. All I could do now was put on my seat belt and brace for impact.

"I'm a searcher, which requires constant movement toward an eventual goal of inner peace and equilibrium," said Avi. "If I could stand still, I wouldn't need this class."

"Before you seek and search, you've got to prepare by settling down before your voyage," said the instructor. "The results will be exponentially more powerful."

"I think it's about harnessing and focusing the energy one has, not trying to bury it," said Avi, who was now gesticulating wildly.

"We're not trying to bury anything here," said the instructor through gritted teeth. "I'm just pointing out that your constant jittering is indicative of an unstable mind."

"But what does a stable mind really look like?" asked Avi. "The kind of stable you're talking about is where I'd put my horse."

"LOOK, YOU NEED TO CALM THE FUCK DOWN AND SHUT THE FUCK UP!" screamed the instructor. "GET WITH THE GOD-DAMN PROGRAM!"

The tension in the yurt was tight as piano wire. The other attendees looked like they needed peeling off the tented ceiling.

I signaled to Avi that it was time for a massage. Avi stood up slowly, solemnly put his hands together in a prayerful pose, and bowed.

"Namaste," said Avi.

We both headed to the front gate of the property and made reservations for a massage. Afterward we waltzed down to the hot springs to unwind and wait for our masseuses.

The baths were divided into two areas by signs that said QUIET TUBS and SILENT TUBS, both with arrows pointing in different directions. We chose the QUIET TUBS, considering our tendency to blabber.

Like most first-timers, Avi was speechless at the beauty of the place. The massage tables were next to the baths on an elevated deck that perched over the ocean, all the better to flood the senses with aquatic sounds while the masseuses worked out all those troublesome, emotional pus balls in our backs.

As we sank into the waters, I saw two young minstrels—dudes with man buns playing Aboriginal didgeridoos—coming down the path. *Hmmmm, hoooowa, hmmmmm, hoooowaaaa.* The sounds were rhythmic and calming as each musician huffed and puffed on his ancient device.

When they got to the tubs they plunged their instruments into the center of each bathing group, blowing hot air on to the chests of several women. They looked higher than helium and were probably on some kind of psychedelic.

I was about to tell them to back off when they turned and saw a ninety-year-old naked man lollygagging against a wall at the edge of another tub. They switched gears and unloaded the full power of their musical gadgets on the elder's flagging man stem.

They danced and played, like snake charmers trying to coax some life into a half-dead cobra. The man was amused and played along. Soon enough, his pecker began to wiggle and show signs of life as it began to slowly rise. After a minute or two it reached half-salute, hovered for a few seconds, and then collapsed.

The man shrugged, the minstrels laughed. Then they abruptly disappeared, taking their circus to another part of the property.

"This is such a place of extremes—the coastline, the people, the weather. I can't get enough of it," said Avi.

We saw two more figures descending toward us carrying a load of towels, water bottles, eye masks, incense canisters, peanut oils, squirting lubricants, and mop-up sponges. One of them was a classic Esalen spirit beauty—covered in turquoise with perfect posture, a confident gait, and long, flowing tresses that spilled onto her sun-kissed, tawny skin. Her male companion was a gnarled, bandy-legged, hunched munchkin, about a head shorter and forty years older, with leathery skin and a mane of flowing white hair.

Please God, I love Avi, but let my masseuse be this tall, all-natural, wunderkind of sandy-blonde goodness. I just can't handle a grumpy old guy working my joints right now. I looked at Avi and I could see we were thinking parallel thoughts.

Soon this unlikely duo arrived near our tub.

"Avi, Avi," proclaimed the goddess. "I'm looking for Avi for a 1 PM massage appointment."

I doubled over in disappointment and felt my nut sack retracting.

"Right here, right here!" shouted Avi, waving his outstretched hand a little too enthusiastically while launching himself full-frontal out of the tub.

"Oh, hi there, I'm Pam," said the goddess solicitously. "Follow me, right this way."

"And you must be Adrian," said the gnarled one, looking directly at my plump body, already calculating what he planned to do to me. "I'm VILGOT, and I'm your tension reducer today."

More like tension enhancer, but I kept a tight mask on my feelings and dutifully followed him to the far end of the massage deck.

"Lie on your back on the table, keep your towel over your mid-section, and just soak up the surroundings," he said with a raspy voice. He dropped his drawers and fronted up to the table behind my head.

I tried keeping my eyes open but kept seeing his grizzled upside-down beard and carpet of white chest hairs directly above me. I closed my lids and began sinking into his rhythmic strokes as he worked my chest and the front of my neck and shoulders.

There was a long pause. *Oh, shite*, I thought. *He's going to take a ten-minute break while charging me ninety dollars for the full ninety minutes. Or maybe he's just slathering some more oil on his hands.* I kept my eyes closed and tried to meditate on passing whales.

I felt the table lurch slightly and a much stronger pressure on my chest. I finally opened my eyes wide. I saw a sight that to this day I'm still processing.

Vilgot (pronounced *Vil-goat*) had jumped up on the massage table with one foot planted on each side of my head looking toward my upturned feet. He was now compressing my chest with the powerful strokes of his flat hands while squatting over my face.

My visuals went from zero to a hundred in a split second. One moment I was dreaming as a castaway on a faraway island. The next I was staring up into a kaleidoscopic cornhole—a winking, pink, star-fish anus rimmed with tufts of white, wiry pubes just inches from my eyeballs. Is this what the gates of hell look like?

His two wizened, toad-skin testicles hovered a half-inch above my chin.

I'm told a couple of friends eating at a Chinese restaurant in San Francisco heard my scream.

PART IV

PUSHING LIMITS

Curbing Larry's enthusiasm.

17

UPPING MY GAME

I ALWAYS MADE A MENTAL NOTE when I heard or witnessed a particularly creative method of gatecrashing. Often the most difficult entries spurred outrageously inventive schemes. Other times, spur-of-the-moment opportunities sparked innovative backdoor capers.

Without a doubt, the most restrictive and exclusive annual party in Hollywood is the *Vanity Fair* Oscar party, held after the awards show. I covered a few of them while a reporter at the *L.A. Times*, when it was held at Morton's, a lush eatery in West Hollywood. Only the most A-list stars are invited, and security around the venue is always oppressive.

Even as a reporter, I was kept at a safe distance from the restaurant entrance, along with hundreds of photographers from the world's media. As each star walked the red carpet, thousands of flashes would go off, barraging each celeb in a surreal machine-gun flicker.

Graydon Carter, the editor of *Vanity Fair*, and the magazine's publisher, Sy Newhouse, would often stand outside the front door and personally greet each invitee. Jackbooted security was everywhere, and Clipboard Nazis (CNs) roamed the nearby roped-off streets, confronting intruders by demanding names and identification.

One of my favorite stories was when Fred Karger, an openly gay former Republican consultant, crashed the affair in 2007. He went out and purchased a fake Oscar and waved it furiously on the red carpet, claiming he'd won for Visual Effects. He accidentally dropped the statuette at the entrance but still walked right in.

Back in 1996, a female reporter from the supermarket tabloid *Star* brought a pig on a leash and said the cute swine was the main character in the award-winning film *Babe*. Both were let in.

I previously noticed Morton's back kitchen entrance flowing in and out with chefs in white smocks and top hats. While in crasher mode in later years, I thought about suiting up as a chef and making a grand side entrance, stripping off my faux outer garments in the bathroom and reappearing in the party with a different outfit.

But the grand irony is that the most exclusive parties are often the most boring. They're not well populated. They're cliquish, formal, and tight. The grand and powerful guests are always on their best behavior and talk only to people they know (and they often don't know me).

As my crasher experiences accumulated, I noticed technology becoming more imposing. Surveillance cameras seemed to pop up everywhere. Instead of trying to read names off a manual clipboard, I observed more and more check-in personnel were armed with iPads. Guest list names were visible for only seconds at a time.

Some of my trespassing brethren began fighting tech fire with tech fire. They'd thrust a selfie stick with their attached iPhone past the check-in table and take pictures from behind the check-in clerk of the respective iPad and hope to cadge a name.

Social media also became an increasingly useful tool for the intrepid crasher. One evening I got tipped off to an exclusive sit-down dinner for about fifty Microsoft employees at a high-end restaurant in Venice, near the beach. The Microsofters had flown in from all over the country, and the gathering was a chance to meet each other, bond, stuff themselves with great food, and savor an extensive wine list.

The event info came from a verbal tip from a friend of a friend of a friend who worked at the company. Barton Whitaker and I both found mention of the gourmet powwow on the web, but after several hours of digital scavenging and innumerable phone calls, we couldn't nail down the start time or the restaurant. All we knew was that it was in Venice.

Around 7 PM, I started driving up and down Abbot Kinney Boulevard (recently called "the coolest block in America" by *GQ* magazine), looking for any sign of foodie festivities. I did a drive-by down side streets scoping out-of-the-way eateries. Finally, I exited my car and walked around the beach area, pressing my face up against restaurant windows. After an hour of obsessive prowling, I threw in my bib.

As I walked back to my car, I checked my Instagram account by typing in "Microsoft dinner Venice" in the search function. Up popped several real-time pictures of the party. I instantly recognized the interior of a restaurant I knew on Abbot Kinney. I also opened the geographic locator function attached to the pictures. It gave me the exact address of the sender.

Within ten minutes I was at a VIP table, hoisting some robust red, nibbling on rockfish fillet, and making friends and influencing people at Microsoft.

I'd encountered many crashers over the years, but some brought a level of moxie, creativity, and sheer personality to social proceedings that upped the game for all of us. I first met BETHSHEBA at an environmental fundraiser at a tech warehouse in Culver City after slipping through an adjacent catering tent. We impressed each other with our commitment to green causes, and I won points by bidding on a guitar at the event's auction. She was in her early forties and an aspiring script doctor in Hollywood with a master's in fine arts from New York University. We hit it off and began a romantic relationship that lasted for

Adrian and Bethsheba at a Saint Patrick's Day party.

several years. It was only after our third or fourth date that we both realized we had each crashed the green event of our initial meeting.

Bethsheba, it turns out, was an inveterate interloper and used her backdoor skills to network and advance her career. She had all the attributes of a stellar crasher: chatty, well read, and expert with Hollywood jargon and name-dropping—a big help when called out at the wrong garden party. With an enormous helmet of lustrous hair, pretty profile, and ample cleavage (what she called her two "entry tickets"), she was the ultimate Tinseltown chameleon.

Bethsheba wearing a fascinator hat before a British
Consulate party.

We soon started partner-crashing galas together. She provided a
significant uplift to my side-door efforts. Solitary middle-aged men
with darting eyes, a thin film of chin sweat, and a hunted gait are
always prime targets for overzealous bouncers. But having a winsome beauty with superlative intruder skills on my arm diverted the
white-hot security gaze.

For years my main reason for crashing parties was to find the "one"
amid L.A.'s numbing anonymity. It was nice to share my adventures

with a romantic partner after so many years of flying solo. The taste of the food and wine was enhanced and the events seemed more thrilling.

Bethsheba also bore an uncanny resemblance to the daughter of Raquel Welch, Tahnee Welch, an actress with minor roles in films such as *Cocoon* and *I Shot Andy Warhol*. But in Screenland, sometimes having a tangential connection to a B-list name is enough to propel you through the front party door.

One evening we found ourselves at an after-party at a nightclub in West Hollywood for an independent film. As we milled about outside, we spotted Clement von Franckenstein, one of the party circuit's most outrageous characters. He was descended from a noble Franconian family that traced its lineage back to the thirteenth century; author Mary Shelley adapted the family name for her 1818 classic gothic novel *Frankenstein*. Clement's father, Georg Freiherr von und zu Franckenstein, was Austria's ambassador to Britain for eighteen years, and when Hitler took over Austria in 1938, Georg renounced his nationality and was knighted by King George VI.

Now in his midsixties, Clement was a true bon vivant and ladies man, and an omnipresent partygoer at Tinseltown's most opulent galas. He'd worked steadily as a character actor since arriving in Los Angeles in 1972, with debonair turns in more than eighty films. He portrayed the president of France opposite Michael Douglas in *The American President* and played bit parts alongside stars such as George Clooney, Melanie Griffith, and Jean-Claude Van Damme.

A lifelong bachelor, "His Clemness" or "the Baron" or "Clem" acted his own part well, often outfitted in monogrammed black velvet slippers, waistcoat, pocket handkerchief, pinkie ring, and a multitude of eye-blinding suits, some in turquoise and purple. He was bombastic, witty, impish, and self-deprecating, and he often ended parties at the bar by regaling attendees with tales, in his plummy Eton-educated accent, of his time as a lieutenant in the Royal Scots Greys.

His Clemness in full regal splendor. *Courtesy of Laurent Malaquais*

He had the whiff of an aristocrat on hard times, horrified by the thought of paying for anything. But his sheer bonhomie and dash, majestic title, B-list acting credentials, and promiscuous use of business cards got him into the best premieres and parties from Hollywood to Cannes. Whenever I saw him, I thought of what comedian Wayland Flowers said about manic partygoer and actress Sylvia Miles—that she would "attend the opening of an envelope."

Soon enough, as we strolled near the event entrance, the Baron spotted Bethsheba's bosoms and made a beeline directly for her. "Oh, hello there, darling," he said admiringly, in his posh, silky baritone. "And what are youuuuuuuuu about?"

Bethsheba hadn't the heart to remind him they'd met more than a dozen times previously, often with Clem's trademark salutation. They slipped into easy conversation for a moment, and then the Baron heard a clarion call: an announcer introducing various B-list actors as they strutted down the red carpet and posed for the usual cluster of photographers. Von Franckenstein politely excused himself and vanished.

An officious Clipboard Nazi herded guests into a waiting line but suddenly turned solicitous upon the arrival of each "name," who was quickly leapfrogged to the head of the queue.

"And here we have Mr. Steven Bauer, the unforgettable actor who played along Al Pacino in *Scarface*," intoned the announcer in a deep baritone.

"Up ahead is Parker Posey, one of our great unsung film actresses!" was the next intro.

"And we are honored to host one of our favorite character actors, Clement von Franckenstein, a Mel Brooks regular in such films as *Young Frankenstein* and *Robin Hood: Men in Tights!*" Wow, that was quick.

Taking my cue from the Baron, I boldly approached the CN.

"I'm with Tahnee Welch . . . you know, daughter of Raquel . . . new film is *Body and Soul*," I said, pointing to Bethsheba a few feet away, who confidently gazed into the distance. "Where should we go?"

"Oh right, come over here and I'll let the announcer know," said the CN, who gave Bethsheba a quick once-over and deemed her legit.

Soon enough, we heard the modern-day version of heralding trumpets.

"And on our left, we have Tahnee Welch, beautiful daughter of Raquel Welch and recent star of the film *Body and Soul!*"

We walked arm in arm to the designated spot on the red carpet, pivoted, and faced the onslaught of paparazzi. Multiple flashes went off, and I was temporarily blinded.

"Tahnee, Tahnee, over here!" screamed one photog.

"You look amazing, Tahnee, give us a quick smile!" said another.

"Tahnee, can we get a serious look now?" said another, and so it went.

Suddenly I felt a tugging at my elbow. It was a diminutive Cockney photographer.

"No offense, mate, but cud we 'ave a few pickies with just Tahnee?" he asked.

"No problem. Whether or not I end up in *Hello!* magazine doesn't matter much to me," I responded with a chuckle.

The frequency of photos picked up considerably once I was out of the picture. Bethsheba/Tahnee vogued, posed, and pivoted for several moments. There was a break in the action, and I went over and returned my sturdy hand to her hip.

"Mate, puh-lease, could you just STAY OUT!" screeched the Cockney at me, beckoning me to move off the red carpet.

For years afterward, whenever Bethsheba needed to remonstrate me for something she'd yell, "Just STAY OUT!"

The Tahnee Welsh act on the red carpet that evening was emblematic of what we called "the daily impossible" in crasher world. We'd arrive at an event with seemingly impossible barriers and be momentarily stumped at methods of entry. We'd try all kinds of tactics and techniques and when on the verge of giving up, a spontaneous solution would miraculously appear. It might be a scalper with an extra ticket, a case of mistaken identity, or in one case, a lanyard chucked off a rooftop party and landing at our feet on the sidewalk. This paradigm appeared over and over despite the mathematical odds. It was a quirk we noticed that puzzles me to this day.

———————

I participated in an uproarious series of improvised crasher incidents at the annual *Los Angeles Times* Festival of Books on the
UCLA campus, the largest gathering of book readers and authors
in America.

I always loved the book festival, as the panels, readings, and author
signings never failed to surprise. I remember once seeing Oliver Stone
on an open-air stage preparing to read from his early novel, *A Child's
Night Dream*, which he wrote at nineteen years old. Whole families
had crowded the courtyard to hear the literary musings of the famed
director. The crowd rustled with anticipation as Stone ambled up to
the microphone, greeted the audience, and gave a short introduction
about his long-ago work.

He adjusted his glasses at the podium, looked down, and began
reading the opening lines: "Do come. With your erection. It may
wish to emote."

Soon, dads with kids on their shoulders, moms pushing strollers,
and sorority girls began streaming to the exits.

Several years later, I went to the festival with one of my usual
scamps, Duane Flanigan, who by this time had returned to L.A. after
a second debacle teaching English in China. He was a man of the
word and loved a good story. Though Flanigan and I were virtually
the same age, he looked years older, due to his love of vodka and
decades of hard living. His proboscis was a mass of broken capillar-
ies, his hair snow white (without his usual brown dye job), and his
face looked like a map of the hedgerows of Ireland. Though only in
his midfifties, he walked with a cane.

We were particularly interested in seeing a panel on biographies
hosted by Walter Isaacson, the author of brilliant biographies such
as *Steve Jobs*, *Einstein*, and *Kissinger*. Unfortunately, one needed an
advance ticket that we didn't have. Not to be denied, Flanigan and I
tried entering through a lower-floor back entrance.

"No, no, you can't come through here. You've got to enter up on the ground level," said a woman security guard as I tried shouldering through.

I was momentarily and uncommonly at a loss for words. I looked back at Flanigan, who was always extremely quick thinking in cornered situations. He was lumbering along with his cane and his glasses at that moment were askew.

"But my dad . . . Alzheimer's," I stammered, while shuttling my gaze back and forth between the guard and Flanigan.

Flanigan immediately picked up the cue and started flailing his cane, gulping for air, and looking around in a state of confusion. The guard became newly attentive.

"Uh, OK, why don't you both come right this way," she said, as she escorted us into the auditorium to front-row seats. To this day I still feel guilty about that caper.

At the end of the festival, Arianna Huffington, irrepressible talk show host and founder of the *Huffington Post*, often threw a huge shindig for the literary elite at her home in Brentwood.

Before driving there from the UCLA campus, Flanigan and I changed out of our sweaty shirts in the parking garage and slipped into cocktail attire—starched white shirts with nautical blue blazers. I always kept a sartorial upgrade on hangers in the back of my car for such occasions. I also had a small box with pocket handkerchiefs and ascots when I needed to ramp up my look to the manor-born.

As we made our way west on Sunset Boulevard, we decided I'd avoid the valet parkers out front of the mansion and drop Flanigan off farther down the street for him to double back on foot and reconnoiter the situation. Soon enough he'd call me with real-time info on wristbands, security situation, check-in tables, and potential methods of entry.

I never liked dropping off my rickety wheels with valet parkers right in front of the entrance, risking rejection at the door and then trying to negotiate the return of my vehicle from the valet staff in full view of guests and security.

Flanigan was uncharacteristically nervous in the car. Maybe it was seeing all the great literary figures hold forth during the prior two days at the festival. He showered me with questions about what he should say if cornered at the entrance. I remembered that Arianna was the featured speaker at a Heal the Bay foundation environmental fundraiser up in Malibu the previous week.

"Just say you're with Heal the Bay and Arianna invited you and a few other volunteers from the event to come to her signature party," I said. "You'll be fine."

Flanigan nodded glumly as we turned off Sunset Boulevard and headed into north Brentwood, one of the most exclusive neighborhoods in Los Angeles. The hedges got bigger, the architecture more ornate, and the tennis courts more numerous. When we arrived at the house, vintage cars were already lined up on the street and a covey of blue-vested valet parkers scampered about, opening doors for the parade of celebrity guests.

We drove by slowly and rubbernecked for any visual insights. As agreed, I dropped off Flanigan a block north, drove another block, and waited for his call detailing what color wristband to bring and any other salient tips.

I waited for five, ten, fifteen minutes. No word. I tried calling Flanigan, and his phone went straight to voice mail. Maybe he was being detained and interrogated in a poolside cabana or waterboarded in the basement? Maybe he flipped out and decamped from the area? Or maybe, what I most suspected, he made it in and had his head stuck in a champagne magnum.

Finally, my impatience and curiosity got the better of me. I locked up my car and walked down the street to the party. The entrance gates were open and the horseshoe driveway packed with guests checking in at a front table. No wristbands were needed, and I saw no sign of my fellow rule-breaker.

I noticed a pathway on the left side of the house, hidden with some foliage. Without breaking stride, I headed in that direction, and but for a few scratches, was soon sipping Dom Pérignon in the back garden. Once fortified, I ventured inside.

The eight-thousand-square-foot Italianate mansion was bright and airy. The living room was warmly furnished with colorful couches, throw pillows, and family photos and had books to the ceiling. This was the kind of party I hoped, someday, would send me an invite.

I locked eyes with Gore Vidal, who was leaning back in a sofa, a cane by his side. He gave me a solid, leering once-over from head to toe. Wow, the man was in his eighties and still had an urge. I kept thinking of his famous observation "Never miss a chance to have sex or appear on television."

I saw Larry David in animated conversation with someone who looked like former presidential candidate Gary Hart. Tom Hayden chatted with a young woman.

Arianna appeared with a retinue of attendants and flitted from guest to guest, and with her nasal accent, impeccable coif, and regal air, hovered above and directed the din. She seemed in her element—the perfect Greek host tending to her courtiers.

As I watched right-wing web impresario Andrew Breitbart talking with New Age author Deepak Chopra, I kept thinking of Chopra's recent comment that one should not fear death, because "you are dead already."

I soon saw Flanigan, in conversation with *New York Times* columnist Maureen Dowd, one of his heroes. He was already stewed, and Dowd was wearing a perma-grin. I went over and snatched him away.

"What the hell happened? You were supposed to call your driver and provide directions in," I snorted.

"Sorry, I just got carried away by the whole spectacle, and the bubbles went to my head," he said animatedly. "I was going to call but got caught up in conversation with Deepak and Dowd. But you wouldn't believe how I got in."

It turns out Flanigan was standing nervously in the front driveway apart from the line of invitees, trying to figure out a way in. Suddenly a beige Jaguar roared up and stopped right in front of him, almost taking off his shins.

Out popped Arianna. "Oh, hi there! And who are you?" she said, greeting Flanigan with an outstretched hand, a wide smile, and boisterous Greek hospitality.

"Heal the Bay," he exclaimed, momentarily forgetting his name and blurting out the only thing that came to mind.

"Oh, Heal the Bay, great organization!" she said. "Well, great to have you here, let's join the partaaaay, dahlink!"

She clasped Flanigan's hand tightly in hers and they both walked in the front entrance together. Arianna briefly introduced her new friend to a coterie of guests as "Heal the Bay," then flitted off, tending to more important matters.

Flanigan also peeled off and made a direct run to the bar to cool his nerves. Once stabilized, he started accosting celebrity guests and introducing himself as Heal the Bay, a nervous tic he couldn't seem to shed.

By the time I pulled him off Maureen Dowd, the whole party knew him as Heal the Bay—quite a moniker for someone not particularly interested in environmental issues.

Suddenly an older, frizzy, bespectacled green-activist type wearing a Grateful Dead T-shirt approached us. "Hi there, I'm a board member at Heal the Bay and I didn't quite get your name," he inquired edgily.

"Oh hi there. I'm Cousteau . . . Philippe Cousteau . . . Jacques Cousteau's son," said Flanigan.

Within minutes, Flanigan and I were both back out on the street.

18

SPACEX LAUNCH

"THIS IS SPACEX POLICE. This is SpaceX Police! Please halt. We need you to halt!"

My co-trespasser Shane Kerch and I had just slipped in through a slightly ajar fence onto the grounds of SpaceX headquarters at 1 Rocket Road in Hawthorne, California.

We weren't seeking trade secrets, hunting for aliens, or hoping to ride a rocket. All we wanted was entry into one of the most propulsive, explosive, and spectacular social events of the year: the SpaceX employee holiday party.

"Do not move. Show your hands!" barked the lead officer in the aeronautics security detail. He sat behind the wheel of a typical cop cruiser, but the vehicle was colored brown with large white letters on the side spelling it out for us again: SPACEX POLICE.

"What are you doing here? Why are you coming in this way?" demanded the officer as he and his partner ejected from the vehicle and strode toward us.

"We're kind of lost in space," I said.

My humor didn't go over well, considering we were trespassing on one of the most secure compounds in Southern California.

"Actually, just looking for the holiday event," I added.

"Well, you're quite a way from the entrance to the party. I don't know what you're doing over here," squawked the officer. "I need you to immediately redeploy back outside the fence. Check-in for the event is about a mile up the road."

Indeed, we knew exactly where the entrance was, but with drones, omnipresent cameras, and hundreds of security personnel inspecting chip-encrusted employee IDs at the front, we thought our chances better through a side entryway. Now, we needed another launch plan.

Shane and I had partnered in many previous capers, but even he was speechless by the spectacle in front of us. For weeks, rumors had swirled on the party-crash circuit about the upcoming gala. Only the weekend before I'd shot out to SpaceX headquarters among the endless aerospace hangars in south Los Angeles on a false tip, and after circling what seemed like mile-long city blocks, I was unable to find any festivities.

This time, I had a classified tip from a crasher cohort Brenda Stevens, who was a close friend of an employee inside who confirmed we had a "load and go." I was ready to light this candle.

SpaceX was started in 2002 by tech wunderkind and space visionary Elon Musk to reduce space flight costs by developing reusable rockets and spacecraft, create an interplanetary transport system, and build a global telecommunications satellite network.

But SpaceX's most grandiose plan is its most idealistic: to colonize Mars. Not only will the expedition provide a great adventure but could also ensure the long-term survival of mankind facing threats from global warming, nuclear annihilation, artificial intelligence, and/or man-engineered viruses.

By 2024, the company hopes to launch its first manned voyage to Mars, with a goal of colonizing the planet with up to eighty thousand people by 2040.

"I want to die on Mars," said Musk. "Just not on impact." In his office, Musk is rumored to have two large posters of Mars—one before human colonization and one after.

After I got launched back on to the sidewalk on that cold December night, I couldn't help marveling that a forty-four-year-old immigrant from South Africa, by way of Canada, had built such an enormous complex, much less several revolutionary companies.

The SpaceX factory is an imposing and gargantuan facility. At one million square feet, it's one of the largest manufacturing plants in California. The three-story aerospace hangar seems to go on for miles and houses the company's office space, software development, and engine, mission control, rocket, and spacecraft manufacturing.

As I retreated back to my car after this initial launchpad detonation, I took a big gulp and wondered if this expedition was beyond my reach. Over the years I'd been pushing and probing many limits, and maybe I'd reached my own orbital boundary.

Shane and I sat on the hood of our car and watched as more than five thousand guests arrived at the massive, floodlit entrance and began running the security gauntlet.

The entryway guest list was thoroughly digitized. No upside-down list reading on this one. After passing through several rings of security, including metal detectors, each employee was eventually granted entry with a swipe of his or her circuit chip ID, with only one guest allowed. I could see giant slides and pulsating laser shows in the background.

The obstacle course before us was overwhelming and intimidating. For the first time, I thought of chucking in my space helmet. It was all too much—too much tech, too much aerospace, way too much money and power. Then I thought, *What would Elon do?* He wouldn't just hop back in his Tin Lizzie and head for home. No, he'd say, "Let's go to Mars!"

I had a brainstorm. I called Sam Brody, my embedded caterer friend, and asked if he could check his contacts to find the catering company handling the event. At the south end of the facility was a huge conglomeration of food tents and cooks that might provide some anonymity and Swiss cheese entry points.

I also asked him to come to the site and bring a bunch of black catering aprons and ties. Shane and I were already dressed in black and just needed the extra accoutrements. Soon Sam arrived with all the above, including some silver trays. We silently and nervously duded up. We took a collective breath, bumped foreheads, and headed for the catering entrance.

We walked single file toward a guard shack that sat behind a thirty-foot-high sliding gate/fence that was slightly open.

"Catering . . . we're with catering!" I bellowed authoritatively.

A guard fronted up and blocked the opening.

"What catering company are you working for?" he asked.

"We're with Très L.A. Catering," I quickly answered, grateful for Sam's stealth intel.

"Oh, OK, c'mon in," said the guard.

We walked about a hundred yards across the tarmac and followed some of our black-clad brethren into the back end of the enormous hangar. Inside was a space-geek Wonderland. There were glowing acrylic Foosball tables packed with guests wielding Day-Glo headbands, sunglasses, and neon wands. Scantily clad women spun from giant rings on the ceiling, Cirque de Soleil style, and manned Texas hold 'em poker tables on the ground floor.

There were dozens of fully stocked bars sprinkled everywhere, some revolving. Giant buffet stations stacked with every kind of ethnic food lined the far walls. A SpaceX logo had been constructed on large silver panels using donuts. There was a SWEETS room crammed with head-sized, planet-shaped desserts. If Willy Wonka had gone to space, it might have looked like this.

SpaceX holiday party ceiling acrobat.

At first, all three of us stood stunned at the outrageous display of creativity, resources, and space-gizmo technology. We were standing on a factory floor the length of multiple football fields that hosted multiple Falcon 9 rocket manufacturing stations, nine depots for the final assembly of the Merlin engine, and several construction hubs for the Dragon spacecraft. I kept thinking, "Only in California."

"Hey guys, you've got to quit standing there and gawking," screeched an officious-looking catering manager at us. "We need you all to get back to work and right now!"

We jolted out of our stupor and tried to make a show of staying busy. I picked up a couple of used glasses, discarded plates of food, and trash on my silver tray and returned them to a nearby station. I grabbed a trash bag and bolted to a nearby bathroom. I practically

Shane and Adrian, catering imposters, at SpaceX holiday party.

rent the door off my stall and ripped off my tie and apron and stuffed them in the bag. Sam and Shane soon followed behind me and performed the same frantic ritual.

We all briefly tidied up in the mirror and burst out of the bathroom in thirty-second intervals, ditching our bags under a nearby covered table. Then we hopped on the indoor train, the SpaceXpress, fled our catering duties, and journeyed deep into the bowels of the factory.

We saw groups of people playing beach volleyball on several courts. Tons of sand had been trucked in for the occasion. A few took selfies while standing, squatting, and "hanging-ten" on several surfboards. We passed a cowboy saloon with guests dancing on the bar. Go-go dancers gyrated to disco music behind a diaphanous curtain on a large stage. Up ahead was just one of several DJ and dance floors illuminated with pulsing neon lights.

After riding for several minutes, I saw the UNCLEAN room, a bizarre *Andromeda Strain*-style quarantine facility with white walls and large glass windows. Inside were dozens of guests cloaked in white hazmat suits holding paint guns and spraying the walls and windows, creating figures in every color as a means of artistic expression. A long line of attendees waited to suit up for their fifteen-minute turn inside the chamber.

I got in line and soon I was stepping into a large jumpsuit, putting on a head wrap, gloves, and goggles. I was given a propellant paint gun and told to have at it. Some civilians outside were staring in a window, and I meandered up and blasted them with a Jackson Pollack flourish. They flinched and retreated while laughing uproariously.

Other space artists created strange landscapes, sprayed phrases like "MARS OR BUST!" or whipped up cosmic themes—swirling galaxies, bursting supernovas, and black holes. One guy next to me stumbled and blasted my backside with red paint. I was going to retaliate but realized the whole thing could quickly devolve into a paint war game. Better to keep the emphasis on peaceful exploration and artistic pursuits. It was a surreal fifteen minutes.

The SpaceX UnClean room

I ejected from paint quarantine and wandered over to a revolving bar covered in tinfoil and other space-age ornaments. A group of engineers were downing vodka shots and toasting Russian Soyuz rockets, the Mir Space Station, and even Sputnik. SpaceX employees often work in project-based teams and are notorious for their ninety-hour-a-week work schedules and impossible deadlines. The holiday party was definitely a chance to blow off some propellant steam and build morale.

After downing a couple of Moscow Mules, I wandered to a nearby dance floor and watched more than a few tech-dorks gyrating awkwardly with their beautiful dates. It was *Revenge of the Nerds* in space.

Nearby was the BALL PIT—a large swimming pool–like structure filled chest-high with rubber and foam balls the size of baseballs. I waded in, flopped down, and sank below the surface. I briefly panicked, as I was buried in a cascade of them. But I soon relaxed and shimmied back up to the top. Dozens of other heads were poking through the mini orbs, some with cocktails balancing in raised hands.

Adrian fighting space balls in the SpaceX Ball Pit. *Courtesy of Shane Kerch*

In the midst of the mayhem, my cell phone started going off. It was RALPH, Brenda's crasher boyfriend. They had both tried to bum-rush the entrance as self-inviters, but only Ralph had made it in. I had earlier texted both of them about my successful catering disguise in a fit of boasting, and now I was being called to account. Could I go back out in my catering outfit and help Brenda get in?

I try to live by the credo: never leave a crasher on the battlefield, especially out in space. After all, Brenda had confirmed the party for all of us through her SpaceX contacts. Though she was exceedingly skittish and carried a perpetual look of wide-eyed apprehension, I knew I had to go back out and retrieve her. I texted Ralph saying I would meet her at the catering entrance.

Luckily my tie and apron were still in the trash bag under the table. I stood behind a fake palm tree, slipped them back on and returned to the fray outside. I saw Brenda pacing back and forth on the sidewalk directly in front of the guard shack. (Couldn't she have paced down the street?)

"Hey, hey, you finally made it. We're going crazy with work in there!" I yelled at Brenda (and the watch guard) as I approached the gate entrance. "Where the hell have you been?"

"I couldn't get a parking place. I'm so sorry I'm late," said Brenda picking up my cue.

"She's with Très L.A. Catering, too," I said to the guard.

"We've got your catering outfit in the locker room," I said to Brenda, who was wearing a Flying Nun–type outfit with a huge white-collar bow. (Again, what was she thinking? Or maybe she hoped for a moon launch from the factory floor?)

The guard nodded and motioned Brenda in. We got inside and I repatriated Brenda with Ralph. I told them they needed a romp in the Ball Pit. That would ease their anxiety . . . or possibly increase it.

I reconnected with Shane, who rhapsodized about another out-landish space playpen on the far side of the factory floor. It took us a solid twenty minutes of walking through throngs of drunken engineers, would-be cosmonauts, and acrobatic ceiling twirlers before we arrived. It was a portable, medium-sized swimming pool, and floating on the water were several large, clear plastic bubbles. Each one had a party attendee inside desperately trying to stand upright and keep his or her balance. The effects were hilarious, as every wannabe astronaut flipped, flopped, and face-planted repeatedly, simulating a bad space walk.

"Maybe it's time to put *the* boy in the bubble," said Shane, poking me in the stomach.

Soon I was standing on a perch, climbing through a zipper into a big plastic orb. I got launched into the water, where I tumbled like a rag doll inside a washing machine. Once my weight was centered, the bubble stopped spinning. I slowly stood up and miraculously kept

SpaceX aqua bubble balancing act.

my equilibrium—must be all the years of surfing. A crowd formed and began rhythmically clapping. I began to vogue, thrust out my chest, and flex my biceps. I started drifting to the side of the pool. Shane crept up behind me and shoved my bubble back into the center of the pool. I began tumbling mercilessly and could never right myself again.

Soon I noticed everyone fleeing. There must be a happening or an arrival of a noted personage. Elon Musk was speaking somewhere on the factory floor. I missed the whole speech trapped in my bubble.

The fun continued for hours. I rode a giant slide from inside the third floor to the ground-floor tarmac outside. I watched a laser show. I sang along with a headbanger tribute band.

I talked with one guest who'd lost her date in the crush of activities. "I'm just hoping my boyfriend doesn't wake up and find himself welded inside a Falcon 9 propellant tank or sealed inside a Dragon spacecraft," she said. "Can you imagine finding him on Mars in a few decades, his bones trapped inside a contraption but still holding a champagne glass?"

By 4 AM the space party was still raging but my circuit board was fried. I was suffering from sensory overload. I'd been placed in an enormous orgasmatron simulator, launched into orbit, and after an eight-hour journey, arrived at splashdown in the parking lot. My head was still spinning with expanding and contracting visuals.

As I took a last look at the giant space juggernaut across the street, I thought of all this enterprise represented: the hunger for exploration, the technological innovation, the insatiable curiosity, the communal initiatives, the torturous engineering details, the creativity, the corralling of capital, the vision. Whether or not the future billions spent on the endeavor to Mars would be better used in saving our own planet is a contentious issue best discussed in another book.

As I drove away, I was filled with an overwhelming sense of awe that has stayed with me to this day.

19

A NIGHT AT THE
PETERSEN MUSEUM

"**A**NYTHING AT THE PETERSEN TONIGHT?"

It was an early spring evening in 2013 and I was checking in with Barton Whitaker in search of excitement. I'd already scrubbed the web and bird-dogged my daily contacts for any kind of function. I was exhibiting signs of desperation by considering a Beverly Hills Chamber of Commerce coffee klatch, a Veteran of Foreign Wars gathering downtown, and/or an Elks Lodge reception in the San Fernando Valley.

"There is a fun event—city councilman Eric Garcetti is holding a good-sized fundraiser for his mayoral campaign this evening at Petersen, and it should be a rollicking time," said Barton. "Starts around 7 PM and should be well-stocked with Puck finger food and palate-pleasing wines. I'll see you there."

Thank heaven for the Petersen Automotive Museum. It was always the go-to venue on a slow night and was almost guaranteed to be hosting some kind of bash, a foundation for adrenaline-starved party seekers. It's the utility player of crasher world, always there in a pinch and providing needed backup on lonely nights.

The Petersen takes up a whole city block on Wilshire Boulevard's Museum Row, also known as the Miracle Mile, the epicenter of Los Angeles's social geography. Most notable functions and galas in L.A. occur in the dense swath of urbanity on the city's Westside, stretching from Hollywood to Santa Monica and including such municipalities and communities as West Hollywood, Beverly Hills, Culver City, and Venice.

The Petersen Automotive Museum is at the physical crossroads of the Westside's swirling nightlife and is a stalwart pit stop on the way to or from bigger adjacent events.

Robert E. Petersen founded an enormous car-themed publishing empire in 1948 that grew to include more than thirty-six monthly titles, including *Hot Rod*, *Motor Life*, and *Car Craft* magazines. In 1994, Petersen assembled one of the finest vintage vehicle collections in the country and transformed a former windowless department store into a thriving auto museum.

The three floors of the Petersen host a revolving gallery of about 150 cars, including Ford Model Ts, Ferraris, Dodge Storms, McLarens, hot rods, custom-made autos, racing cars, and motorcycles. In the "Vault" below the main exhibits, recently opened to the public, are another three hundred notable vehicles, including President Franklin Roosevelt's 1942 Lincoln, a 1939 Bugatti that belonged to the shah of Iran, and a 1952 black Ferrari Barchetta once owned by Henry Ford II.

A large "Hollywood Star Cars" collection includes famous roadsters such as Thelma and Louise's T-Bird, a DeLorean from *Back to the Future*, a 1968 Dodge Charger from the film *Dukes of Hazzard*, the VW bus in *Little Miss Sunshine*, and Steve McQueen's 1956 Jaguar XKSS.

Car buffs say that Detroit made the automobiles, but Southern California is where many of the cultural inspirations and design ideas originated. The Petersen Museum captures all that local car history, industry, and artistry with detailed galleries and creative dioramas that include some of the most exquisite cars ever manufactured. It's a glittering hood ornament to L.A.'s sunny lifestyle that attracts up to two hundred thousand visitors a year.

It's no wonder that it's a popular place for weddings, corporate parties, conferences, product launches, concerts, fashion shows, and political confabs. Crashers love the venue for its perpetual events, panoramic rooftop views, gorgeous architecture, and multiple stealth points of entry.

The museum's one brush with infamy happened on March 9, 1997, when rapper Christopher Wallace, a.k.a. Notorious B.I.G., was killed after a party there. He hopped into a large SUV with his entourage, and he was fatally shot in the passenger seat at a red light fifty yards from the parking entrance. It remains one of L.A.'s most prominent unsolved murders.

I wasn't thinking about Biggie when I entered the ground floor of the museum's multilevel parking structure and climbed up the fire stairwell to an upper floor. There's a skyway there, usually unguarded, that connects to the second floor of the exhibit. The ground floor had lots of hustle and bustle with political funders, guests, and other bigwigs arriving down below. But up above, all was quiet.

I walked hastily across the bridge and noticed that the second-floor car exhibit ahead was completely dark, which was unusual. Due to the inactivity I figured the door was locked, but when I grabbed the handle, it popped open.

I entered into near darkness and tried to get my bearings. I gingerly tiptoed between the multimillion-dollar cars trying to find the main escalator down.

"HEY, what are you doing in here? Stop right there!" yelled a beefy bouncer at the other end of the emporium. I figured he didn't get a complete look at me due to the dimness. I was also wearing what I called my Viet Cong outfit: buffed black shoes, black pants, shirt, and blazer—easier to blend in with the shadows.

I made a split-second decision to flee, figuring I could outrun my chubby chaser. I began sprinting through an obstacle course of vintage automobiles. I dodged a Meyers Manx dune buggy, almost tripped over a 1956 Chevrolet Corvette SR2, and smashed my knee on a 1929 Ford Roadster.

"Second floor . . . running . . . trespasser . . ." were several words I heard crackling over the walkie-talkie behind me.

As I sprinted, I kept looking behind me at my pursuer and to the side for an exit. I couldn't seem to find that damn escalator. I must have ridden the thing a hundred times and never gave it a thought.

Then I caught my groin on one of the shark fins on the back of a 1959 Cadillac Series 62. I doubled over in agony, realizing my days as a sperm donor were probably over. I was so hampered I ducked behind a 1989 Batmobile. I lay flat under the rear bumper like a crazed Joker gripping my privates as the chubster hoofed by, flailing his flashlight hither and thither.

After a minute or two of hyperventilating, I caught my breath and my eyesight acclimated to the darkness. I then saw my lifesaver—a small green exit sign that I hobbled toward. I nudged open the door and half-stumbled, half-fell, and half-hopscotched down two levels to the ground floor. I jimmied open the door and popped into the center of the party.

I could see security was in a state of high dudgeon, and a few of them were scampering up the inert escalators to help their brethren upstairs. I looked over and saw Shane and Barton chatting amiably nearby. I relieved Shane of his beer and briefly said I needed it as a prop as security was after me.

There's a joke that crashers sometimes tell. What happens when three or more crashers get together at a party? Answer: They immediately disperse.

Adrian with the Batmobile in calmer times at the Petersen Museum.

It's a good chance at least one of you is known to one of the guards. I've seen many a peripheral interloper get caught up in a security dragnet just because they're talking with a target.

I took a quick beer sip and by the time the bottle was off my lips, Shane and Barton were gone, fleeing like rats from a sinking crasher. I couldn't blame them.

I began circulating and trying to make small talk with attendees, an assortment of big-ticket donors, small-time political aides, schedulers, ragged community activists, and reporters. But I was still in considerable ball-pain, sweating buckets, and jabbering incoherently. I was definitely off my game.

A security guard stuck to an earpiece kept talking into his lapel and eyeing me. Or *was* he? My paranoia was bubbling over. Why didn't I just leave? On some level I couldn't—it was a great soiree, and I didn't want to miss the fun.

Finally Eric Garcetti, the mayoral candidate himself, ambled within range. I had occasionally interviewed him over the years in my reportorial duties. He was always a charming and respectful guy. Maybe I should just grab him by the horns, pay my respects, and in the process, face down the enclosing security detail. Or would that escalate the whole situation and end up with me on the floor in restraints wearing a bite mask?

I decided to stick my head into the maw, reach out and greet him with a hail-fellow-well-met backslap and handshake. He seemed to vaguely remember me and couldn't have been friendlier. We were all smiles, and that put security back on their heels. I had one of his aides use my iPhone to take a commemorative photo of the two of us.

After that I was untouchable, and all kinds of friends and acquaintances popped out of the mist. Even Shane and Barton circled back.

"Nice move. I thought you were done," said Shane. "I had to remove myself so I'd be able to bail you out of County."

Adrian and future L.A. mayor Eric Garcetti.

"Appreciate that I'm always in your thoughts," I said.

We lingered another hour, inspected some hot rods, American race cars, and customized drive-in automobiles and watched the soon-to-be-mayor give a speech. But by the end of the night, my fight-or-flight adrenaline was wearing off and I was in considerable pain.

I left the museum limping and lowered myself into my bucket of bolts two blocks away. When I got home I unbuckled my belt, loosened my knickers, and noticed a baseball-sized purple hematoma on my right groin canal. It's been a few years, but I can still see a remnant. I refer to it as my crasher car scar.

20

INCREASING MISHAPS

IN ALL THINGS there's an ebb and flow—seasons, cycles, rhythms, looping sequences. When all was well on the crasher circuit, when I'd have month after month of seamless entries, stimulating events, and lively new acquaintances with nary a disputation or confrontation, I'd get nervous. I knew trouble beckoned—a stretch of good crasher fortune can only last so long. And then, when shit hits, you're up to your neck in it, a never-ending deluge.

I'd been humming along nicely with a tight core of gamesters, making new friends, taking numbers, and soaking up all L.A. had to offer. Then I started stumbling into an escalating series of collisions, misadventures, and social fender-benders. I'd begun another bad run.

One late night I got pulled over by a cop for gliding through a right turn. I signed off on the ticket and was about to bid the deputy adieu when he stopped me.

"Excuse me, but what's in that black bag you've got in the front seat?" he queried. "That's one helluva bunch of doohickies you've got there."

I glanced down and, to my horror, realized my party bag was splayed open on the passenger seat with all my tricks of the trade—wristbands and pens and markers and name tags, even an eye patch—sprouting in full view.

"Uh, I was just at a kid's birthday party. You know how it is—just a mess of games and stuff—musical chairs, pin the tail on the donkey, unicorn piñatas, Snakes and Ladders," I sputtered.

"That's a lot of kiddie games—all at midnight?" scoffed the cop, looking at me like I was John Wayne Gacy with a clown suit in the trunk.

There was a long pause. I thought I was on the verge of a car ransacking and strip-search. I got a hard stare, followed with a wave back into traffic and a reprimand to drive more carefully.

The next night, I jumped into an overly packed lobby elevator heading to the top of the Sunset Tower on the Sunset Strip for a movie premiere after-party. A lobby guard saw my sudden move and probably radioed up to the guardians at the top.

I burst out of the elevator and tried to bum-rush the entrance.

An officious-looking woman stopped me cold. "Are you with Benedict?" she asked. "You in Benedict's group?"

"Yup, that's me, I'm with Benedict, and he told me to just mention his name," I answered quickly while pushing resolutely ahead.

"Sorry Beavis, there's no Benedict here," she snapped. "Now get the hell out of here."

The following night I was standing at the bar of another industry soiree. I had arrived by carrying a potted plant through the entrance. I was nuzzling a gin and tonic when an amped-up bouncer fronted up beside me. He thrust an iPad right next to my head and started scrolling through several large mug shots—a veritable rogue's gallery of other crashers with dour expressions.

"Is this him . . . is this him . . . this one?" he urgently asked another manager who stood in front of me scanning intently between my face and the endless stream of degenerates scrolling by. I grinned manically to throw them off. Luckily there wasn't a direct hit. I couldn't believe how many they'd digitally pegged in my inner circle.

"Sorry about that sir, false alarm. Someone thought they saw you bring in a potted plant," said the lead security manager. "You're free to drink up."

I gulped my remaining tonic and fled.

Adrian and friend arriving at a party incognito. *LAPhotoParty.com*

My sisters believe I'm like my uncle Brian, always dancing on the edge of a bonfire, drawn to flames. Maybe a little too much curiosity and lust for adventure. They think it's in the genes. My uncle was a veteran commercial pilot for the Australian airline Qantas. His near misses are legendary in family lore.

In the early 1980s, at the height of the Cold War, he and his crew flew into Moscow. They had a three-day layover and thought they'd start their hiatus right. They began making the rounds sampling the local jungle juice, vodka with a dab of pineapple. On return to their hotel late that night, they piled into my uncle's room for a nightcap.

One of the crew noticed a large hump under the carpet behind the main couch in the living room.

"For Kriss-sake mateys, we're being bloody bugged," bellowed one of the crew, probing the bump with his hands. He quickly grabbed his extensive, portable tool kit.

My uncle and his remaining troupe soon swarmed the swatch of carpet with knives, scissors, and pliers. They peeled it back to reveal four large vertical rods bolted into the floor, all crested with a horizontal steel plate.

"It looks like a bunch of bloody antennae," screamed one. "We're probably transmitting live as we speak!"

Off came the plate, and soon after the bolts on three of the rods were removed. Finally, the last bolt on the last rod was unscrewed. Suddenly all four rods disappeared into the floorboard below. There was a pause, followed by a deafening crash that shook the whole building.

"Serves them right mateys. They'll think twice about ever trying to bug the good first officers of Qantas airlines ever again," said one of the chief engineers.

A couple of minutes later came a loud banging on their hotel door with demands to be let in. The door opened and six KGB types barged in and quickly overran the room, inspecting the spot behind the couch.

"Do uuuuu reeeealize wot u heff done?" asked the lead commissar. "Uuuuu just unscrewwwwed the chandelier, which came crassshhing down and almost keel several people in lobby!"

I wasn't thinking much about my uncle's exploits or my recent bad turn of crasher luck when I agreed to return to the Golden Globes, slated for the coming weekend. Duane Flanigan had never attended and implored me to take him.

On the way to the Beverly Hilton hotel, Flanigan insisted we stop at a 7-Eleven. I thought he wanted alcohol, but he darted in to grab a sixteen-dollar throwaway instamatic flash camera.

"I'd like to nab some pics of a few celebrities," he yammered excitedly.

"Oh no, Flanigan. This is a recipe for disaster," I said. "I'd rather have you drink neat Absinthe than start stalking celebrities."

He protested, and I eventually relented. That's what happens when you bring Flanigan—a million detours and surprises—we call them "Flanigan's shenanigans."

We arrived just as the awards ceremony ended and the after-parties were beginning. Our top target was the Weinstein Company extravaganza, held in a giant white tent, a temporary abutment on the west end of the Hilton property. As hundreds of attendees streamed into the tent, we jumped into the throng and bypassed the distracted guards with ease.

There were the customary live bands and dozens of buffet stations, and the place was raining vodka. Flanigan began pouring and lit up quickly. I beseeched him to slow down—we had all night. But whenever the firewater was free, Flanigan insisted on dousing himself, drinking like Prohibition was starting on the morrow. Suddenly, I noticed Harvey Weinstein ambling along, surrounded by his security retinue.

"Oh, there's Harvey," I said under my breath, more to myself than anyone in particular. But Flanigan heard me.

"Where? Where is he?" asked Flanigan excitedly. I stupidly pointed Harvey out.

Flanigan bolted and broke into a near sprint toward Harvey. He ran right by him, stopped, twirled, crouched down on one knee, and lifted up his cheap instamatic right in Harvey's face.

Flanigan clicked off several full-frontal flash photo bombs, and Harvey flinched violently. He looked like he'd been shot or suffered a mild heart attack. Not for nothing is Harvey considered one of Hollywood's most paranoid.

Harvey quickly recovered his composure and ordered his guards to set upon Flanigan. Soon they had him on his hind legs with his arms pinioned behind his back. They marched him toward Harvey and offered him up as the first sacrifice of the night.

I was off to the side watching intensely, as Harvey began the impromptu interrogation. Flanigan repeatedly blanched, went weak in the knees, and then slowly lifted a crooked finger, rotating it slowly in my direction.

Suddenly I was surrounded by goons and brought into Harvey's impromptu, mobile interrogation chamber. He gave me a quick once-over, not recognizing me from our encounter at the Riverhorse on Main at Sundance several years prior.

"Who are you guys with?" Harvey growled.

"We came with my entertainment attorney, Greenberg . . . Stephen," I said, making up a quick placeholder name. "We're all family here tonight."

Harvey stared bullets right through me for a few seconds. He looked ready to land a haymaker across Flanigan's jaw. Then he glanced over at his goon squad.

"GET THESE CLOWNS THE FUCK OUTTA MY PARTY," he half-snarled and part-shrieked with a cock of his head.

Flanigan and I were hoisted up by the elbows and, with feet dragging, hustled up to the tent entrance and hurled outside. We dusted ourselves off and sought our bearings.

"I'm sorry I pointed you out. I just panicked," yelped Flanigan. "That guy's a friggin' beast."

"How could you photo bomb him, especially at his own party!" I said. "The goal is to *avoid* security, not bring it down on our heads."

"I'm really sorry. Here's a cigar as atonement," said Flanigan sheepishly.

I didn't know if Flanigan had purchased it at 7-Eleven or had ripped it off from a Weinstein table. At that point, all I could do was shrug.

I missed Avi, my great pal and fellow adventurer. We'd had so many amazing capers together, especially each year at the Globes. This was a special place for us, and memories of all the super times came flooding back. We'd always worked in lockstep, and his street smarts and loyalty always kept us both out of trouble.

Avi had been gone for several years. He'd fallen for a beautiful Russian Israeli woman, relocated to New York City, and had a young daughter. He was happy, content, and settling in with a growing family.

I was now outside, after being expelled from my favorite event, and left looking at Flanigan. We stood in the hotel courtyard's cross-party traffic, and after a few minutes we both decided to go back in.

Now we'd be trespassing.

I felt careless and somewhat dissipated. Again, we blitzed the entrance inside a throng of attendees and rode the crowd in.

After walking around for about thirty minutes inside the party tent, with all eyes on constant alert for Harvey, Flanigan and I stopped at a central table. There was an enormous promotional bottle of Ketel One Vodka atop it, and Flanigan started prying it open with a toothpick. I absentmindedly sat down and looked over at a large name card lying face down. I reached over and flipped it.

BOB WEINSTEIN'S TABLE. (That would be the other cohost of the party—the cochairman of the Weinstein Company—Harvey's brother.)

I jumped up violently and grabbed Flanigan by the neck, pried him off the Ketel One bottle, and pushed him ahead, zigzagging through the crowd until we found an exit.

———————

The next morning, I still felt frazzled from the surges of adrenaline dodging the Brothers Weinstein. But I was on a roll, a bad roll, and like a gambler unable to quit, I invited myself to a large art gallery opening, part of a group of exhibits in the West Hollywood art district.

Over the past few decades the Los Angeles art scene has exploded, with more than four hundred blue-chip galleries and private museums, several internationally recognized art schools, and an influx of young, ambitious painters, photographers, sculptors, and ceramicists.

I know some crashers who only do the art scene—they appreciate the asymmetrical faces, the hang-back security, the bizarre clothing choices, the unpredictable hygiene, the offbeat exhibits, and the dynamic and quirky community.

I'd been tipped off by "the Professor," Al Barrios, which seemed odd initially, as there's rarely a meat buffet at an art event. But his voice mail gave me the coordinates, and the affair promised to be well populated and lush with food and drink.

I put on a colorful Mao jacket and a felt fedora and hopped in my clunker, making a dash for West Hollywood. While cruising down Melrose Avenue, I saw throngs of art denizens pouring out of a gallery. The address seemed off, but this had to be it.

After circling the area for twenty minutes, I finally found a parking spot about a half mile away. As I disembarked, I noticed a couple strolling to their car with gold sparkling wristbands. I rifled through my bag of tricks and couldn't find a match.

Before I was even aware, I compulsively approached the couple.

"Hi there, friendlies," I said with a dry-lipped grin. "Are you two leaving that big art gallery opening on Melrose Avenue? My cousin's inside and I've got to pick him up, but he won't answer his cell phone. Any chance I could borrow your wristbands?"

Best to always ask for *all* wristbands, as you may need to pay it forward to another intruder stuck outside the event and hope that person reciprocates the next time you're stuck out in the mud.

The middle-aged couple looked like typical L.A. art patrons. The male had slicked back hair, a whiskered soul patch under his lower lip, and a white T-shirt that said EVEN I'D DO ME. His female spouse had mounds of frizzy hair, loud eyewear, and nursed an irritated expression.

"*Borrow* our wristbands?" she huffed. "Don't think we'll see you again. Why don't you just take 'em. But how the hell do we get these things off?"

"Piece of cake," I countered and took her hand lightly, leaned down, bit into the wristband, and followed with a quick rip. "Voilà!"

"Ewwww, that was a little invasive," she barked. "I don't like strangers biting my wrist."

Her husband quickly followed my lead, bit off his own wristband and flung it at me.

"Hey, thanks so much. My cousin will be most grateful," I said.

Both of them grunted, turned, and walked toward their purple hybrid Prius.

I cantered up to the art gallery but upon arriving was told that the exhibit had just ended. I had the wrong address. My correct target was three blocks up the street.

My misfire set me off a bit, and I broke into a run. Soon, I got to the next gallery, and this one was packed with hundreds of guests. There was only one chute-like entrance, partially blocked with a desk manned by two chipper checkers and amply fortified with security muscle. My gold wristbands were useless.

I got in the long check-in line and started carpet-bombing the Professor with texts and calls for back door, ink-stamp, or famous name suggestions. No answer. After another twenty-minute wait I was at the desk and fell back on my tried and true—the upside-down list read.

I quickly picked off the name Peter Coyote, a solid character actor known for his roles in *Erin Brockovich*, *Bitter Moon*, and *Patch Adams*.

"Your name?" said the chipper checker.

"Coyote, Peter," I responded knowing that last names were usually first on check-in lists.

"Oh, right, here you are," she said. "Head on in."

I was thankful she wasn't familiar enough with decades-old movies to recognize this particular celebrity. I felt the usual relief as the ripples of anxiety slipped off my back. I wedged past the two guardsmen, who stared impassively straight ahead.

Just as I got inside the door, I again heard the check-in lady offering her typical salutation.

"Your name?"

"Peter Coyote," said a very familiar voice.

I whirled and there he was standing several feet away—Peter Coyote! He must have been standing behind me the whole time in line.

I froze momentarily but quickly ducked into the embrace of the party, hiding behind sculptures and strange paintings while peeking back at the front door. Coyote seemed to be talking earnestly with the checker, and I wondered if he was trying to convince her he really *was* Peter Coyote. I couldn't watch anymore and fled to the head.

I ditched my felt fedora, slicked my hair back with water, and after a few minutes ventured back out. All was well. The musclemen weren't hunting for me, the Professor was at the meat buffet piling up his plate, and Peter Coyote was staring intently at an obscure Chinese painting from an inch away.

Maybe the checker hadn't realized the difference between "Coyote, Peter" and Peter Coyote? The rote rituals of the job had thankfully dulled her name-detector skills.

Again, the pulses of anxiety left me drained, and a stiff one was in order. In the bar line I started conversing with an attractive blonde, middle-aged lady by the name of Katie. I talked too much and bombarded her with information about my birth in Montreal, my surfing skills, and my upcoming documentary projects. Then I got direct.

"Look, I never ever give out my cell phone number, but this one time, and only this time . . . I'll take yours," I said.

She laughed nervously and suggested tactfully that she'd be happy to take my business card instead, if I had one. I promptly handed her my MAHER PRODUCTIONS card with all my coordinates—cell phone number, e-mail, website, and office address. I offered to write down my organ donor status and next of kin to be contacted in an emergency . . . There was nothing left to the imagination I didn't try to provide.

But she did giggle when she saw the phrase under my name on the card:

Adrian Maher
Since 1959

"I assume 1959 is the year you were born?" she asked.

"That's the year I was born to do business," I said. "That's when the empire began."

We exchanged a few more pleasantries, and then I grabbed my whiskey sour and drifted into the crowd. I perused some of the impressionistic paintings, talked with the Professor briefly, and tweaked the nose of a sculpture.

"Sir, please do not touch the works of art!" snapped an exhibit minder.

"Sorry, it just looked so real," I said.

Then, as I continued my exuberant walkabout, I ran into another familiar face. Her name was Debbie. She was about five foot ten, had lustrous blonde hair, and looked like a central blocker on a local college volleyball team. I thought I'd seen her before, but I just couldn't place her. We started talking about art, key workouts to build "core" strength, and documentaries. At the end of the conversation, I offered her my MAHER PRODUCTIONS business card.

"If you ever want to get into documentary television, feel free to give me a call!" I exclaimed with a parting handshake, a little too enthusiastically.

I wandered the rest of the gallery, trying to decipher some of the list prices. One of the pieces was titled *It's a Boy!* and was nothing more than a giant splotch of red paint on a white canvas. The gallery wanted $2,500. *Hmmm*, thank God I'm in the documentary business. I can sit in an editing bay and figure out what works and what doesn't. Here, I hadn't a clue.

After one last whiskey sour, I meandered toward the exit. I even shook Peter Coyote's hand and complimented him about his acting work and documentary narration skills. I didn't have the heart to break it to him that I'd used his gold-plated name in backward fashion to get in.

As I walked out to the sidewalk, there were Katie and Debbie—the two similar-looking blondes, waiting at the valet together for their car. No wonder the younger one looked familiar; she was the *spitting image* of her mother.

"Well, look at the mother/daughter art duo," I said. "Were any of the pieces up to your exacting standards? Maybe the two of you should sit for a regal portraiture yourselves sometime!"

Both of them laughed a bit nervously, and I kept up my friendly banter until I felt a hot gaze scorching the side of my face. He was about six foot four, middle aged but still heavily muscled with a high and tight buzz cut. Probably had lettered on the crew team at Harvard in days of yore.

"Adrian, this is Kingsley, my husband, and also the father of my daughter," said Katie.

Their car pulled up to the curb. Kingsley cracked a thin smile, reached out, and gave me the most bone-crushing handshake I'd ever experienced. I felt my knuckles popping, my pinkies buckling, and a possible wrist sprain.

He held his grip for what seemed an eternity, staring right through me and seeming to push me back on my heels. Finally, he loosened his titanium clamp and wordlessly turned, heading to the driver's side of his car.

But something was off. He had released something into my hand. He'd left me with a message, something to ponder on my long drive home. I stood pigeon-toed on the sidewalk and looked down at my spongy right hand that was slowly springing back to life.

In my now-opened palm were two crumpled, tattered MAHER PRODUCTIONS business cards.

21

CRASHER CANNIBALIZATION

H INKY HANK WAS BESIDE HIMSELF. We were outside a restaurant opening in Santa Monica and his gray hair was frizzed out, his eyes buggy, and his forehead stuck with sweat.

"I can't take it anymore," he confessed. "How can I make it stop?"

The Hinkster was usually the coolest of trespassers, but he'd just been pointed out to security by another crasher at the event. It was the latest in a series of expulsions that had him rattled.

I couldn't blame him. I too had once been targeted by the same finger-pointer. It was an unnerving experience. Here you were, relaxing inside a local bash, and then the security tap on the shoulder, the pummeling questions, and the public perp walk through the party as several bouncers deposit you on the sidewalk. It is humiliating, embarrassing, and a potent public shaming.

The confrontations came out of the blue. You hadn't argued with anyone, you hadn't swiped a platter of food, and you hadn't cut into the bathroom or bar line. The next instant you were stopped in mid-conversation, separated from friends and acquaintances, deprived of the night's entertainment, and hustled to a side exit. Afterward, there's that long walk back to your car, trying to figure out what happened.

That's not to absolve trespassing crashers of blame, most of whom deserve a launching. As noted, you pay a price in skyrocketing anxiety and ceaseless hypervigilance. It's just that when targeted by another insider, you feel defenseless. Other crashers know all about you. They've got the goods on all your routines, activities, your likes and dislikes, your favorite events, foods, wines, and bath soaps. They know way more about you than security or even your own mother will ever know. They've got your number. When they turn on you, they wreak havoc.

Most crashers are solicitous, generous with information, and share a bond from innumerable adventures, pileups and crack-ups, bizarre mishaps, and priceless anecdotes. But several harbor a strange compulsion to perpetually tattle on their brethren.

Some snitches do it to curry favor with security. Others squeal out of deep self-loathing—they're ashamed of their own petty crimes and trespasses and hope to lessen their own guilt by calling out the dreadful misdeeds of others.

While in conversation with the most hypocritical crashers, I'm always amused when they launch into a jeremiad about another crasher and all their immoral infractions.

I've noticed these canaries love the feeling of power and fear they wield over other interlopers. Some of them are complete nonentities—no skills, no careers, and no deep friendships. They're society's invisibles, and their only chance at nabbing attention is to fink on others. Sometimes the snitchers will try to extort money, tickets, or swag from their vulnerable crasher targets, who sometimes agree just to halt the vicious harassment.

I've had my own problems over the years with several of them. They hide in the shadows behind pillars, curtains, or security personnel and start their pointing and whispering. Then they approach you seeking favors and, if that doesn't work, increase their threats and up their snitching.

I sat Hinky Hank down and suggested the best defense was no defense. Just ignore the tattler and deny any of the attention he or she so desperately seeks. You'll get lofted out of several parties in a row, but eventually the snitches turn their sights on new targets. They want a craven reaction, and with none forthcoming, there's no fuel to feed their pathology. By paying no mind, you should get a year or two of respite before the attacks ramp up again.

I once watched a notorious stoolie go after another friend of mine. My buddy was a tough, stubborn, resourceful guy, and he fought back with everything he had. Soon the two of them took their bruising battles of reciprocal ejections all over the L.A. party circuit—from beach parties in Malibu to Pilates studio openings in Redondo Beach to Hollywood mansion shindigs. Sometimes both got ejected at the same time and ended up jawboning with each other on the street.

Unfortunately, their epic altercations created collateral damage that spilled out on to the crasher circuit—warring sides, destroyed friendships, vicious blog posts, increased surveillance, and a security crackdown.

Sometimes I'd shake my head at the bizarre aspects of this subterranean world. Several years ago I accidently attracted a crasher stalker. She was a big German and looked like an Olympic swimmer, about six feet tall with wide shoulders and a fierce expression. Her name was GUNDALA (pronounced *GOON-da-la*), and after meeting her at an event, she wouldn't leave me alone.

"Ver ist der partaaaaaay?" she'd scream into my cell phone, sometimes a dozen times a day.

Gundala was an émigré of rough beauty with international movie star aspirations and a relentless belief that by crashing every red carpet event and unleashing her Teutonic charm, she'd will her way to stardom. Her tactics weren't a bad idea. Paris Hilton had found fame using the same gambit with no discernable talent or personality. But Paris had a catchy name and the famous Hilton pedigree. Gundala was, well, Gundala.

My first sign of trouble occurred at a big pre-Oscar party at a producer's home in Beverly Hills. Security was stifling, but I managed to slip in the front gate among a group of VIPs. Once on the property, there was a line up the walkway to get into the front door.

I was standing patiently when I heard my name screamed over and over with a heavy guttural accent. I turned to see a crazed Teuton with her head stuck through the railings beseeching me to come over to her. Ignoring her only drove her into paroxysms of waving and screaming.

I turned around and gave a slit-to-the-throat gesture to cut the theatrics. I motioned that I'd call her once in. But she couldn't let it go.

"AAAAdrian, AAAAdrian, how deed you get eeen?" she screeched. "Vat is bist vay in?"

I tried to look ahead, studying the bald spot of a studio executive in front of me. At that, Gundala went ga-ga.

"AAAdrian, AAAdrian, I know uuuuuu!" she shrieked. "Don't pretend you don't know me! Yes, you, you, you . . . Adrian in the blue blazer and gray pants. Turn around, turn around! Ver you invited to dis partaaaay? Are you on der list?"

Soon, I had some of Hollywood's most powerful swiveling and staring at me with quizzical expressions. Security began murmuring. I finally broke rank and fled back outside as Gundala chased me up the street back to my car.

It was quite a scene. My crumbling 1984 Toyota Corolla pulling out with tires screeching and engine smoking amid a train of Bentley Continentals and Maseratis, with a fanatic, howling German in high heels trying to grab my radio antennae.

She hounded me for a couple of years afterward. I used my own advice and tried ignoring her. Other times I ignored my own advice and tried to feed the beast and throw her some good events that I couldn't attend. I even broke down once and took her to a movie premiere after-party. I soft-talked her, appealing to her peaceful side, her dormant rationality, at times begging for social détente. Nothing worked. The texts and calls were incessant. She had a bottomless need for information and party access and believed I alone held her ticket to global celebrity.

One day she disappeared. Maybe she got an acting gig in a Romanian horror film or went to join her brethren in southern Brazil or became an East German swim coach. Gundala, wherever you are, stay planted. No need to return to La La Land or "Gundalaland" as you once called it. It's hard out here for a crasher.

Over the years, I'd built up a thick hide from all the friction, affronts, and strife that comes with a risk-taking, social lifestyle. Of course, there were perpetual payoffs in camaraderie, strong friendships, and all the excitement and good times. But the moments I felt weariest involved crasher cannibalization—when the uninvited turned on each other. Maybe there is no honor among petty trespassers, but I'd always hoped there was.

One night, after a particularly irksome month of party squabbles, I got invited to a big poolside event at a home in the upscale community of Encino in northern L.A. County. The fete was to be hosted by a successful public relations agent, a woman in her early seventies named BONNIE who was omnipresent at Hollywood events. She was rumored to also self-invite on occasion.

A good Russian financier friend, Victoria Silchenko, was the cohost, and for once I got a legitimate invite. As she and I drove from the Westside over the hill into the San Fernando Valley, I felt at ease for once, without that constant queasy feeling of the infiltrator.

It was a well-heeled crowd, and it felt good to turn the knob of the front door. Soon Victoria and I were clinking glasses, nibbling on quiche, and chatting up the local denizens.

A large Hells Angels–looking guy abruptly came up to us. He was bowling-ball bald with a goatee and wraparound sunglasses (it was 10 PM), wearing a leather vest, chains, and chaps—a definite outlier at the party. He looked as if he'd finished a long beer run with his local chapter and was hankering for trouble.

"Were you invited to this party?" he asked me aggressively. "Because you're eating all my food and drinking all my gin."

Before I could answer, Victoria jumped in and said yes, I was invited to the party. She was the cohost and I was her date. She followed with a zinger.

"And who are you?" she asked. "Why are you hiding behind those sunglasses? Isn't it a little dark out here?" She then reached over and tried to swipe the glasses off his face.

The somewhat embarrassed thug grunted and lumbered away. I didn't think much of the encounter until about two hours later. I was chatting with a half-dozen guests in a semicircle when Mr. Hells Angel appeared again, reeking of booze.

"I really don't like you, and it's time for you to leave the party," he blurted out, as he stepped forward and prodded my chest with several nail-bitten fingers. Soon he began shoving me, and I began retreating with my back to the pool. No doubt he was a big dude—about six foot six and close to three hundred pounds. But I suspected his alcoholic bluster masked cowardice—or indicated it.

I quickly reviewed my options: wrassle this big gator into the pool with the help of his heavy leather vestments, head-butt him and run, or yelp for assistance.

Suddenly, Victoria ran over and accosted him.

"What are you doing, you big idiot!" she shouted.

He took a step back and hesitated. The whole party stopped, startled by the unfolding scene. Then the hooligan reached out, grabbed Victoria by her frills, and threw her into the pool. He quickly fled with his leather belt between his legs.

I grabbed Victoria and hoisted her out of the water. Her summer finery was drenched and her hair a chlorine-tangled vine. But she kept her cool.

"My clothes are destroyed, but at least that hooligan is out of the party," she said.

"And I'm alive to fight another day," I said. "Thank you so much, Victoria."

We got her dried off with a new change of clothes from Bonnie, the cohost and owner of the house. While Victoria recuperated, I started enquiring about the thug. Who was he? What was he doing at the party?

An acquaintance took me aside and said that Bonnie had hired the goon as a bouncer. Maybe she took her inspiration from the Rolling Stones hiring Sonny Barger and the Angels at the notorious and lethal Altamont concert in 1969. When Bonnie saw me at the party, she immediately went over and informed the thug that I was a crasher. He quickly confronted me.

I was astounded by the info. I'd never met Bonnie, although I'd seen her many times at events over the years. I'd always given her a smile and a nod. But she herself was rumored to crash, and obviously my appearance at her party set off a deep resentment and disdain.

This was a new danger—I was a known crasher to other crashers I didn't even know well. And because of their twisted psyches and contorted motivations, I was now a target. This simmering hostility could erupt at any time, anywhere. It was a stealth threat that could blindside me poolside.

It was not security and all their intel that posed the biggest threat, it was other crashers. My paranoia spiked markedly going forward, and put a dent in my carefree views of the uninvited.

22

SHAME AND
DISILLUSIONMENT

─────────

WAS INSIDE A SMALL DIGITAL STUDIO PRODUCTION LOT in Culver City on the Westside of Los Angeles. There was little security, and I'd pierced the gates easily. It was an intimate charity affair of some sort with a couple of food stations sandwiched into a busy cocktail hour.

A couple of crashers already had their snouts buried in the seafood section when I arrived. I kept noticing several young children whizzing around in mobile wheelchairs. As I chewed on a fresh delivery of Maine lobster, I asked one of the female volunteers the purpose of the night's charity event.

"Oh, this is our annual fundraiser for pediatric cerebral palsy," she said.

I almost dropped my crustacean. Do you mean to tell me I just crashed your most critical function of the year on behalf of society's most vulnerable? That I'm standing here mooching off your finite food budget? That I didn't even know the cause of tonight's fundraiser?

A boy rolled up behind me to talk with the volunteer, and I was introduced to him.

"Thanks for coming and for really helping us out," said the boy.

I flushed deep purple with shame. All those hopeful kids, dedicated staff, and big-hearted funders were gathering for the very best of causes. And here I was, like a giant aphid, feeding on their limited largesse.

I promptly took my debit card over to the funding desk, clocked in for $100, and bolted.

It was these moments that gave me pause. Over the years, I had growing pangs at inadvertently crashing such small fundraisers. Sometimes I'd find myself at a charity sale for a Mexican orphanage, gobbling down food at a battered women's shelter, or mistakenly sidling into an event benefitting homeless Hollywood youth.

In between my work in documentaries, I'd spent more than a decade helping my sister's small nonprofit, Pogo Park, in Richmond, California. Her organization reclaimed abandoned and dilapidated inner-city parks and transformed them into magical play spaces for children, employing innovative recreational equipment and stimulating sporting activities. I'd written grant applications, organized community events, and managed fundraisers. I knew better. I knew the finite resources, the daily struggles, and the good people fighting for sometimes hopeless causes at these tiny nonprofits.

While never completely excusable, it's one thing to crash an awards show, a corporate holiday party, an extravaganza at the Playboy Mansion, a movie premiere after-party, or an art museum spectacular lush with resources. It's another to self-invite to a backyard fundraiser for autistic kids.

Some other interlopers had no compunction about hopping the fence of even the smallest fundraiser. It was dispiriting to watch, and I began studiously avoiding such affairs.

After repeated experiences and exposures in any profession or subcultural activity, there occurs the inevitable erosion of idealism, curiosity, and sense of adventure. Age deadens the senses, skepticism morphs into cynicism, and the candle begins to flicker.

As a reporter, documentary filmmaker, and storyteller, I'd repeatedly hunted for the backstory, the real tale, seeking all below-deck activities everywhere I went. After years of watching how the basement sausage is made, I began flinching at the packaged kielbasa on the store shelf. And so it went in crasher world. Pulses of disillusionment began occurring with increasing frequency.

One year, I attended a massive fundraiser at the Century Plaza Hotel for multiple sclerosis hosted by Nancy Davis, the daughter of petrol zillionaire and Hollywood mogul Marvin Davis. The annual event raises millions of dollars and is attended by hundreds of wealthy socialites. It's a particularly lush affair with a multicourse sit-down dinner, bands, dancing, and a slew of comedians. The attendees skew elderly. Pearls, furs, and bad wigs pepper the ballroom.

The big attraction is one of the heftiest swag bags on the charity network circuit, dished out at the end of the night. It's an enormous carryall weighing more than eighty pounds and stocked with every conceivable powder, perfume, lotion, and ointment meant to halt the aging process.

Once the lights came on, the last Scotch slurped up, and coffee spilled, there was a mass exodus of the bewigged and bejeweled toward the gift bag counter in the lobby.

As I ambled up to it, I could already see several klepto-crashers feeding at the trough and lugging several treasured duffel bags away. Soon there began a slow, unfolding pileup as throngs of the plumed and pomaded began surging toward the counter. Apparently, someone yelled out that the supply of gift bags was running low.

Almost instantly, a crush of elderly millionairess matrons began pushing and shoving to get to the front, *anything* to get the promised cosmetics. Elbows flailed. There were shin kicks, slaps, and stealth pinches.

Two well-heeled hags got into it.

"Don't you cut in front of me!" screamed one.

"I was already standing here!" yelled the other.

Some initial shoving was followed by the two of them clawing and scratching at each other with velociraptor talons and screeching. One had a strong grip on the other's frozen hair helmet. Then, with a final tug, she dewigged her adversary, and pandemonium erupted.

Security waded in to break up the geriatric rugby scrum. Once order was restored, high heels, broken necklaces, and several purses dotted the floor. I couldn't see the wig anywhere and figured it was back on the head of its owner, who had disappeared into the crowd.

I retreated to the hotel bar to collect my thoughts and marvel at what I'd seen. The rich really are different from you and me. They never feel they have enough.

After about an hour, I returned to the garage to collect my auto. I looked over and saw a stooped crone with hair askew and glasses askance, heroically dragging two of the hefty bags by their leashes along the concrete floor.

"Can you help me get these into my car, young man?" she chirped.

Many other scenes of depravity and social havoc ensued. In July 2015 I attended opening day at the Del Mar Racetrack in northern San Diego County. All the local blue bloods were peacocking in their summer finery. My crash partner Shane and I managed to scalp some tickets in the parking lot and successfully penetrated the paddock area for a close look at the horses. We infiltrated the members-only Turf Club, sipped some tropical cocktails, and watched the initial races from the club's panoramic viewing seats. We became bored with the upper-crust palaver and descended to a different enclosed VIP area near the finish line, right at the railing at ground level.

Suddenly there was a significant commotion between one of the races. I looked up into the bleacher seats, and roughly forty thousand people were brought up standing. They seemed to be looking right at us. Mere feet away there appeared an incredible phantasm—an impossibly athletic lady with rectangular shoulders and a bold stride. She was fashionably decked out in a wide-brimmed floppy hat and bright red frilly dress. With high heels, she looked about six foot four.

It was Caitlyn Jenner making a dramatic entrance in one of her first public outings, just after her dramatic speech the night before at the ESPY Awards in Los Angeles. Both Shane and I rushed to snap off a few pics but were stopped by a cordon of San Diego County Sheriff deputies who blocked our lenses with their hands and threatened ejection if we didn't halt our digital rubbernecking.

The blockade continued as Caitlyn took in the next race. Then she made a move to leave and set off another stampede as the crowd pressed close for a gander. It looked like the final scene in *The Day of the Locust*. She was now within five feet of me, but I dared not raise my cell phone camera, even amid the bedlam. That is, until I glanced over and saw the backs of several of San Diego's finest badge-men, who were firing off their own photos of Caitlyn.

Though not completely cognizant at the time, I was becoming a crash junkie. Instead of finding a quiet seat at the Del Mar event, betting on a few races, and rooting for some well-chosen nags, I kept pinballing around, penetrating one exclusive section after another. It brought back memories of my time at the Sundance Film Festival. A daily dose of adrenaline was not enough. It now had to occur every hour or even by the minute.

I'd seen the trait in many other crashers. After piercing an elaborate security apparatus and luxuriating at an opulent event, they'd start getting restless within moments. They'd ravenously check the

Caitlyn Jenner at Del Mar Racetrack, Opening Day 2015. *Courtesy of Shane Kerch*

web, peruse their text messages, and make incessant phone calls. Their minds were already on the next event. They needed another dopamine hit. Once in, they were bored, unable to engage in their immediate surroundings or with people around them. They all suffered from the "grass is greener" syndrome or FOMO—fear of missing out—on another event across town. They lived for the grim satisfaction of piercing security rather than the joy of social interaction.

I knew one middle-aged Scandinavian woman, ERIKA, who was ubiquitous. On particular frenetic nights I might visit up to four different venues. I'd see her at every one. The great puzzle was she didn't drive in L.A. She was instead a bus-schedule savant—she had all times, city blocks, and transportation vectors memorized. Somehow she was able to hopscotch from place to place, always arriving before the rest of the crasher throng, who were mired in traffic or parking problems. And she always did it with her pet Chihuahua in tow, snuggled in a strange, jerry-rigged chest harness.

I was exchanging information with her one night, after we'd both just gotten into an event in Beverly Hills. After several minutes, she abruptly gathered her stuff.

"There's another party," she said, cradling her canine. "We must go to Santa Barbara."

It was already nine at night. Santa Barbara was ninety miles north. I noted her use of the phrase "must go," as if it was her duty to quickly trek to the next event. I don't know how she made it to Santa Barbara, but I had no doubt she did.

This bizarre party-pushing compulsion began happening to me. I was once with Avi at Clive Davis's "Night Before" annual pre-Grammy event at the reliable Beverly Hilton. It was an incredibly difficult entry, and once in, we were seated at a table sumptuous with food, drink, and great company. We anticipated great musical acts like Alicia Keys, Smokey Robinson, Lionel Richie, and John Fogerty.

My phone vibrated with an incoming text. It was yet another tip: a big shindig in the Hollywood Hills at a tri-level mansion, attractive women chanting my name, a funkadelic theme with a famous DJ that promised to go all night (although neighbors in such environs usually start their 911 calls at 9 PM).

I immediately prevailed upon Avi to ditch our prime seat at the Davis music gala and make a beeline for the hills. He protested, but with my hyped descriptions of what awaited, he reluctantly agreed.

We'd been at the Beverly Hilton for no more than ten minutes and now got snagged in a ninety-minute traffic jam heading east. We finally got to the "mansion" and were forced to park more than a mile away. After hiking up a long, steep road, we arrived to find a large group of teenagers, many high on Ecstasy and other hallucinogens, with thumping rave music and a couple of beer kegs in the backyard. Some kid had assumed weekend mansion rights from his parents. The party was even announced on AM radio. It was definitely not a scene for grownups, and as we descended the hill we ran through a streaming gauntlet of flash mob pubescents. I absorbed a tirade from Avi.

It turned out I'd been used as a "crash-test dummy" by another social gamester who'd sent me on this wild reconnaissance mission with hyped-up info. It was another harsh lesson.

Besides going on wild forays with dubious information, I also found myself taking more and more risks that made no sense. If I couldn't get in somewhere, it seemed to fan my desire for entry.

One evening I arrived at a simple wine and food event at the Victorian, a popular bar/restaurant that hosts private parties in Santa Monica. Unfortunately, the area around the venue was sheathed in temporary fencing that afforded only two tight entrances. After an hour of circling, I just couldn't make it in.

I remembered an outdoor staircase on the southern side of the building. I galloped up the stairs, but the door was locked. Behind it were the rhythmic thumps and screams of a raging shindig that inflamed my determination. I was exposed on the second-floor landing and needed to make a quick decision. I flicked open a window and, without much thought, dove in horizontally, landing with a thud on the floor.

"What the fuck are you doing in here?" screamed a big, bearded urban lumberjack squatting on the toilet with his pants hugging his ankles.

He tried rising in anger, but I'd caught him mid-pinch. The extra second of hesitation allowed me to bolt out the door and into the party. But once in, I couldn't get the smelly apparition out of my mind. Minutes later, I saw this towering Forrest Hunk hunting for me like I was Montana moose. I quickly self-ejected from the event. Lots of sweat, anxiety, and frustration . . . for what? A few glasses of wine, cheese blintzes, and small talk with some chubby epicureans.

I was also pushing more and more outlandish schemes of entry. During one stretch, the Playboy Mansion was hosting a slew of events.

But the check-in at the bus shuttles had gotten no easier. The name on the list had to match your driver's license. As Avi and I both had androgynous names, I solicited some young college women friends to write short handwritten introductory notes in girly cursive to the Playboy Mansion with their enclosed pictures. Then sign the full names of "Avi Fisher" and "Adrian Maher" to their respective letters requesting to be put on the permanent Playboy Mansion guest list.

I trundled over to the post office to deliver the special package. As I approached, my pace slowed. What was I doing? What was I thinking? Did I really wish to create a fraudulent paper trail just to party with a bunch of old lecherous goats and glassy-eyed, silicone-enhanced habitués? All the planning and intent and effort seemed way overboard and done for all the wrong reasons.

I made a ninety-degree turn and dumped my misguided materials into the nearest trashcan.

Around that time, several of my close crasher friends were graduating from all the subterfuge, getting hitched, assuming mortgages, and having kids. Some, like Duane Flanigan, tired of L.A.'s grind and bustle, moved out of town seeking quieter burgs.

As mentioned, Avi had married and moved to New York City. He called often for vicarious updates and would occasionally visit for a caper or three. But his trips were like the last flashes of a retreating lightning storm. He was now firmly domesticated and in harness, his spare time taken with his daughter's karate lessons, neighborhood co-op association meetings, and couples therapy.

A rough cloak of disillusionment and weariness began enveloping me. I'd had the same fleeting feelings over the years after multiple days of parties strung together around the clock. At times it all became a blur.

Admittedly, I had witnessed scenes over the years that were unforgettable. I'd watched porn impresario and publisher Larry Flynt lowered in his wheelchair from his private jet onto the tarmac at Santa

Monica Airport, then wheeled like a crippled Caligula along a red carpet lined with kneeling, half-naked women into an airplane hangar for *Hustler* magazine's thirty-fifth anniversary party.

I'd stood outside Elton John's Oscar party at the Pacific Design Center in West Hollywood and witnessed the paparazzi swarm an elfin figure. All I could see were some vertical black plastic spikes moving horizontally at chest-high level at a steady pace. Was this an R2-D2 type robot? I rushed the media mob, and in the middle was Elizabeth Taylor wearing an ornate spiked tiara and riding in her electric wheelchair.

Another time I couldn't find my girlfriend, Bethsheba, at a party in a palatial estate in Beverly Hills. I combed the outdoor gardens, ventured into the private quarters upstairs, and checked the maid's rooms. I finally found an obscure hallway, and at the end was a bulky guy talking intensely and hovering over someone with his outstretched arm seemingly blocking the hallway. It was the actor Gary Busey (also known as "Scary Abusey") talking with a wide-eyed Bethsheba. I used some verbal jujitsu to extricate her, and we ended up skedaddling from the premises.

But these surreal moments were increasingly rare, and I instead felt locked in an endless loop of rubber salmon buffets, tired celebrities, irascible publicity agents, silent auctions, security harassment, and bad art openings. The branded vodka promotions, the ceaseless dessert trays, and the cheesy swag bags were becoming indistinguishable. I was tiring of the omnipresent queasiness, the hangovers, the chicanery, the traffic jams, late-night antacids, the yo-yo dieting and weight-gain surges.

I was already in a melancholy mood when I got my summons to crash the Screen Actors Guild Awards.

23

SCREEN ACTOR
IMPERSONATORS

I **MADE A CLASSIC CRASH-BLUNDER.** My girlfriend, Bethsheba, and I were driving east on the 10 Freeway toward downtown Los Angeles to attend Photo L.A., an annual invite-only exhibit featuring more than five thousand pictures from photographers worldwide.

We were uninvited, but that wasn't a problem. We were already tipped off to the means of entry by another crasher on the scene—a cell phone text with a picture showing a zebra-striped wristband. As Bethsheba drove, I rummaged through my large tote bag that carried thousands of multicolored bands, found the correct ones, and strapped them onto our left wrists.

Suddenly my cell phone began popping. My gatecrash partner Shane Kerch was in the south part of downtown and noticed hundreds of people congregating around the Shrine Auditorium. How could I be so remiss? Tonight was the Screen Actors Guild Awards, one of Hollywood's big five annual events along with the Oscars, the Grammys, the Emmys, and the Golden Globe Awards—catnip for crashers.

Though the SAG Awards show is relatively young, begun in 1995, it provides an important bellwether for the Academy Awards. The full membership of more than 165,000 actors, the largest union in Hollywood, votes for the best acting performances in multiple categories. It's a simple, tightly orchestrated event that discourages the bloated format and distracting sideshows of the other industry awards ceremonies. And the after-party, held in a large outdoor tent adjacent to the Shrine, is a bacchanal of beautiful people, endless buffets, and drinking stations.

"Get down here now!" Shane screamed. "It's chaos with so many people, and we shouldn't have any problem riding the wake in!"

But there was a problem. I was dressed for an arty photo exhibit—black turtleneck, neon-orange corduroy pants, a brown beret tilted at just the right angle, and black wingtips. I looked like a bad Picasso painting, one even he couldn't sell. Bethsheba was no better. She wore a flowery dress, with bright red rectangular eyewear and a garish pink belt. We were colorful bull's-eyes headed for a black-tie event.

As we approached the awards gala downtown we saw all the tell-tale signs of a celebrity-packed extravaganza—circling helicopters, swishing searchlights, hundreds of idling black Suburbans, and cops everywhere.

The Shrine Auditorium was built in the 1920s in a Moorish revival style and over the years has hosted some legendary moments. The famous audience scene in the 1933 movie *King Kong*, where Kong is manacled on the stage, was filmed at the Shrine. In 1956, Elvis performed his first L.A. concert there. And in 1984, Michael Jackson fled the stage with his hair on fire during the filming of a Pepsi commercial.

We parked blocks away and proceeded to run the ringed gauntlet of security toward the Shrine's ornamented turrets.

After a few blocks of zigging and zagging through a warren of expressionless security personnel, we saw another noted crasher, wild-eyed Bradley Bleat, in the clutches of a security detail. They were force-marching him at a fast pace toward the event perimeter. He was protesting wildly that they were making a big mistake, he was on the list, had been coming for years, that this had never happened before, and so on.

On a nearby street corner stood another crasher acquaintance undergoing intense questioning by security. I felt a sense of foreboding. We were only minutes into our approach, and crashers were getting methodically dispatched.

Then Bethsheba broke the heel off one of her Blahniks. We had to retrace all our hard-earned steps back to her car to retrieve another pair of footwear.

In the trunk, all she had was a pair of purple-glitter pumps. She snapped them on but looked like Dorothy in the *Wizard of Oz* to my Toto.

We made another assault on the Moroccan citadel. Just outside the main entrance, I noticed "the Crab," one of Hollywood's most cunning crashers. Middle-aged, furtive, and relentless, he employed an ingenious technique: hunched over with his back to security and embedded in a crowd of surging guests he pressed his cell phone against his ear and carried on an imaginary conversation with someone in the industry. He belched out all the right phrases: "green light," "on the studio lot," "in turnaround," "Weinstein may go for it," "five-year first-look deal." He did all this in a crouch, crab-like, while slowly backing past security.

Most security guards, being human and often paid subsistence wages, unconsciously and unwittingly make a quick decision to let him pass. To stop the Crab requires multilayered actions: physically halt him, make eye contact, stand him up, turn him around, cut off his phone conversation, request his name and identification, and call in additional security if his answers seem dubious.

Sure enough, the Crab made it in. I initially thought Bethsheba and I should try the same tactic but realized that two crabs backing in together right after an initial crab entry would be mega conspicuous.

I also noticed the ubiquitous Clement von Franckenstein breezily approach the check-in clerks at the front desk. There was a momentary delay, and I thought His Clemness might be caught in that Hollywood twilight zone of B-list celebrity pushing for A-list entry. But his impeccable dinner jacket, accent, and panache, along with a few tossed calling cards, soon opened the gates, and he was escorted in.

We retreated and decided to try the northern entrance to the auditorium. Suddenly I ran into Shane, who always had a knack for inappropriate outfits. He was wearing his typical T-shirt with a drawing of a large gun across his chest, a shabby blazer, black Levis, and cowboy boots. His hair was unruly, and he hadn't shaved in days.

"You've done it again," I squawked at him. "There's no way we're all going to get in with your attire. We might as well just hand ourselves over to the LAPD right now."

"What about you?" he countered. "I saw your orange pants from five blocks away. You're a walking sandwich board. And where's your jacket? And my God, look at Bethsheba's shoes!"

He was right. We looked like a traveling circus troupe preparing for a junior high juggling performance. At least I'd ditched the brown beret.

Shane considered the situation and redeployed to fetch a burrito outside the security perimeter, asking me to call him with an update.

Bethsheba and I forged ahead. We entered the huge courtyard abutting the north side of the building and saw our chance. Guarding one of the doors was a young African American dude in his early twenties, probably a freelance hire for the big event working for minimum wage. I always marveled at the way Hollywood producers hired large, scowling black men to man the gates at these grand entertainment spectacles, always cynically playing on the fears of uninvited skinny white guys trying to thread security. And behind the lines, they layer the second and third rings of security with officious, marble-eyed white managers.

"Hey, we've already been in," I shouted to the guard as we barreled through the door.

"No, no, you guys got to use the other entrance," he yelled back.

We both kept moving fast, and just as the guard was about to give chase, another crasher couple appeared at the door. The guard gave us an exasperated look and turned back to deal with the new duo.

I began to feel a familiar sense of welling relief. We'd made it in. That momentary surge of queasy adrenaline quickly faded.

Suddenly, we found ourselves at another roped entrance. A large, hump-necked, blonde bouncer with an earpiece confronted us.

"Uh, where are you two going?" he calmly asked.

This time, we were forced to halt—a death kiss when dealing with inquisitive security personnel. We repeated a series of lame excuses, and his questions narrowed. Bethsheba tried using her purple shoes as an excuse, explaining that a heel on her other set of shoes broke and she'd had to fetch a new pair.

"Why on earth would I wear these eyesores to an awards show?" she insisted. "We're just getting back from our car!"

After a moment, he gave us a baleful look and tilted his head into his earpiece.

"We've got another," he barked.

Almost immediately, four of LAPD's finest were at our elbows.

"We need to bring you both to our office and ask you a few more questions," one of them said, now gently guiding me by the arm as another escorted Bethsheba. The blond bouncer gave me a lengthy smirk and went back to scanning the lobby for other notables.

We were now in the clutches of the police, not just some part-time, absentminded guard. My mind reeled, my body turned rubbery, and my armpits were instantly drenched. *I'm an accomplished guy! I've got a master's degree in journalism from Columbia University! I've worked as a reporter at the* L.A. Times! *I've written and directed dozens of television documentaries! I am in the Business! Why am I in this situation?*

Bethsheba handled the situation no better. She began to jabber. She was an accomplished script doctor! She was already an attendee! How could she be treated so badly? This was one colossal mistake! She hinted at a lawsuit. She whipped out her Writers Guild Card and began waving it violently.

Our sense of entitlement faced a smackdown.

The cops remained silent as I wished Bethsheba had. As we descended in lockstep down a hallway into the bowels of the building, I saw a shimmering silhouette moving toward us. It was a gorgeous blond woman in a floor-length, pink, diaphanous gown with a stylish silver necklace. Who was this? Could it be a guardian angel sent to pluck me from this disastrous predicament?

As I got closer, she came into focus and we locked eyes. She was confident, winsome, and her beauty seemed to increase with each step. She gave me a slight smile. It was actress Cate Blanchett heading to the stage to receive her Screen Actors Guild Award for best actress for her film role in the Woody Allen movie *Blue Jasmine.*

I had the sudden urge to call out "Cate! How are you? You look great! How's Woody? Congratulations, I knew you'd do it!"—all while enveloping her in a loving bear hug. Nothing beats back security better than a connection to an A-list movie star.

But I was not in the custody of security. I was in the custodianship of the LAPD. A quick move might have stalker implications. Maybe Cate would start screaming and her smile would turn to horror. I imagined myself going down in a hail of gunfire, courtesy of a trigger-happy cop. Or being dragged into a dark corner, hog-tied and billy-clubbed below the awards stage, my cries for help deafened by the accolades above.

I let my insane urge pass. I grimly smiled back and gulped. Here was Cate Blanchett, ascending to receive an award at the pinnacle of her career. And here was I, as we crossed paths, descending into a career-ending arrest and potential physical reprimand below deck.

My sense of alarm skyrocketed when we arrived at the security office door. As we entered, I saw RICHARD WEINBERG, a crasher in his late fifties, handcuffed to a bench and still immaculately outfitted in his tuxedo. He was hunched forward, and his toupee had slipped and was now nestled, Trump-like, just above his eyebrows, giving him a look of permanent subterfuge.

Weinberg squirmed next to another accomplice, who was also tethered to the bench. They both looked miserable and doomed. About a half dozen other detainees lined the opposing wall in varying states of restraint.

I averted my gaze as Bethsheba and I were marched to the end of the room and plunked down on metal chairs. It was more of a war room. Dozens of security personnel milled about, responding to the constant chirp of walkie-talkie traffic and girding for the arrival of more hapless trespassers. Monitors hummed above with the comings and goings of guests inside and outside the building. I tried to focus on the peeling wall paint, but it didn't help.

"There's one. . . . I think we nailed him last year," barked an officer into his two-way radio as he scanned the streaming visuals on the wall monitor. "I can't believe he's back. OK, let's move on him, but wait till he's alone."

Out of the side of my eye, I saw a beady-eyed interrogator with a high and tight haircut officiously approaching. He stood about five foot five, even with his elevated boots on.

"I don't recognize you two," he said. "Most of you crashers are always advertising your exploits on Facebook or Instagram."

"We are not crashers. We were invited, and we need to attend the after-party," sputtered Bethsheba in her best mock outrage.

"I think your after-party is going to be in Twin Towers," he said, referring to the L.A. County jail downtown.

Turned out his working name was John. He demanded our identification and took it down the hall to run our records and search for
any outstanding warrants.

For a moment, the security emptied from the room.

"We're fucked," said Weinberg in a morose tone as he looked
down the bench at me.

"Should we make a run for it?" I murmured to Bethsheba.

"God, no. They have our IDs!" she rightly pointed out.

Obviously I wasn't thinking clearly, but that changed abruptly as
John strode back in. He had that jacked-up persona of a second-string
linebacker on a high school football team, the type who was never
good enough to play on the field. A character who overcompensated
by frenetically pacing the sidelines, pumping his arms, and howling
at each tackle. He always seemed to have his helmet on but never
got in the game.

John approached us, grabbed a chair, flipped it around, and sat
facing us like an interrogation scene out of a 1930s detective movie.

Bethsheba began her usual protestation, and John quickly cut it
short.

"You guys know where you are?" he blurted out in an irritating
staccato. "You're in my house, and I don't like it when people trespass in my house. Those guards you breezed by outside . . . they're
family . . . and you've seriously pissed off members of my family."

John told us to stand up and began taking multiple pictures that,
in his mind, passed for official mug shots. He started with different
angles—looking up, faraway, from the side, up close and personal.
Then he left.

With a break in the action, I tried calling my entertainment attorney, Denny Cline, on my cell phone. I made multiple attempts and
ended up leaving a foggy voice message that I needed his advice, was
in a jam, and needed his help *now*.

"So why do you guys do this?" asked John with a tap on my shoulder. I hadn't realized he'd come back in and was listening behind me as I was hunched over making frantic appeals to my consigliere. I bolted upright as my phone slipped out of my greasy hands and clattered across the floor.

"Look, we are not crashers. You've made a huge mistake," proclaimed Bethsheba for the twelfth time. "We are members of the industry, in good standing, and this is just outrageous." She waved around her Writers Guild card again.

"Oh yeah, sure, of course you're not crashers. You probably were invited to accept an award . . . that's why you're here," said John with a snort. "Just level with me. You guys tried multiple times and different ways to get in, and you got caught. Just admit it and we can move on."

An officer appeared in the doorway. "Hey John, the paddy wagon will be here in a few minutes—just a heads-up!"

Bethsheba upped her protestations. I looked at her with an imploring gaze to shut up. I remembered legal advice that one can only be arrested for trespassing if you're sufficiently warned that you are trespassing but proceed anyways. Sure, we'd breezed by the guard, but we hadn't been formally warned or kicked out of the event and returned. I realized any type of admission would result in arrest, like all the other poor souls sitting there watching us intently.

John slapped his thigh, abruptly stood up, and left the room.

"Keep quiet and we'll be OK," I hissed to Bethsheba, who also finally began understanding John's strategy.

A moment later, one of the largest officers I'd ever seen—about six foot eight and 270 pounds—strode in and stood in front of us.

"I just want to let you know," he said calmly, "you're both under arrest."

24

DETONATION

THROUGH MY YEARS on the crasher circuit, I'd experienced my share
of incidents and accidents, confrontations and accusations, highs
and lows. I'd had champagne glasses ripped from my hands, been
assaulted, denied entry, had food and wine thrown in my face,
been called a social leper, a mooch, and a degenerate. I'd been hounded
by security, snitched on by other crashers, locked in fire stairwells,
and escorted out of innumerable parties. I'd climbed through thorny
canyon chaparral, hiked along miles of private beachfront at night
wearing black wingtips, climbed concrete walls, wrestled through
hedges, and suffered physical injuries in innumerable backdoor pratfalls and capers.

But this was another level. I was now in the custody of hostile
security guards and surrounded by LAPD jackboots in a dank bunker
at the Shrine Auditorium during one of Hollywood's biggest awards
shows. Should I have assumed this might happen someday? Yes. But
that realization didn't lessen my shock.

It was now nearly two hours since my girlfriend, Bethsheba,
and I had been detained. We'd been interrogated, relieved of our

identification, threatened with arrest, pressed to confess, and photo-graphed more than the royal family. We'd watched our fellow gate-crashers corralled and manacled to benches.

Luckily, Bethsheba finally began trimming her protestations. The waves of questioning by John, our chief interrogator, began petering out. We were left to sit and stew in our own malfeasance. Occasion-ally, there'd be a burst of activity as more wild-eyed intruders were brought in and others shepherded out. We assumed the cops were methodically filling up the paddy wagon and that it was only a mat-ter of time before Bethsheba and I were read our rights, cuffed, and perp-walked to the big bus outside.

We were sweat-stained, bleary-eyed, and resigned to having a permanent blotch on our records. Would this determine our future job prospects? Could this affect Bethsheba's custody of her teenage son? How long would we be incarcerated in the Big House downtown? How many cellmates would we have? What charges would we face? What were the legal costs? How much was bail? Would we have access to organic, vegetarian food and jailhouse yoga classes?

Our despondency was heightened by the periodic bursts of wild applause and the good times upstairs, as waves of awardees mounted the stage to accept their SAG trophies. We could hear their muffled speeches playing on a television down the hall, slightly out of sync with the real-time applause in the auditorium.

We both continually flagellated ourselves over the ignominy of our arrests. We imagined conversations with friends after we'd been sprung.

"Hey, so where were you this weekend? None of us could get a hold of you."

"Uh, we were behind bars downtown after getting arrested at the Screen Actors Guild Awards show for trying to crash the after-party."

If you go down, wouldn't it be better to go down in more dra-matic fashion for a worthy reason? More like the final moments of

Butch Cassidy and the Sundance Kid surrounded by federales in a tiny Bolivian village amid a hail of bullets? Or like Mel Gibson choking on his rope in *Braveheart*? Or Sydney Carton's closing lines while facing the gallows in Charles Dickens's *A Tale of Two Cities*, "It is a far, far better thing that I do, than I have ever done; it is a far, far better rest that I go to than I have ever known"?

Yes, our imminent arrest was for the most unheroic and pathetic of reasons. On the other hand, we weren't facing torture and oblivion. My thoughts drifted back to an earlier visit to Moscow when I stood outside the Lubyanka prison—Joseph Stalin's notorious local torture chamber. Tens of thousands passed through a ground-floor door just off a side street, never to appear again. In those days, the wrong trespass or minor political offense ended with a gunshot to the back of the head while kneeling in the basement.

All Bethsheba and I faced was fingerprinting, some barked instructions, and white bread and bologna sandwiches. Still, our apprehension was palpable.

Another police sergeant stuck his head in sideways through the doorway. "The first bus is filled and heading downtown and we've got another on the way," he announced, to no one in particular. "We should be able to clear the room shortly."

After a few moments the gargantuan LAPD commander appeared. "I thought you two might need this," he said, offering us two cups of coffee. "You've got a long night ahead of you."

He sat beside us and engaged us in some pleasant chatter—querying us on potential winners of the upcoming best dramatic television actress award (upstairs), our favorite movies of the year, and what Sean Penn was up to these days. He slyly pivoted.

"For years I've watched people bite, scratch, and push to get in here," he said. "As for me, I'd rather be home with my wife and kids rather than deal with this circus. I just don't get it. What's the appeal? All this for a free eggroll?"

"We like these shows and parties because we are in the industry, we like networking and seeing all our friends, which we can't do because we're stuck down here," said Bethsheba. "And besides, *we're* invited!"

"Look, you're not fooling me, and it's time to stop fooling yourselves," said the commander, abruptly handing us back our IDs. "You *are* actually the uninvited. Yet, we've decided to let you both go. But if we ever see you here again, I can assure you that you'll both be arrested."

With that, the commander stood up and was quickly joined by three other deputies who were at our elbows.

As we walked out of the room toward the building's exit, I could feel my anxiety lifting in coordination with the steady drumbeat of jackboots beside me. Relief ran through me.

"HEY, WHERE THE HELL ARE YOU TAKING THOSE TWO?" screamed John, who bolted out into the hallway as we passed his security office. "They are NOT to be released! They are under arrest! Bring them back here!"

Oh shite. I turned and looked back at his contorted face. He was relentless. He kept screaming at the officers to return us to his custody while he cantered a few feet behind. My anxiety re-spiked. We'd almost made it out, and now this, one yard from the goal line.

I looked up at the large commander and noticed he was expressionless, staring straight ahead. I looked at the other officers who also paid John no attention, with no break in their purposeful march with us toward the exit.

I realized that John had set up this last little scare tactic to rattle us on the way out the door. It worked. By the time Bethsheba and I were delivered outside, we were like jelly, our emotions whipsawed. As we walked back to our car, we turned on each other in a screaming row that lasted for the next hour.

She was outraged I didn't stand up for us.

I was infuriated that she hadn't the sense to stop yapping.

"I'll go get the car," I finally said.

"Don't bother. I'm taking an Uber home," she responded testily.

I didn't see her again for many months. Our relationship was over. We'd met crashing, and now our union was ending on a bad crash. Those who live by the wristband, die by the wristband.

As I drove home, I noticed my cell phone piling up messages. Word had probably gotten out on the circuit that I'd gotten nailed—actually, a catch and release, but I still felt the sting of a life-changing stumble.

I again considered the compulsions I'd witnessed in many of my crasher brethren that were becoming more apparent in myself. The constant quest for new events, the dopamine hit from every sliver of intel, the smartphone addiction, the posing, the misrepresentations, the bad accents, the gluttony, the chicanery, the inability to stop.

After a couple of decades of purposeless jaunts across the L.A. basin, my nights often ended like they did now—in my car, alone, listening to the blabber of a bad AM radio sports show.

Soon after, I heard that Burt Goldenberg had died. At eighty-four years young, Burt was a legend in the crasher world, having started invading backyard barbecues, Hollywood mansion soirees, and swinger parties in the early 1970s. He was immortalized in an iconic picture from the time, walking poolside at a Beverly Hills bacchanal that he attended courtesy of a self-invitation.

In the early days, he lived a libertine lifestyle and was known as quite the ladies' man. Into his eighties, Burt still tooled around L.A. in two cars. The Camaro was for errands around the neighborhood, but the red Corvette was for special occasions. I'd see him backing up at different functions, knocking over trashcans, denting fences, and grinding the undercarriage on elevated curbs.

A younger, svelte Burt Goldenberg (left, wearing sunglasses) prowls the party scene circa 1977. *Brad Elterman, Dog Dance LLC*

For years, I encountered Burt at events of all shapes and sizes. He was always alone, wearing his trademark baseball hat and white sneakers and always a fiend for new party tips. He once lifted up his pant leg to show a gout-like growth on his leg. When one of my friends offered to drop by his home and periodically check in on him, Burt declined.

"Just call me regularly and let me know what's going on," he said. "That's all I ask."

Burt would disappear from time to time, but we thought he was just pacing himself for the next big event. I hadn't seen him in a couple of months and heard that he'd been found dead in his home in West L.A. Apparently no one had checked in on him for weeks. He was discovered only after neighbors noticed flies swarming the inside of his windows and newspapers piled up on his driveway.

When LAPD officers broke down his front door, they found a hoarder's paradise—books, magazines, piles of boxes, and hundreds of gift bags jammed up to the ceiling. His bedroom was barricaded with party-crasher detritus.

"He was alienated from his family back east and didn't have many close friends," said Brad Elterman, the Hollywood photographer who knew Burt for more than forty years. "He'd spend all day on the phone calling people for party tips and calling women he'd met the night before. By late evening he'd peel out of his driveway headed to an event—he just couldn't be at home alone. For years, many of his neighbors thought he was a Mafia hit man—home all day, gone all night."

An extraction team from the L.A. County coroner's office was sent in to remove his remains.

"He was typical of many of these crashers—kind of misfits by day and then a mini-celebrity on the circuit at night—he knew everyone, but in the end really no one," added Elterman. His body lay unclaimed in the county morgue for weeks.

Burt's death—ironically on February 14, Valentine's Day—gave me serious pause. Was this the typical fate of an aging, lonely party crasher? To anonymously leave your house toes and tits up, hoisted by a group of first responders? To be undiscovered for weeks because no one cared enough to check in? It was a dark end to a sunny, sybaritic style of living. I saw the parallels to my own life and the direction my train tracks were heading. It made me shudder.

The night after I learned of Burt's passing, I lay in bed thinking about what drew me to the crasher lifestyle. Initially, it was an attempt to escape the clutches of depression and seek some form of community in the most anonymous city in the world. It was a search for adventure and camaraderie among fellow outlaws. It was the exploration of hidden locales and events that pumped my adrenaline and quenched my curiosity. It nurtured my hope of finding love and intimacy in an alienating dystopia.

As I stared glumly at my bedroom ceiling, I resolved to go cold turkey. I was done with all crashers and the crasher lifestyle. I would delete all interloper numbers in my cell phone. I would cancel my subscription to the Master List. I would chuck out all my colored pens, ultraviolet inks, name stickers, lanyards, and headgear.

I even contemplated the unthinkable—scooping up my large black tote bag filled with thousands of multicolored wristbands collected over many years and discarding the whole shebang into a large dumpster in my alley.

I curled into a fetal tuck, buried myself with pillows, and drifted off into a fitful sleep. I awoke midday with a heavy head and ignored the blinking messages on my cell phone. I tried distracting myself with a *Family Feud* television rerun, a new Mao biography, and cleaning my electric shaver. Nothing helped. I kept thinking of Burt in a bag.

Nevertheless, I had new resolutions, errands to do and chores to complete. I trashed the few swag bags left in my closet, ditched some earpieces, and gave my clipboard collection to a neighbor. I retrieved my wine glasses and champagne flutes from my car trunk and returned them to my kitchen closet. Then I reached for my black bag of wristbands, and my hands rummaged through the paper, plastic, vinyl, and silicone bands that came in all shapes and sizes, logos, and graphics. I just wanted one last look, touch, and feel.

For a moment, all the memories came flooding back—the hazy dazzle of mountaintop homes, nameless nightclubs, dressed-up wineries, spa closings, and unidentifiable restaurant openings. This bag had provided one helluva chariot ride. I picked it up and headed to the dumpster.

I got yet another call, the third in ten minutes, from Sam Brody, the embedded crasher-caterer, and I finally answered. "Hey Adrian, there's a massive shindig up in the Hollywood Hills at a ginormous mansion tonight off of Mulholland Drive!" he yelled excitedly. "Great crowd. Catered by super chef José Andrés. Definitely will be going late."

There was a solid twenty-second pause.

"What's the cross street and the wristband color?" I asked.

NOTES

Introduction: The Pink Palace

Elizabeth Taylor spent six honeymoons: Ann O'Neill, "Marilyn Monroe Slept Here," CNN.com, November 30, 2011, https://www.cnn.com/travel/article /beverly-hills-hotel-history/index.html.

1. Who Are These People?

story I never got to complete: Adrian Maher, "Gunplay," *L.A. Weekly*, September 9, 1998.

His department still used: Adrian Maher, "Culver City Confidential," *L.A. Weekly*, September 9, 1998.

2. Navigating Crasher Codes

the cautionary tale of Terry Bryant: Kenzie Bryant, "The Frances McDormand Oscar-Statue-Caper Gets Weirder," *Vanity Fair*, March 6, 2018, https:// www.vanityfair.com/style/2018/03/oscars-2018-frances-mcdormand -stolen-award-terry-bryant.

7. Playmates at Play

"Everything in the Mansion": "Celebrity Homes: Inside the Crumbling, Sorry State of the Playboy Mansion," *Realty Today*, October 21, 2015, https://www

.realtytoday.com/articles/44772/20151021/celebrity-homes-inside-the
-crumbling-sorry-state-of-playboy-mansion.htm.

a fever and other flu-like symptoms: Rong-Gong Lin II, "Mystery Illness May Be
Tied to Playboy Mansion's Famed Grotto," *Los Angeles Times*, April 22, 2011,
https://www.latimes.com/world/la-xpm-2011-apr-22-la-grotto-bacteria22
-story.html.

tell-all about life inside the sex castle: Holly Madison, *Down the Rabbit Hole:
Curious Adventures and Cautionary Tales of a Former Playboy Bunny*
(New York: Dey Street Books, 2015), 38–39.

12. King World Knockout

"confused hurt": David Remnick, *King of the World: Muhammad Ali and
the Rise of an American Hero* (New York: Random House, 1998), 33.

a fight against Swedish boxer: Remnick, 6–7.

"Only in boxing": Remnick, 32.

14. Pumped Up with Paltrow

"You sit on what is essentially": Daniel Summers, "For the Love of Goop,
Don't Steam Your Vagina," *Daily Beast*, January 29, 2015, https://www
.thedailybeast.com/for-the-love-of-goop-dont-steam-your-vagina.

"increase sexual energy": Brianna Sacks, "Gwyneth Paltrow's Goop Will Pay
$145,000 for Misleading Customers About That Vagina Egg," *BuzzFeed
News*, September 4, 2018, https://www.buzzfeednews.com/article
/briannasacks/goop-vagina-eggs-settlement.

15. Side-Door Sundance

"didn't have anything to do": "Robert Redford Admits Sundance 'Not as Much
Fun,' Complains Paris Hilton Shows Up," *Page Six*, January 18, 2013, https://
pagesix.com/2013/01/18/robert-redford-admits-sundance-not-as-much
-fun-complains-paris-hilton-shows-up/.

16. Esalen Interlopers

the site was known as Slate's Hot Springs: Jeffrey J. Kripal, *Esalen: America and
the Religion of No Religion* (Chicago: University of Chicago Press, 2007),
32; Peter Hockaday, "Hippies, Nudity, and Don Draper: Inside Big Sur's
Esalen Institute Featured in 'Mad Men,'" *SF Gate*, May 18, 2015, https://www

.sfgate.com/tv/article/Hippies-nudity-and-Don-Draper-Inside-Big-Sur
-s-6271471.php; David S. Wills, "Hunter S. Thompson—Gonzo Fron-
tiersman," *Beatdom* 11 (September 22, 2012): https://www.beatdom.com
/hunter-s-thompson-gonzo-frontiersman/.

"the most beautiful meeting": Jean Allen, "The Greatest in Golf," *Sun-Sentinel*
(Fort Lauderdale, FL), December 26, 1993, https://www.sun-sentinel.com
/news/fl-xpm-1993-12-26-9312150705-story.html.

"It is a region where extremes meet": Henry Miller, *Big Sur and the Oranges
of Hieronymus Bosch* (New York: New Directions, 1957), 4

"Jive shit for rich white folk": Jeffrey J. Kripal, *Esalen: America and the Religion of No Religion* (Chicago: University of Chicago Press, 2007), 401.

17. Upping My Game

"the coolest block in America": "The Coolest Block in America," *GQ*,
March 20, 2012, https://www.gq.com/gallery/abbot-kinney-boulevard
-shopping-venice-california.

"attend the opening of an envelope": Anita Gates, "Sylvia Miles, Actress with
a Flair for the Flamboyant, Dies at 94," *New York Times*, June 12, 2019,
https://www.nytimes.com/2019/06/12/movies/sylvia-miles-death.html.

"Never miss a chance": Ned Sherrin, ed., *Oxford Dictionary of humorous
Quotations*, 4th ed. (Oxford: Oxford University Press, 2008), 319.

"you are dead already": Suzanna Andrews, "Arianna Calling!," *Vanity Fair*, October 17, 2006, https://www.vanityfair.com/news/2005/12/huffington200512.

18. SpaceX Launch

the company hopes to launch: Dave Mosher, "Elon Musk Revealed a New Plan to
Colonize Mars with Giant Reusable Spaceships—Here Are the Highlights,"
Business Insider, September 29, 2017, https://www.businessinsider.com/elon
-musk-iac-mars-colonization-presentation-2017-9; Brian Wang, "Elon
Musk Statements and My Own Extrapolation of Developments Toward
an Eighty Thousand Person Mars City by 2040," *Next Big Future* (blog),
August 9, 2014, https://www.nextbigfuture.com/2014/08/elon-musk
-timeline-and-extrapolation-of.html.

"I want to die on Mars": Elien Blue Becque, "Elon Musk Wants to Die on
Mars," *Vanity Fair*, March 10, 2013, https://www.vanityfair.com/news
/tech/2013/03/elon-musk-die-mars.

The SpaceX factory: Sandy Mazza, "SpaceX Makes Deal to Keep Headquarters in Hawthorne Through 2022," *Daily Breeze*, October 29, 2012, https://www.dailybreeze.com/2012/10/29/spacex-makes-deal-to-keep -headquarters-in-hawthorne-through-2022/.